Praise for *When the Dust Settled*

"The prose and lessons in *When the Dust Settled* by Tamara Littrell are stunningly crisp in their delivery and unassailably authentic. Whether you have lived around the ranch life of the Northern Rockies and Plains or not, you will smell sage and sweat. You'll feel the stiff weave of a lariat in calloused palms; remember its burn on young skin. Soon you'll hear the lonesome fullness of quiet wind against your heart and taste the blood of a horse in your mouth. Yet those are but an eddy in the river of sensation where Littrell floats this vagabond, coming-of-age story. We watch Littrell and her sister grow from girls to women in the wake of their tough and stoic cowboy father and his adoring but subjugated wife, who deeply loved him.

When the Dust Settled is proof that cowboys grow old, but their pain is "guaran-goddamn-teed" to stay fresh. It's proof that a man's daughters are still daughters, even when the reins are ripped from his aged hands, and that finally finding the trail is all that matters. Littrell bares her well-earned scars without shame, showing them with toughness, humor, and honesty. She is a woman and author-in-full. But perhaps most of all, Littrell proves a human of extraordinary grace as she examines her life-long oppressor and hero. She is our mentor. She is the real deal."

—William C. Pack
Author of *The B̶*   est Book Award Finalist and
Pulitzer Nominee

"Tammi L̶   ̶k that is both heartbreaking and soul se̶   ̶orous and poignant. Before you're done reading it, yo̶u̶ ̶ll̶ laugh out loud, crave a stiff shot of whiskey, and wipe away tears that refuse to stop flowing. Raw emotion, searing angst, and gut-wrenching drama rise from *When the Dust Settled* like a Montana sunset on a winter-washed prairie. This is a story of a little girl, a tough old cowboy, and the bond that held them together through a life that attempted to tear them apart."

—Jane Wells
Writer, Essayist, and Former Book Critic, *Louisville Courier Journal*

"In the tradition of Mari Sandoz and *Old Jules*, Tamara Littrell's portrayal of a family in the American West at mid-century is as heart-wrenching as it is surprisingly tender."

—Mary Clearman Blew
Author of *Jackalope Dreams*

"I so enjoyed *When the Dust Settled*. I can appreciate the early sadness in Tamara Littrell's life, and so enjoyed the way that she found humor to replace it. The duty she felt for her father is hard to explain, but I sure can relate. I know this will be a compelling read for anyone."

—Buck Brannaman
BUCK, Winner of the Sundance Film Festival Audience Award, 2011
Inspiration for *The Horse Whisperer* and Author of *The Faraway Horses*

"This book will go right to your heart. It is so powerfully written, you won't be able to put it down. Tammi pulls no punches and gives us the gift of insight into her life, and what it really means to grow up cowboy in the American West."

—John Douglas Wood
Author of *The Adventures of Blondie Magoo and Puddles Pinkerton*

"Tammi Littrell is a great storyteller, captivating readers from the start with tales from her past. This book is easy to relate to in so many ways, especially when the author talks about her need for her father's approval, even as an adult. This is a challenge that many people face in their lives. *When the Dust Settled* is a great read for anybody!"

—Chris Linnares
Author of *Beautiful Women of North Dakota*

When the
DUST SETTLED

A Memoir

[signature: Tamara Littrell]

Tamara Littrell

BROWN BOOKS *small press*

Lyrics from Trent Wilmon's "Good Horses to Ride" reprinted with permission from Trent Wilmon.

When the Dust Settled

Brown Books Small Press
16250 Knoll Trail Drive, Suite 205
Dallas, Texas 75248
www.BrownBooksSmallPress.com
(972) 381-0009

A New Era in Publishing™

ISBN: 978-1-612547-62-6
Library of Congress Control Number 2011928035

Printing in the United States
10 9 8 7 6 5 4 3 2 1

For more information about Tamara or the book,
please visit www.WhentheDustSettled.com.

This book is dedicated to my sister, Valerie.

There just aren't words, so I won't make up a bunch.
The truth is that I could not have gotten through Mom's
death and Dad's life without you.

You have made me laugh, have kept me sane, and have taken on
way more than you should have had to. (I think we deserve a trip
to the Bahamas—you bring the kidney stone this time.)

I'm sorry for a lot of things and I love you more than
I have ever had the guts to tell you.

*May you always walk in beauty and may a
rainbow touch your shoulder.*

This is a true story and in telling it I have done my best to recount it as accurately as possible. However, it is subject to the imperfection of memory. Some people in this story may remember shared experiences differently than I did and I respect that. The truth is always subjective to the person's impression of it and I have told the truth as I perceived it at the time.

All the little towns that no one has ever heard of are real. All the names of the people who lived in those unheard of towns have been changed, except for those of my immediate family.

Contents

Part Three: Dirt Roads

Part Four: Ashes to Ashes

Part Five: One Year Later

Part Six-Last Call

About the Author

Acknowledgments

I am so blessed to have an amazing family and circle of friends. The fact that they know me well and like me anyway always astounds me. The following are VIPs who have read my manuscript in part or in its entirety at various stages. Their support and encouragement kept me writing.

My dear friend, Jane Wells, who was the first person to read the rough draft and who offered up this stellar advice: "Be careful about telling people that you are writing a book. It's kind of like being pregnant—pretty soon folks are going to start asking where the baby is." Well, Jane, it's taken me almost ten years, but I have finally delivered. Now if I could just lose that baby weight. . . .

My love and appreciation goes out to my loyal friends who read my early work without being forcibly tied to a chair: Elvis Parsley, Robert and Ashley Farnum, Karen Schreffler, Hannah Kopicky, Linda Schmidt, Risa Scott, Dennis Driskill, Jamie Scott, Shelly Doty, Julie Davidson, Tammy DeLong, and Rosemary Welter.

I also offer my love and gratitude to those who read excerpts of the *almost* finished draft—Wanda Johnston, Sierra and Aaron Wright, Brenda and Chris Case—and to those who gave me their unbiased and unpaid opinions on the interior and cover design— Savannah and Shane Rice, Suzy Anfield, Rod Lang, Matt and Melissa Neidlinger, and the zealous members of the "Bruise Cruise." I sincerely appreciate your judgment, your feedback, and your input. You can stop squirming— I'll untie you now.

Thank you *all* for your honesty, your comments, and for listening, but mostly I thank you for the dirty job of being my friends.

A special shout-out to the following: My girl, Risa Scott, who has been a great example of how to handle grief. Risa, you could have written the "how-to" book and I wish I had been paying attention sooner. I thank you for sitting up with me all those long, lonely, late nights and for sharing those bottles of wine with me over the telephone. You got me through an incredibly rough time and I can't begin to thank you enough. I'm sorry you're in the club now.

Boy, did I get lucky when they were handing out in-laws. Joe and Shirley Littrell are the best that a girl could hope for! Thank you for always being there for me and for your never ending love and support.

My adopted daughter and my friend, Julia Thee. You will always be a part of our family and I thank you for cheering me on throughout this project and for offering to be my European connection.

I cannot begin to express the depth of appreciation I have for my family.

Larry, my husband, who has read only bits and pieces of this book, but who knows all of the story by heart. I offer up on a silver platter my undying love and adulation—you are my oxygen and my ocean. Thank you for always being my number one fan, even at times when I wasn't worthy. Also, I thank you for sticking with me through the years, the hot flashes, and throughout this really long process. God knows you deserved better. I love you more than you can possibly ever imagine. I know you said you were waiting for the movie to come out, but c'mon, read the damn book, would you?

Sierra, who has been my biggest supporter from the beginning and who was the person who encouraged me to keep writing when I had doubts about being able to complete this project. She said, "I laughed, I cried, and I was shocked, all on the same page." Sierra, you never knew it, but that single sentence was my catalyst. Thank you for always believing in me. I am so honored to be the woman you call mom!

Savannah, who has always been the calm in every storm. Vanni, just being near you puts me in a peaceful place. When I started this project you were only fourteen years old and now here you are, all grown-up with a daughter of your own. I wish Paisley could have met her Grandpa Coyote and her Grandma Di. They would have adored her! Thank you for "dreaming" up the title. It is such a privilege to be your mother!

Valerie, my sister, who shared with me her own memories of various events and helped me with certain facts. Val, I know telling this story has been hard on you and I am truly sorry for that. Putting it on paper has probably saved me a shit-load of money in therapy, so I owe you one. You, Saul, Dustin, and Hannah will always be in my heart.

Now, I'll say it one more time for you all: "OK, everybody act like we are a nice, normal family!"

My sincere gratitude to Ryan McCollins for his early editorial work. He helped to organize and shape this story from the very beginning.

Heartfelt thanks to Buck Brannaman, Bill Pack, Mary Clearman Blew, Doug Wood, Chris Linnares, and Jane Wells for reading the finished copy and offering me such beautiful endorsements. "Thank you" doesn't even begin to cover it, so I'll just say I'm honored and humbled that you would all give so generously of your time to read this and to write a few lines for me.

My appreciation to Doug Wood, for his wealth of information and for insisting that I make that call to Brown Books and the amazing Cynthia Stillar-Wang. Thank you for the push, Doug; I needed that!

Speaking of the amazing Cynthia Stillar-Wang, director at Brown Books Small Press—thank you for being so patient with me and for taking my hand and leading me through the exciting labyrinth of publishing. When I placed this baby in your very capable hands I knew that I had found someone who could make it walk and talk. Thank you for that. I'm not sure I'm ready to let go yet, so would you please hang on for just a little while longer?

A very special thanks to the brilliant Auburn Layman, my editor, who is wise beyond her years and whom I admire greatly. I don't know what I did to deserve you, and I can't begin to tell you how much I appreciate your insight. It's like you were in my head at times, which I know is a scary place to be. What a privilege it has been to work with you!

Thank you to the talented Jessica Kinkel for her genius design work and for going the extra mile to get it *exactly* right. When the girl nails it, she nails it to the wood!

Cynthia, Auburn, and Jess, it's been a privilege; you have my respect and appreciation always. Thank you so very much!

Finally, thanks to God for the breathtaking view, for the gift of life and forever.

Dad and Mom,
I love you and I miss you every day.

Mom and Dad, late 1960s

Author's Note

Valerie and I are complete opposites. The obvious difference is that she is a skinny one-hundred-pound blonde and I am a meaty 135-pound brunette—with boobs. The not-so-obvious difference is that she's a liberal agnostic while I am conservative and a Christian. I rarely attend church and I don't care for organized religion, but not a day goes by in which I don't pray or thank the big guy upstairs for all the blessings in my life.

Val is an environmentalist with sorted recycling bins, a compost pile, and an herb garden that even Martha Stewart would envy. The only things I recycle are last season's shoes—and that's only if they're *really* cute. She has custom-made New Balance sneakers and has run a few marathons in her life. The only way I can do 26.2 miles is if I'm in a mall and Neiman Marcus is having a clearance sale—then I can do them in my Jimmy Choos.

Valerie can arrange flowers, faux paint, and sew her kids' Christmas stockings and Halloween costumes. I hire florists and painters, and I have been known to hem my kids' pants with a stapler. The most creative I have ever gotten at Halloween was when I cut out a head-hole in a kitchen garbage bag and told my daughter to go as white trash.

Val is sensitive to the world around her and would never hurt someone's feelings, even if she had to tell a lie to avoid doing so. I wouldn't deliberately hurt your feelings, but if you ask me if your butt looks big in those pants and it does, I am going to have to tell you like it is, no matter who you are. I'm only good at lying to myself.

For most of her adult life, Val owned a hip boutique with overpriced, high-end artisan goods, where she spent her workdays showing vases, candles, handmade jewelry, and the like to wealthy housewives. These days she is a registered nurse taking care of babies in the NICU. I own a trucking company. I manage millions of dollars and deal with tough-talking men who are twice my size. I know as much about Cat engines as I do about kitten heels.

Valerie's home is in the city and mine is in the country. Hers is aged and filled with antiques and vintage furniture while the oldest thing in my house (besides the cat) is probably a leftover sauce *du jour* that has made its way to the far corner of the refrigerator.

She is a vegetarian. I like my filet mignon medium. Her family cars are a Subaru and a VW and it takes a court order to get her to drive on an interstate. Mine are a diesel 4x4 pickup and a Mercedes SUV and I love nothing more than cross-country road trips.

Valli wouldn't be caught dead wearing real fur and her handbag is vintage. I look fabulous in fur and I wouldn't be caught dead without my Fendi bag. She's Birkenstocks and Crocs. I'm Manolos and cowboy boots. She's at the "Y" every day, packing her Nalgene. I'm downtown, packing a .38. You get the picture.

Even our choices in husbands were on the opposite ends of the man spectrum. We both married tender, loving, big-hearted men who worship us like the queen biatches that we are, but that's pretty much where the similarities end.

Valerie's husband, Saul, is highly educated with a master's degree in one of the sciences that starts with a *b*—biology or botany, I can't say for sure which one. During the day, he is an industrial hygienist, doing something that involves the cleanup of hazardous chemicals or the prevention of nuclear spills. We're not *exactly* sure what he does. If he told us, he'd have to kill us.

Saul is always immaculately groomed and with his stylish look, he could fit right into the pages of *GQ*. He is the closest thing to a metrosexual that our family has ever seen—and I mean that in a nice way. Did I mention that when he's not reinventing the wheel or stopping the greenhouse effect, he is a maestro who composes masterpieces on the piano *and* the guitar? He has even written a rock opera that I happen to think is good enough to be on Broadway. Saul's body is lean and athletic—kind of Lance Armstrong-ish. He's a marathon runner, an avid skier, and, at one time, was a nationally-ranked tennis player—and he rides his bicycle to work *every single day.*

On the other hand, my husband, Larry, is built like a brick shithouse—more Hulk Hogan-ish. His biceps are like bone-in Easter hams and he can probably bench-press a pool table. I know that he can lift the front end of a farm tractor off the ground because I saw him do it on a bet. He has a twelfth-grade education, a full head of beautiful pewter-colored hair, a few tattoos, and a Harley. Larry's idea of athleticism has more to do with how many keg stands someone can do after a hotdog-eating contest. If life is good, said contest takes place at a NASCAR race.

Behind his tough exterior is a pushover who has a hard time saying no whenever one of our daughters sidles up to him, wraps an arm around his neck, and says, "But, Daaaaddd, I really *need* a new (insert whatever it is that she *really* needs)." Then he does what they refer to as "the secret handshake," which means that a credit card or a Benjamin covertly slides from his hand to one of theirs. He probably wouldn't admit that most renditions of "The Star-Spangled Banner" make him tear up, but I'm here to tell you that it's the truth.

Saul can change $(\varpi)r^2$ into an isosceles triangle, to the tenth power. Now I don't really know if that is mathematically possible, but my point is that if it *is* possible, Saul is the genius who can do it. Just don't ask him to change a lightbulb. On the other end of the brilliance continuum, Larry can change oil, transmissions, rear ends, and tires. He can overhaul a diesel engine over the telephone in the middle of the night, and there is not a piece of equipment that he cannot operate, take apart, or weld back together.

On top of all that, there is no one—I repeat, no one—who is up for a good time like my Larry is. I swear to God he is the only person I know who would be up for a shit-eating contest in a mall after being forced to shop all day and camp out in Macy's home section all night. If I'm in, he's in! Truth be told, if Val wanted in on the shit-eating, shopping, camping adventure, well, then you could count Saul in too. They are just those kind of men and they wouldn't dream of calling, "Not it." They would follow us to hell and back. We know. They already have.

Val and I may be opposites, but we do have more than a few things in common. Besides having wonderful, loving husbands, we each have two great kids who have never done drugs, gotten knocked up, or been in therapy, jail, or any real kind of trouble. We are both loving mothers and we are pit bulls when it comes to our relationships, our work, and our commitments. We can laugh at each other and at ourselves.

We both love to entertain and we throw killer dinner parties. When we do, we can count on our husbands and kids to get in on the act. Saul is the best *sous* chef I have ever worked with. Larry doesn't do a single thing in the kitchen, but put him at the grill with a basting brush and he can do to ribs what Michelangelo did to the Sistine Chapel. My eldest daughter, Sierra, and Val's son, Dustin, are the go-to team—running last-minute errands, arranging chairs, taking out garbage, and carrying trays of food to their designated spots. Hannah, Val's youngest, sets a beautiful table and can fold a napkin to perfection. By the time my youngest daughter, Savannah, was six years old, she could set up a bar, tap a keg, and make a perfect Grey Goose dirty martini.

Val and I both hate fast food, non-dairy creamer, flying, and white zinfandel. We sing off-key, sleep with eye masks on, and carry wine openers in our purses. We both have soft spots in our hearts for stray animals and we cherish gourmet food, fine wine, dark chocolate, soft linens, and jazz. We like our coffee strong, with quiet and cream, and—oh yeah . . . we have the same mother and father. That's what really ties us together and that's what this story is about.

Prologue

I'm forty-nine years old and I'm afraid to pick up the phone and call my father. I picture him sitting in a wheelchair in a nursing home with his back to a TV that is tuned to *Fox News*. He is staring at the wall and his mouth is hanging open as if someone has just said something that he can't believe. He is wacked out on Ambien, Xanax, Prozac, Trazadone, Hydrocodone, and God knows what else. He hasn't bathed or brushed his teeth in a week and he probably has crap in his pants. Yet I'm afraid to call him because he might tell me that I'm "not smart enough to pour piss out of a boot"; or he might tell me to get my ass over there and get him "out of this shithole"; or he might go on and on about his breathing, his pain, and his meds; or, even worse, he just might not want to talk to me.

My sister has been stuck with all the minutiae since my dad moved into this place a week ago. He has been mean and uncooperative—with her and with his nurses. She is torn between sympathy and hatred. I know that she cries most nights when she leaves him. When she gets home, she calls me and she cusses him.

"Maybe I could bring him to a nursing home here, in Wyoming," I suggest.

"Why do you want him?" she asks. "Why have you always wanted him?"

I deny it. "I don't want him."

"Yes, you do. You've always wanted him. God, you need therapy."

"That's not true," I reply, unsure if I'm referring to the not wanting him part or the needing therapy part.

"Yes it is. Your whole life it's been that way. You've always wanted him. You dote on him, you wait on him hand and foot, and you are still waiting for his approval."

I don't know what to say, so I say nothing.

I call him. I say, "How are you?"

He says, "I don't feel like talking right now."

So I do what I always do. I pack a suitcase full of courage and clothes and I go to him.

When I arrive, I peek my head into his room and find him sitting there just as I had imagined. He doesn't see me so I quickly step out of the room and take a moment to let go of a few constrained tears. Then I buck up and step in, bracing myself for a storm.

He's happy to see me, but I feel sick to my stomach and it kills me to see him like this. He wants me to spend the night with him.

"Dad," I say, "are you kidding me? That means that neither of us will get any sleep."

"Would it kill you?" he asks, and because the answer to that is obviously no, I decide to run back to my sister's place to grab some dinner and my pajamas.

Valli is about as supportive as the chair I'll be sleeping in that night. "That's just stupid," she says when I tell her my plan.

"It's only a few hours, not the rest of my life," I reply defensively.

Again she tells me that I'm stupid, and I agree, but I head for my chair anyway. Dad and I stay up late talking and I say things to him that should have been said years ago—things that I have been afraid to say. Gently, I tell him that he is addicted to drugs and alcohol. I tell him that he has been under the influence of one type of mind-altering drug or another for so long that he doesn't know what normal feels like anymore.

"Twenty years, at least," he says, agreeing with me.

Dad and I have a rough night. He demands coffee at three in the morning. I pretend to be asleep and he demands it again at four o'clock. The nurse who gives him his breathing treatment says that the coffee has not been made yet. Dad is pissed. I have to remind him that since she didn't grow up in our house, she doesn't know that she is supposed to jump when he tells her to jump.

At five, his jitters force me to get up and I go off in search of coffee. At six, I think about Googling the question, "Is mercy killing legal in Idaho?" At seven, I kiss him on the cheek, wrap my arms around him, and tell him that I am proud of him for getting through the night without Hydrocodone, Ambien, and Xanax.

At eight, he says he's had enough of this bullshit and wants me to get him the hell out of there. Breakfast comes and he fidgets and glares at it until it goes away. I contemplate retrieving my .38 from under the driver's seat of my car. At nine, I think about pulling the trigger.

Part One

One

My earliest memory is of an ass-kicking. Well, actually it's of my dad's eyes—dark and angry—as he was pulling me out of an irrigation ditch just before the ass-kicking. I was about three years old and was already marching to the beat of my own drum. Though I had been forbidden ever to cross that irrigation ditch, I still did it every day. I would sneak away from our house and tiptoe across the long, skinny plank that would lead me to a wonderful old lady who rewarded my efforts with illegal amounts of candy.

Although it was no more than ten inches wide, I had gotten quite good at "walking the plank," so to speak. At least, I was good until that day when I fell off of it. The water was fast, deep, and cold, and it instantly tried to suck me under. Here my memory gets foggy; there was a scream, but I don't remember if it came from me or from someone who had seen me fall. In my recollection, my dad was both *the rescuer and the abuser. It's the same dual role that he has always played in my life so that's how it went down into the book of my memory*

That was also the first time that I heard my mother frantically screaming, "Gary, Gary!" It was a cry that I would hear many more times from her throughout my childhood. It always meant one of two things: either one of us girls was doing something that could get us killed and she needed him to come to the rescue, or he was disciplining one of us and she was pleading with him to stop.

Feeling sorry for me after my fall and the subsequent ass-whipping, the old lady next door gave my mother a fancy crystal cake plate, along with instructions that it should be passed along to me when I grew up. If she grows up, *the old woman was probably thinking.*

I always thought that it was kind of strange for a kid to have a cake plate, but I also liked knowing that I had it. Whenever I saw it, I was reminded that I had a future, or at least something to look forward to. To this day, I still have that cake plate.

My earliest memory of my sister, who is two years younger than me, is much clearer. We were sitting at the dinner table one night when Valli, who had yet to reach her third birthday, spilled her milk. Dad barely looked at her; his eyes gave away nothing. He just got up from the table, pulled her out of her chair, tipped her upside-down, and used all twelve inches of her thick, blonde hair to mop the floor. He held her by the ankles and swung her back and forth, her *head occasionally bumping the floor. Her body remained stiff, as if it was the handle of a mop.*

Mom kept begging the whole time, "Gary, Gary! Stop!" He did eventually, but not because of her pleading. He stopped when the milk was pretty well mopped up. And when he was done, he just sat Valli back in her chair, just like you would stand a mop in a corner. He never said a word. He didn't even wring her out. I kept right on eating, refusing to notice what was happening. I just pushed my own glass of milk a little farther from the edge of the table.

Years later, this incident was still something that my Dad liked to tell other people about. Mom laughed along, but she always seemed kind of sick when she did.

Dad was born in 1940 in Sidney, Montana, and spent most of his early childhood there. His mother was just fifteen years old and his grandmother was barely over thirty at the time of his birth. Dad loved his grandmother, a heavyset, hard-working, cow-milking, tough-talking woman. He has often bragged that she was just as handy with a paring knife as she was with a broom. Not only does he claim that she could peel an entire apple in one, long, continuous strip, he swears—and I shit you not— that he once saw her knock down a runaway horse with a broom. Dad also adored his granddad who, conversely, was quiet, kind, gentle, and deeply religious. No swear word ever passed through the man's lips and he saw to it that Dad attended church with him every Sunday.

When Dad was about six or seven years old, his parents moved to Billings, Montana. His mother was a waitress then, working two jobs and living off of her tips. His father, a womanizer, was rarely home. His job kept him on the road most of the time and when he did come home, he didn't *really* come home. He cruised the streets of Billings in his new Caddy and when he saw his kids on the streets, he pretended not to notice them, even if they called out to him. Dad once said that his father had told him he didn't want the dirty little bastards in his new car.

By then, the streets of Billings were raising Dad and they didn't care that he dropped out of school when he was in the eighth grade. As he tells it, his teacher sent him home because he had shown up at school without a belt. He left, supposedly to go home to put one on, but he never went back.

He also told us that when he did go to school, he rode a new bicycle every morning because he stole one every afternoon on his way home. When he needed new clothes, he went into a store, tried them on, put on his old clothes over the new ones, and wore them right out of the store. When he and his brothers wanted a new basketball, they would simply dribble and pass one out the door of the store. He got everything he wanted or needed because he stole it—everything except for love or discipline, that is. His mother was busy working and his dad was busy pretending that he didn't have kids. No one cared how—or even if—he survived. He just did.

By the age of fifteen, Dad had already been in jail six times and was on his way to becoming a felon. He had been kicked out of Billings for some type of petty crime that resulted in him suffering a gunshot wound to the wrist. He was about to be sent to the "bad boys" school in Miles City when his granddad intervened and talked the judge into letting him take care of his juvenile delinquent grandson. Granddad never reprimanded Dad. He just climbed into the passenger side of his brand new '55 Ford truck and told Dad to drive them the 275 miles back to Sidney.

There, Dad had his grandparents, as well as two uncles, who had no trouble administering discipline. He also had a bunch of cousins who were just as tough and ornery as he was and were in no way intimidated by the scars and tattoos of their city-boy cousin.

Mom grew up poor, living with her mother, brother, sister, and grandmother. She was twelve when her father died of multiple sclerosis. She used to say that he was mean but she never knew if it was because of the MS or if he just was. One of the little mean things he did was hit her with his cane whenever she walked by him. The biggie was serving her pet rabbit for dinner but not telling her until the meal was over.

Most of her life was spent with her mother and grandmother in a little house on Tenth Street in Billings. During the summers, she would go to Boyd, which was about forty miles away, to an aunt and uncle's place in the country. This was where her love of the outdoors, the sun, and horses turned into life-long passions. There, she was a carefree kid with her playmates, away from the day-to-day poverty, her mean father, and her mother, who suffered from mental illness.

When the summers were over, she would go back to the city and the little house on Tenth Street, where she cared for her two younger siblings. Her mother would often go off the deep end and get taken away to the state mental hospital, where she would remain for several months. In her absence, Mom and her grandmother developed a close bond and a great deal of love and admiration for each other. Their devotion was mutual and it lasted for their entire lives.

When my mom was about to marry my dad, she found out that her abusive, crippled dad was not really her father. While looking for her birth certificate to apply for a marriage license, she discovered that she had actually been born in a home for unwed mothers in Helena. Her mother and grandmother refused to talk about it, but years later, while discussing her birth with some aunts, Mom discovered that her biological father was also the father of one of her childhood playmates—her first crush was her very own brother!

I was about thirty years old when I learned that the "dead" grandpa I had never known was very much alive and living in Butte, Montana. I was shocked! I had to double-check our family tree to be certain that this bit of news didn't mean that I was adopted—or worse, abandoned by wolves and found beside the road, as I had often been told.

My mom was a naïve sixteen-year-old kid when she first met my dad. After a couple years of "fetching up," Dad had gone back to Billings and swept my mom off her feet. Fresh off his work sentence at granddad's farm, he returned tougher, buffer, and cockier than ever. He was handsome in a way that only movie stars are. At night he cruised the streets of Billings in his '49 Chevy while Mom and her best friend, Celia, walked the streets or hung out on the corners. Celia had been crippled by polio and used two walking sticks to get around.

One night, Dad saw them walking and stopped to talk to them. Mom ignored him, looking at the ground and refusing to laugh at his jokes or accept his offers for a soda or a ride, but whatever Celia lacked in physical mobility she made up for in confidence and sociability, so she made friends with Dad immediately. Mom was skeptical, figuring that Dad was going to pick on her and Celia or that he was there on a dare or a bet. She was afraid that he would tease Celia about her disability, as a lot of kids did. Mom had been protective of her friend for years and she certainly wasn't going to trust this Don Juan. She wondered what a guy like him could possibly want with a cripple and a skinny girl. Celia didn't question fate. She was flattered that a good—no, make that *great*-looking—guy was being nice to her, even if he was using her to get to her friend. These drive-by encounters kept up for a few more days until Mom finally let her guard down, talked to Dad, and made eye contact, which immediately sealed her fate.

For a poor girl like Mom, finding Dad must have been like winning the man-lottery. He was so worldly compared to her. He'd been outside of Yellowstone County and he had a car. At sixteen, Mom was thin with thick, beautiful, unruly auburn hair and bad teeth. Dad looked like James Dean, only darker, more mysterious, and more handsome. He had charisma, bad boy tattoos, and an attitude.

Dad says Mom played hard-to-get. Mom says she was afraid of Dad and wondered why a guy like him would want a girl like her. He liked the challenge and she loved the attention. She was also impressed that he didn't notice her friend's disability, or at least that he didn't mention it. What Mom mistook for compassion was probably nothing more than plain, old-fashioned teenage lust. Maybe it was the thrill of the chase, but Dad had his eyes set on Mom. Celia could have been walking on all fours and he wouldn't have noticed. A sensitive side is something my dad never had. It just never occurred to him that he couldn't have whatever he wanted. They dated for about a year and were married within a couple of weeks of Mom graduating high school. But before she said, "I do," she said OK to a tattoo and let him carve a small "Di"— short for DiAnne—on her inner leg. She was seventeen and he was nineteen in July of 1959 when they got married. I was born eight months later.

After they were married, Mom went to her first-ever dentist and Dad bought her a brand-new set of teeth. She was barely eighteen and had a full set of dentures.

Mom refused to let Dad ever see her without her teeth and she claimed that in more than forty years, he never did. I can remember them wrestling and Dad saying that he was going to take her teeth out. Mom would be screaming, "Gary, Gary, don't you dare!" He could have his hand in her mouth, thumb hooked under the top front teeth, but at the last second he would always let her win. Her teeth seemed to be the one line that Dad respected enough not to cross. I know that if one of us kids happened to walk into the bathroom while she had them out, brushing them, she could slap them back in her mouth so fast that Houdini's head would have spun. For the rest of her life, she had perfect teeth when she flashed that big smile.

Mom was always a bit afraid of Dad and she continued to play a great game of hard-to-get whenever Dad did something bad enough to require sucking up, but they really were madly in love with each other. It was obvious in the way that they looked at one another. I could tell from the early pictures of them that Dad was very naughty and *very* mesmerizing. His dark eyes could trap someone into a place that was impossible to escape.

I could also tell that Mom had something very special about her. I couldn't put my finger on it. It wasn't obvious like Dad's good looks were, but there was something about her that attracted people to her, something that made them love her forever, tell her everything, and trust her with their deepest secrets. It lasted for her entire life. Dad's good looks faded with age but his ability to make people try to please him never did. Mom spent over forty years under his spell. As did I.

Two

Married life morphed Dad from a petty criminal into a cowboy—not the trophy-buckle-wearing, PRCA-card-carrying kind, but the on-horseback-365-days-a-year kind. He fixed fences on horseback and brought baby calves into the world in the freezing snow. He went where pickups couldn't go—and he did it all with a roll-your-own cigarette between his teeth.

Though he had very little to call his own, he was always generous. Fellow cowboys could come to him with old saddles, silver bits, or spurs to hock and Dad would give them whatever he had in his pockets. He was also the kind of cowboy who loved his horses and dogs as much as his wife and kids. Dad may have loved animals but he was anything but sentimental about them.

I recall one horse that lay down too close to a fence and got its legs stuck underneath. It lay there all night struggling until it broke one of its own legs. By the next morning it was so spent that it could barely move, but Dad had better things to do with his day than waste it trying to get twelve hundred pounds of horse flesh out from under the two-by-twelve planks that made up the corral fence. I saw the big bay horse lying there helpless and exhausted. His body was drained, but his eye that faced the heavens was wide with fear, like my own. Dad sent me to the house, but I had barely made it out of the corral when I heard the gunshot.

Dogs that had the misfortune of being in the way of moving vehicles usually suffered the same fate. If one ran off yelping and limping, packing a front leg, it usually got to live. The ones that got up dragging a hip were not so lucky. He cussed them as he went to get his gun—damn that the dog was so dumb and damn that he had to do it and, "Tam, get to the house." After the shot, I would come back out and do whatever I could to avoid looking into the back of the pickup as I climbed into the cab.

Some of these animals never got proper burials but were instead discarded in the dump, which was really just a cutbank out in the hills that we unloaded our garbage into. One of the only times I recall seeing Dad show any sorrow over an animal was when his beloved cow dog, Sandy, died. His expression and body language communicated true sadness as he wrapped her in one of his winter coats before giving her to the earth.

Dad was a self-taught, accomplished horseman who was able to get a horse to do just about anything or go almost anywhere—that is, if it survived his breaking process, which was sometimes brutal and downright cruel. I wouldn't say that he was ever intentionally cruel but rather it was just the method and the era, or sometimes the outlet for his frustration. I saw a few particularly stubborn young horses tied down on the ground with big, black tarps thrown over them, roasting in the summer heat for the better part of a day. Buckets, tires, and gunnysacks were tied to all of them at one time or another and some were left saddled all night with their heads tied around to their tails. He may have inflicted the torture, but he was also the one who relieved the pain and discomfort, so they ended up trusting him and working hard to please him. He believed, and told me many times, that the best thing for the inside of a man was the outside of a horse.

Dad disciplined the dogs and us kids in pretty much the same manner. He usually had a rope in his hand, and he didn't put up with any whining or fighting. A quick lash was the most convenient way for him to punish us, so we all learned to duck our heads whenever we heard the zing of a rope. If Dad didn't have a rope in his hand, he always had a cowboy boot on his foot, so a good, swift kick in the butt was another way to silence kids or dogs that were whining, barking, or fighting. I can tell you that the knot end of a lariat hurts much more than a big stick, and I know that the toe of a Tony Lama can fit up a child's rectum.

The thing that I hated most though was when Dad would knock our heads together. Sometimes when he heard Valli and I fighting, he wouldn't say a word. Without warning, he'd just walk up to us, put a hand on each of our heads, and BAM! One thing about head-cracking is that it's an instant fight-stopper—as fast and sure as flipping a switch. Lights off, fight over. We didn't dare cry; we just rubbed our heads and tried not to pee our pants. It may have stopped the fighting, but it made each of us even more mad at the other because we blamed each other for the newly-sprouting goose eggs. When Dad had walked away, we would glare at each other with "I wish you were dead" eyes and rub our heads, silently hating each other as our headaches set in. I don't believe the dogs ever had their heads cracked together, but they had felt the sting of a rope and the kick of a boot, so we empathized with each other whenever we were in trouble.

There were two types of dogs—dumb dogs and cow dogs—and we always had at least one of each. The dumb dogs stayed home, lay in the shade, and barked whenever someone or something moved. The cow dogs followed Dad everywhere he went and actually tried to be one step ahead of him, much like I did.

If Dad headed for the ranch truck, they beat him to it and jumped in the box (I knew enough to already be in the cab, waiting). When we went to move cows, the dogs trotted alongside our horses, ears pricked, eyes always watching Dad, waiting for him to point them in the direction of a cow or to say those two little words that they loved to hear: "sic 'em!" When he gave the command, they sprang into action, biting the heels of whichever cow had been singled out, and then biting her nose if she had the audacity to turn and face them before running back into the herd. If they forgot for an instant that they were cow dogs and barked like the dumb dogs, Dad would holler and snap them with his rope. It was their reminder that they were cow dogs.

When the cows had been moved, the gate behind them shut, and we were heading for home, the dogs would follow close behind the horses' heels. Knowing that their work was done, they would trot along, relaxed and happy, their tongues hanging to the sides and their tails swinging back and forth with the rhythm of the horses' clip-clop gait.

We never fed our dogs store-bought dog food. They ate our leftovers—if we had any—smothered in the bacon grease that was left in the pan from breakfast. And they ate horseshit. If there's one thing I know about cow dogs, it's that they are the horseshit-eatingest dogs that I have ever seen. Ours ate more shit than the dumb dogs, which really begs the question, "Who are the dumb dogs now?" After Dad and eating shit, the dogs' next love was rolling in dead cows or deer that they had sniffed out along the trail. That made them about as pet-friendly as porcupines.

When it was exceptionally cold outside and Val and I didn't want to be on horseback all day, the dogs backed us up by not automatically following the horses. Instead, they would have to be coaxed by Dad, talking in a nice voice and bribing them with "sic 'em" promises, because all they really wanted to do was curl up in the barn or the haystack while we curled up in the house.

Dad never offered any sweet talk to us kids. He just told us to "get saddled up," and we got no sympathy from him if we weren't smart enough to dress for the weather or remember to tie our yellow rain slickers to the backs of our saddles. I never complained to him if I was cold or wet. I just learned to curl my toes inside my cowboy boots, tuck my chin into my neck scarf, and breathe out through my nose so that my warm breath blew down onto my bare skin.

The dogs, the horses, and us kids were all loyal to Dad, and all of us respected and admired him—possibly more out of fear than love.

Three

Iconsider my Dad to be a complex man, who was often misunderstood. To say he was a loner or anti-social would be an understatement.

We moved from ranch to ranch, always looking for a little more money and a place a little farther out in the sticks. He was a hard-working cowboy who wanted to better himself and his family, but if he had to put up hay, fix equipment, or irrigate, we would be pulling up stakes.

We always had an old horse trailer and a couple of horses and just about everything else we owned could fit into the back of our pickup truck. We could be loaded up and ready to move in a few hours, so a move was always equated with chaos. Mom packed us up at a frantic pace, wrapping breakables in newspapers and putting them into boxes, then hustling the boxes to the pickup. Dad handled the heavy stuff, but we didn't have big furniture like couches, china cupboards, or a dining room table. We had a small kitchen table with a speckled, red and gray Formica top, and four cracked, vinyl-covered chairs. We had a coffee table made of fake blonde wood, which had a matching end table with a wobbly leg—courtesy of a previous move—and we had our own beds.

On moving days, nothing was more important than getting gone. Valli found that out the hard way—she almost became a victim of a move when we were getting ready to leave Forsyth. Dad had taken the beds apart and had the frames leaning up against the wall while he man-handled the mattresses to the pickup. Val came walking into the bedroom just as one of the frames lost its balance. It came crashing down on her, cracking her head open like a soft-boiled egg that had been whacked with a knife. Blood spilled out like a runny yolk, staining her blonde hair. She probably should have had stitches to patch the gash in her head, but all she got was an order to "get the hell out of the way," or she would be "guaran-goddamn-teed to get hurt." To this day, if she parts her hair down the middle, the scar is still visible.

If we lived in any one place long enough to accumulate more stuff than we could fit in the pickup and horse trailer, we left it. Mom was usually sullen and teary-eyed when we were packing up because she knew that some old treasure of hers was most likely going to be left for whoever moved in next. Val and I helped, but tried to stay out of the way. We kept our eyes on the items being packed up, hoping to see that our stuff was going to make the cut. Cats often got left behind if we couldn't find or catch them when it was time to pull out. The dogs were used to seeing us pack up, so they stayed near the pickup, ready to jump in at the last minute. None of us wanted to be left behind with the cats, an old chair, some books, and a few houseplants—not even the dumb dogs.

Four

Moving was the one consistency in our lives, unless you count being broke. Everything else Dad did was spontaneous and unpredictable. On more than one occasion, Val and I awoke in the middle of the night to the sound of him saying, "Get in the pickup, we're going to Billings." That was where our three grandmas lived, and going there usually meant that we were out of money and Dad was about ready to change jobs again.

When we got to Billings, we would stay with Grandma Wanda, my dad's mother. She was always good for a few bucks—very few, but even a couple mattered. Dad would never ask, but Grandma had a way of knowing. When we would get back home, there would be twenty-five or fifty bucks slipped into a dozen eggs, a pie, or a package of homemade rolls.

Grandma was a stout little spitfire of a woman—beautiful, with dark hair and eyes like Dad's, which made it obvious where he got his looks. She was tough-talking and she had a knack for making Dad seem like a little boy. She was the one person I knew who wasn't afraid of him. Grandma could out-cuss, out-stare, out-boss, out-bully, and out-holler him, and she was the only person I ever saw my dad back down from. I never knew if it was out of fear or respect, but I suspect that it was a little bit of each.

Grandma appreciated the finer things in life and she worked hard to have just a few of life's little luxuries. She introduced us girls to down comforters, feather beds, and 800-thread count Egyptian cotton sheets. She loved fancy table linens, good cookware, heavy stainless steel flatware, expensive crystal, and fine china. She worked her butt off and saved her tips to be able to pay for them. She once coughed up fifteen thousand dollars, mostly in quarters, to buy an old house.

She was also a fabulous cook and we never showed up on her doorstep when she didn't have a ham or turkey, rolls, pies, cakes, and cookies made. We were force-fed all day long. "What do you want to eat?" were always the first words out of her mouth. Even if we said, "Nothing," or "I'm not hungry," she still began piling food in front of us.

Every time one of our midnight trips ended at her place, Valli and I would climb into bed with her, one of us on each side, and she would try to terrify us with ghost stories. Her voice would quiver and she would pull the covers up tight under our chins. Her dark eyes would widen and glow in the dark as she looked back and forth between us, talking through clenched teeth and making her lips so tight and thin that we could barely see them. We hung on her every word and our toes curled with fright as we listened. The visual, however, was another story—Grandma always slept with massive amounts of toilet paper wrapped around her up-do, trying to keep every hair in place until her next weekly hair appointment. There is just something about lying in bed with someone who resembles a giant Q-tip that takes the edge off of a ghost story.

Behind all of the toughness that she showed toward Dad was a soft spot. It broke her heart to see us kids going without Christmas presents or new school clothes, so she always came through when my parents weren't able to. She had a way of making us all feel safe.

Our other two grandmas were my mom's mother and grandmother, who lived together for their entire lives. These two grandmas had nearly nothing to spare, but we could always count on them for one meal of macaroni and ketchup.

My great-grandma had been the oldest child in a family of thirteen children and she was a wonderful old lady who always wore a dress and kept her long, gray hair in a bun at the nape of her neck. For the thirty years that I knew her, she wore the same, sensible shoes—in black Monday through Saturday, and white on Sundays. She slept in the same twin bed, with the same little stainless steel flashlight at her bedside, and every morning she read her daily devotional book using a big, round magnifying glass. Afternoons were spent crocheting plastic bread bags into rugs. Unlike Grandma Wanda, my great-grandma would not have said a swear word to save her own life.

My mom's mom, Grandma Irene, was crazy—certified, double-stamped. She did a few stints at the state mental hospital in Warm Springs, Montana. Some of my favorite memories of her are from the times when she would drag my preschool-aged butt about forty-five blocks uptown to the Spur Bar. I usually whined at about block twenty-five, my little legs tired from running to keep up with this crazy lady who was hell-bent on meeting some loser and having a vodka tonic and a cigarette at two o'clock in the afternoon.

When we would finally get to the Spur, I would feel pretty proud, sitting on a barstool, my legs swinging back and forth, drinking soda through a skinny, striped cocktail straw. I loved everything about the bar scene—the clinking, colored bottles, the dim lights, and the shadows that they cast. I was spellbound, watching the bartenders grab glasses, two at a time, and plunge them into the small, silver sinks, and the pool players as they magically flipped the little, white triangle in their hands. The sounds of the pool balls banging together and the "squeak-squeak" of the blue chalk on the end of a pool stick were music to my ears. I also loved the jukebox, with its fascinating neon colors, and I would drum my fingers on the bar as if sitting at a bar, listening to music, and drumming my fingers was something I did every day.

Grandma never really knew any of the men's names and they never knew mine. She always just said, "This is my granddaughter." She had been deaf for her entire life, due to a childhood fever, so her speech was impaired, which made her difficult to understand. I heard enough at the bar to know that the men she drank with didn't care that they couldn't understand her or that she couldn't hear them. This was a side of my grandmother that I would otherwise have never known—flirting, smoking, and drinking alcohol—and I adored her for it.

It was the walk home that I hated, so we usually stopped at Woolworth's and she bought me a little trinket in exchange for my silence. We never spoke to Great-Grandma or Mom or Dad about our barhopping. It was definitely our little secret.

Whenever my dad decided that these trips to Billings were necessary, my sister and I would climb into the bed of the pickup truck, hunker down in our sleeping bags, and sleep until we got to Billings. This normally took anywhere from two to four hours, depending on where we were living at the time, and they usually occurred in the middle of the night.

On one of the more memorable trips, I woke up to find that I was being choked out by smoke. Thinking that a farmer must have been burning his fields, I pulled the bag tighter over my head and tried to go back to sleep, but I couldn't keep the smoke out of my sleeping bag. I finally stuck my head out long enough to figure out that the smoke was coming from a fire in the back of the pickup!

I began pounding on the window to get my dad's attention. It was dark outside so he had failed to notice the thick, black smoke boiling out from behind the cab. When he finally heard my urgent hammering, he pulled to the side of the road, nonchalantly picked up the smoking spare tire, and pitched it in the ditch. Then he made a few swats at our sleeping bags with a smoldering gunnysack, which he discarded with the tire. Apparently he had thrown a cigarette out the window and it had landed in the back, catching our sleeping bags on fire, which then caught the spare tire on fire. If Valerie even woke up, she never let on.

Most of the time, we had a small camper shell on the bed of the pickup and Val and I were forced to ride in there. We always lived on about a million miles of dirt road, so the dust would boil into the back, through the cracks between the camper and the bed of the truck. It was particularly bad in the summer, as it could also be unbearably hot. At times we would emerge looking like we had been dipped in talcum powder.

Mom always sat in the center of the pickup, next to Dad, rather than on the passenger side. That meant that it was impossible to get her attention. She sat so close to him that they didn't even have to turn their heads to speak. There were two glass windows between them and us, so no matter how hard we pounded, Mom and Dad rarely ever heard us. While we were being forced into the camper, we would beg Mom to look back at us every ten minutes or so. She always said that she would but she hardly ever did. We usually only tried to get her attention for important reasons, like not being able to breathe through the dust, or having to pee.

We usually had a stinking dog or two in the back with us, too. They would immediately jump into the camper when the door was thrown open so that they could stake their places on the little foam mattress. Most of the rest of the bed of the pickup was covered up with stuff like a spare tire, a jack, a cooler, chains, buckets, and tools. We would fight the dogs for position, each of us wanting to be near a window because of the dead cow stench that the dogs always wore. They would always win out and get the best spots if they got too close to us with their hot, panting, horseshit breath.

One time we emerged with a major case of fleas, courtesy of the dogs. Thank God the friends that we had gone to visit had real flea powder. Dad told Mom to douse us with that instead of the kerosene that we usually used to rub down the dogs when they got fleas. That night, we were bathed in Hartz 2 in 1 Flea & Tick Powder.

On another late-night trip to Billings, we went to bed in the camper, only to arrive in comatose states. When the camper door was thrown open and we were ordered to "get up and out," Dad found that we could not be aroused. The strange smell was his first clue that something wasn't right. Digging around, he found a can of ether that was leaking. We were so out of it that someone could have done major surgery on us and we would have slept through it. I am now thankful that this was before the days of kidney harvesting. With four good ones between us, we were prime candidates for that little procedure. Not to mention, our folks were really broke.

Five

Val and I spent our childhood living like gypsies. Being uprooted as often as we were meant that we were always the new kids in town and the interlopers of playground politics. Rather than just ignore the taunting and insults or endure an initiation, I would throw punches. I fought some of Val's battles too—partly to defend her, but mostly because it gave me license to go home and brag to Dad that I had beaten up on someone, preferably a boy. The payoff for me came in the form of his, "Atta girl," a slap on the back, or a shit-eating grin. His ways of telling me that he was proud of me were always unspoken. It wasn't that I wanted to be a bully. It was the one place in my life where I was able to stand up for myself, so I reconciled it by circumstance and the circumstance was that I was always the new kid.

Dad wanted to make me tough and did nothing to discourage my fighting. He bought me Copenhagen or Skoal and I could chew and spit as well as any boy. When I was in the sixth grade in Cody, Wyoming, I beat up a boy for taking a basketball away from me. The teacher threatened to call my parents so I went home and forewarned Dad, who said, "Let the old bitch call me. I'll just ask her, 'Whadda ya expect from a girl who chews snoose?'" I was so relieved and pumped up that I could have whipped the entire sixth-grade class. I was sure, at that point, that I could have taken up cigarettes, bourbon, and poker and Dad wouldn't have cared.

Even as kids, Val and I were polar opposites. She was always the sweet, sensitive kid who cried easily and often. Her feelings would be hurt if someone told her that her shoes were ugly. She was a caregiver—distempered kittens with their puss-filled eyes stuck shut would send her on around-the-clock kitten-nursing missions. Val was a peacemaker and quite a good little negotiator. She used her reasoning powers to get her point across, to defend herself, or to get out of having to help ride if it was really cold outside. She could sometimes negotiate herself right out of trouble.

I, on the other hand, had a brick wall up around my heart. I was insensitive and unsympathetic about everything. Sick kitties or puppies in gunnysacks, destined for the river, didn't even make me flinch—at least, not on the outside. If I had feelings, I pretended not to so that it was impossible to hurt them. I would bite through my lip to keep from crying if I had to. When I was mad, I pouted and refused to speak. I internalized everything so much that I should have spontaneously combusted.

Val made friends easily so she always had many of them, which made her hate the impending moves. After the first day at a new school, she would come home with a new best friend, and by the end of the week she had sleepover invites. I found it hard to make friends and I hated school, so I liked moving and was always ready to go somewhere else and start over.

Being a tomboy and Dad's right-hand man meant that I spent most of my days with him, and most of those days were spent on horseback. I could ride, rope, shoot a gun, roll a cigarette for Dad, pee standing up, hook up a calf-puller and a three-point hitch, run a PTO, post-pounder, and wire stretcher, and identify any tool that Dad asked me to get for him: three-sixteenths ratchet, quarter-inch wrench, half-inch socket, clinchers, nippers, wire pliers—I knew them all. I dug out my slivers with a pocketknife and I blew my nose by placing my thumb on one nostril and firing a snot rocket into the dirt.

Although Valli could ride a horse, most of the time she preferred not to, so unless Dad needed everyone's help, she was left at home with Mom. She did girly things like help Mom clean the house, hang clothes on the line, bake cupcakes, and sew. She knew a loaf pan from a Bundt pan and the difference between a bobbin and a zipper foot. I still don't know what either one is.

Since we had so little in common my sister and I never got along very well. Looking back, I'm pretty certain that I was downright mean to her. Maybe it was just the pecking order or maybe I inherited Dad's mean streak, but I don't recall having any real feelings toward her, one way or the other. It wasn't that I didn't like her, I just didn't care. As a kid, I felt pretty numb toward everyone and everything. To me, she seemed as disposable as the cats and dogs. I'm ashamed to admit that now. I thank God that somewhere along the way she forgave me, not only for being a shitty big sister, but for being a mean one too.

Six

My mother was a 110-pound fireball and the perfect ranch wife—incredibly low-maintenance, never asking for anything and expecting even less. Breakfast, lunch, and dinner were on the table at six, twelve, and six. She kept a spotless house even though most of the houses we lived in were nothing more than shacks equipped with mouse populations that resembled medium-sized prairie dog colonies, some crappy dressers with drawers that were stuck shut . . . and cats. We always had cats—mostly feral ones with squatters' rights that had taken up residence long before we moved in. Dad did his part to keep the inbred kitten population in check by stuffing the heads of any tomcats that we could catch into cowboy boots so he could neuter them. If we ever saw them again, Val was quite good at turning them into cats that wore doll clothes and bonnets.

Mom washed walls, sewed bed sheets into curtains, and turned old Navajo saddle blankets into rugs to cover up ripped-up linoleum. The wind would blow dirt right through the walls of our shanty, but there was never any dust on our plastic flowers.

She milked cows, churned her own butter, made her own cottage cheese, and always had a crockery jar of sourdough starter on the kitchen counter. Mom helped Dad when he needed her to and she could nurse a bum calf back to life, as well as doctor a wire-cut horse and cook for a branding crew, all in the same day—all before noon, if necessary.

My mother worshipped the sun like it was some kind of god and her copper-colored body was proof that she had been baptized as a faithful follower. She would lay stark naked in a lawn chair for hours with little, round, black glasses that I couldn't see through covering her eyes. Her skin would be shiny and slick, covered with oil. She wore so much oil that the little beads of sweat that covered our skin didn't stand a chance of popping up through all the oil on hers. When she turned over onto her stomach, one of us would oil up her backside and then she would read or sleep while she lay facedown, deep-frying in the sun. This was in the late sixties and early seventies, before sunscreen and skin cancer scares, so the browner she got, the more beautiful we all thought she looked.

When she went to town, she traded her Levi's and cowboy boots for mini-skirts and go-go boots and put her hair up in a bun (a "French roll," as she would call it). When I was in elementary school, I knew that I had a younger, prettier mom than anyone in my class, and I'm pretty sure that I was the only kid with a mother who had a tattoo.

For most of the time that we spent on the ranch, Mom was in jeans and boots with her thick, red hair in a braid hanging down her back. She would work all day alongside my dad, wearing coveralls, mud boots, and a cap, or whatever the season demanded. Then she would come home, get all dolled up, and put on something sexy for Dad. I later figured out that lingerie is not—at most peoples' houses, anyway—considered acceptable dinner attire.

In those days, the one thing that we did have plenty of was beef. Every ranch job included it—400 dollars a month and beef. The next job would be 425 dollars a month and beef, and the next would be 450 dollars a month and beef. For 25 dollars, we moved, as long as beef was included.

Dad thought that pork was precious—probably because we had to pay for it—so it was usually only served for breakfast. The only times we had chicken were when we were at a restaurant or Grandma Wanda's house, and we had fish just once or twice a year. One time was always on my birthday, when I got to choose whatever I wanted for dinner and Mom would make me fish sticks. The second time only came if my Uncle Bart went fishing and caught some trout.

As kids, we were forced to sit at the table, under the threat of an ass-kicking, until we cleaned our plates. This usually came with a deadline such as, "Your ass is grass if your plate isn't clean by eight o'clock." I can't begin to tell you how many cold scalloped potatoes, fatty or grisly pieces of meat, soggy chunks of zucchini, and cold, greasy onions I choked down just seconds before the deadline. I always chose the food over my ass being grass. On the upside of that, at least I can honestly say that I never had to go to bed hungry.

One morning I was pushing a big, thick, fatty, undercooked hunk of bacon around on my plate, hoping to stall long enough that I would have to make a mad dash to the school bus and get out of eating it. I should have known better. It wasn't about to go unnoticed.

"Eat your bacon," Dad ordered.

"It's fat," I said.

"Eat it; it's not fat."

End of discussion. I put the fatty bacon in my mouth and held it there, unable to swallow. Having not stalled long enough, I had to keep it in my mouth for what seemed like hours, but was probably about ten minutes. Then I got my books and walked to the bus stop, all while holding that slimy, wet, swollen piece of lard in my mouth. It felt like I had a frog, fresh out of a pond full of scum, sitting on my tongue. I waited about another five minutes for the bus and then, just before I stepped inside its doors, spit the frog-bacon in the snow.

I spent the entire day with my stomach in a knot, worrying that Dad would find that hunk of fatty slime and thump me when I got home. The fact that the snow was powdery and about twelve inches deep did little to comfort me; I still worried myself sick about it all day.

It was during those years that I made a promise to my future children—I would never make them eat things they hated or sit at the table until they cleaned their plates.

Larry and I used to have arguments over the fact that I have let Savannah eat ice cream for breakfast every day since she was old enough to ask for it. It was dairy and at least she was eating, I reasoned. Popcorn for dinner wasn't going to stunt her growth or turn her into a vegan, so I really didn't see the harm in that either.

To this day, I can't waste food—I'm a leftover queen. If I do leave something on my plate, it goes in a to-go box or a container and then is pushed into a far corner of my already overcrowded refrigerator. That doesn't mean that I'm going to eat it. It just means that I can't throw it away until it resembles a science project.

All those days of forced beef-eating probably contributed to Valerie being a vegetarian ever since she got old enough to make her own food choices. Watching our mother cry while she plucked and cleaned prairie chickens and pheasants that Dad had tossed into the kitchen sink after having shot or run over them, probably sealed the deal for her.

Mom would cuss and cry and try not to gag while she plucked feathers and took those little sacks of dirt, or chicken shit, or whatever they were, out of their craws. She would continue swearing while she cut the stinking things up and cooked them, all because Dad didn't want to waste the meat and thought it would be a nice change from beef. I'm not insinuating here that we ate roadkill, but I won't deny that, occasionally, pheasants that had happened to fly up in front of our pickup landed right smack on our dinner table. Those were some of the nights when we sat at the table under the threat of an ass-kicking, until our deadline came.

These days, Valerie is not the only vegetarian in the family. Saul, Dustin, and Hannah also turn their noses up at meat, which just chaps Dad's ass to no end.

Seven

I'm not sure where, why, or how my passion for food began.

Mom never really liked cooking and considered it to be a chore. I think she had a repertoire of about eight dinners that varied little from week to week. Sunday was always roast beef with potatoes and carrots and the next six days consisted of spaghetti, cube steak, meatloaf, and three days of something with round steak, stew meat, or hamburger. The eighth item was lasagna, which she made just once every few months. It was divine and compliments rolled off our tongues like collapsing dominoes as she dished up our plates.

Dad never cooked when we were kids, but by 1985 he was doing all of the cooking. Big breakfasts, long-simmering stews, and soups full of beans were his specialties. He aged cabbage in a huge crockery pot to make his own sauerkraut and he became obsessive about canning vegetables and deer meat. He also helped Mom turn Kool-Aid and berries (that he'd picked himself) into jellies and jams. He and his pressure-cooker were inseparable.

Now I am what you might call "food-obsessed." Before my feet even hit the floor in the morning, I am planning dinner. In my house, "What do you want for dinner?" always follows, "Good morning," and many times I fill every separate request. From Larry's steak and potatoes to Sierra's pasta and cream sauce, Savannah's chicken and dumplings to my own seafood preference, it's nothing new for me to make three or four different entrees in the same evening. I'm like a short-order cook in my own kitchen and I take great pleasure in pleasing every person's palette.

White truffle oil, champagne vinegar, capers, and goat cheese are considered staples in my kitchen. And don't even think about trying to sneak any stinky, polyester cheese in a green can past anyone in this house. They all know real Parmigiano-Reggiano when they taste it! My cream sauces are so rich that they alone could send you to the ER.

Valerie is a great cook and is almost as food-obsessed as I am, but on a much healthier level. Steel-cut oats, granola, hummus, soymilk, and natural peanut butter are staples in her kitchen. If I cook a cheeseburger, it's one hundred percent ground sirloin and it's guaran-damn-teed to bump your cholesterol up and do some damage to your arteries. Angioplasty is served on the side, with the fries. Valerie's Gardenburger is perfectly cooked and beautifully garnished with heirloom tomatoes and organic lettuce, served with a side of homemade baked sweet potato fries. It's definitely healthier—and a lot drier. Still, I do have to admit that her homemade pesto pizza can kick my pesto pizza's butt.

Besides sharing a passion for food, Val and I are both loving mothers with a devotion to our kids like that of the Pope to the cross, but we parent in totally different ways. Valerie is a perfect mother, possessing patience and reasoning powers that I can't comprehend, and she is compassionate and sympathetic about even the smallest boo-boo. I have a much more matter-of-fact approach. My kids know the rules: unless they are on fire or have a bone poking out, they aren't really hurt.

I would bet the farm that Val has never spanked her little darlings and I can say with certainty that she never sat on one of her children with her hands wrapped around a tiny throat, seriously thinking about ending one of their little lives. But then, she never had Sierra for a child. I only did it once, and I did let her live, but still, Val makes me look bad.

Valerie doesn't raise her voice when she's mad—only her pitch goes up. I raise my pitch too, but that's usually when I'm aiming at their heads instead of their behinds, with a shoe, wooden spoon, or Tupperware bowl.

Once when my girls were fighting, Savannah picked up my paring knife and began to chase Sierra with it poised over her shoulder, like in a scene from a bad horror movie.

"Savannah!" I screamed, "Put that knife down right this minute!" She stopped dead in her tracks, deflated, and slapped the paring knife back on my cutting board.

Sierra gloated, "Nah-nah-nah-nah-nah."

"Use this one instead," I said, handing Savannah my chef's knife with an eight-inch blade. Sierra's gloating turned to fear as she ran off screaming. I did catch Savannah by the scruff of her neck before she could actually stab her sister, so no harm, no foul. Valerie would have just put them in time-out.

While Val was giving her kids good advice like, "Don't smoke, don't drink, and don't have unprotected sex," my best parental advice was: Don't take a knife to a gunfight. Don't ever let me catch you putting a tomato in the refrigerator. Don't lick the beaters while the mixer's still running.

I'd like to think that I am a good mother—just in a funny kind of way. Valli may be a little more practical than I am, but the one thing we do have in common in motherhood is that we love our kids passionately and unconditionally. We would kill anyone who ever tried to do them harm—except for maybe Dad, that is. Oh, we'd want to kill him. We would just have to ask his permission first. Or sneak it by him.

Eight

In our family, drinking is almost as important as eating—drinking alcohol, that is. I swear it's in our DNA.

When Val and I were kids, Dad rarely drank, mostly because he couldn't afford to and he didn't have time. If he did drink—usually after a rodeo—he only had a few beers. If he had winnings in his pocket, we would go to the local supper club for dinner and we kids would get to drink Shirley Temples and eat fried chicken. If he didn't have winnings, he would pick up a six-pack and drink it on the way home, and we'd eat whatever Mom had packed in the cooler. In those days, he rarely got out of hand and was a pretty happy beer-drinker.

Whiskey was something he liked but seldom drank. The hard stuff made Dad mean—his dark brown eyes would turn squinty and black and his mouth would take on an Elvis-like sneer. He would light one cigarette off of another and sometimes he would smoke two at a time, tapping them on the edge of the ashtray a little too hard. He usually only went on the hooch when we went to visit his brothers.

Uncle Dean and Uncle Bart were extremely handsome, charming, and quick-witted men who were always very good to us. When Dad got together with them, they always had a great time and the booze flowed like water—it was a safe bet that that it wouldn't stop until it ran completely dry.

"Instant asshole: just add alcohol," Mom would say behind Dad's back, like she was reading the label on some new kind of instant drink mix.

Uncle Bart loved his gin and tonics and when he drank, he got cocky and arrogant and he thought he was funny, cracking jokes and then laughing like crazy. Dad and Uncle Bart would drink until they got drunk and stupid and then sometimes they would try to pick fights with Mom and Aunt Katie. If the girls didn't fight back, they would occasionally end up in fights with each other; they would try to out-smart-ass each other and end up arguing about something dumb—like how many miles it was to somewhere that neither had ever been nor cared to go. I remember a few times when they ended up getting into a full-blown pissing match.

One time after Dad and Uncle Bart had gotten into an argument, Val and I were told to get our butts in the pickup because we were leaving, "pronto," Mom said. Dad was pissed at Mom because he thought she had stuck up for Uncle Bart during one of their dumb arguments. She started to say something to defend herself and Dad reached out to backhand her, but since Mom was sitting right next to him, his elbow connected with her nose. His hand actually reached farther across the pickup than he intended and he accidently smacked Valli, who was sitting next to Mom, right in the kisser. She and Mom both silently cried all the way back to Grandma Wanda's house. I kept myself pressed up against the passenger-side door and pretended to be asleep.

Uncle Dean was a Canadian whiskey drinker, putting away the better part of a bottle of MacNaughton's almost daily. Johnny Cash songs, all starting with the same "I Walk the Line" chords, poured out of his guitar as fast as the hard stuff poured out of the bottle. Dad, with one hand wrapped around a small bar glass and the other one pinching a cigarette, would just watch Uncle Dean, tap his foot in time, and smile. Dad would make song requests, but would never sing along as Uncle Dean played them. In my entire life, the only words I've ever heard my dad sing are the first seven words of "Grandma Got Run Over by a Reindeer" (which, by the way, are "Grandma got run over by a reindeer").

Mom loved music and was always singing—especially when she was cleaning house, which was constantly. She belted out the chorus of every song, like a Cinderella turned Tammy Wynette. If she didn't know all the words, she simply hummed or used her tongue to make a low-pitched clicking noise that resembled a cuckoo clock's ticking. She would sing along with Uncle Dean if she wasn't mad about having just been picked on by the drunken duo. When that was the case, they would feel bad and try to lure her back into the group with her favorite songs.

Mom and Dad rarely fought and he seldom raised a hand toward her if he wasn't drinking. In fact, most of the time they were downright lovey-dovey—pathetically so. Their attraction to and infatuation with each other was powerful. It was nearly impossible for them to walk past each other without touching. I don't think I ever heard Dad actually say those three little words to Mom, but I knew that he was crazy about her and was completely devoted to her. The looks they exchanged were electric and Mom melted like butter when Dad slid his hand up the back of her shirt. His touch always brought goose bumps to her skin and sent a shiver down her spine. Mom's only purpose in life seemed to be pleasing her man.

I never doubted for a second that they loved us girls. With Mom, it was obvious and explicit; with Dad, it was implicit. I learned of his love by reading meaning into the little things, like when I was getting ready to ride into the arena to compete at a rodeo. Dad would casually walk up to the left side of my horse, check my cinch to make sure it was tight, pretend to check my tie-down or curb chain, then lightly tap my left leg twice with his fist, saying, "Come a-jobbin' cowgirl, come a-jobbin'." If he didn't do that little ritual, I would think that I had disappointed him the last time out. On certain occasions, like when I did well in a rodeo or Val baked a really good cake, Mom would gush, "Your dad is so proud of you!" It was almost as good as hearing him say it.

I also always knew that my mom and my dad put each other first. As a kid, I thought that was how love worked when you got married. And it did—until I had kids of my own. From the moment I first held each of my baby girls, I knew that I would take a bullet for either of them without even thinking twice about it. I love Larry too. I love him madly and would probably still take that bullet for him, but I have to admit that for at least a second or two, there would be a good possibility that my husband was going to die from a gunshot wound.

Part Two

The Dead Bed

Nine

I t's cancer," Mom said matter-of-factly.

"Shit!" I spit the word into the buerre blanc sauce that I was frantically stirring. I was mostly referring to the texture of my sauce, not my mom's news.

"Shit, Mom," I said again, adjusting the phone to my ear, this time responding to her bad news—news that I had heard many times over the years. Then I fired off the usual round of questions that I had learned to ask.

"Are you sure? What did the doctors say? Are you going to get a second opinion? Have you told Valli? What does Dad say?"

It was October of 2000, and it had been about five-and–a-half years since the last time Mom had dropped the cancer bomb.

That last time was in the summer of 1995. Mom and Dad were living in Pompey's Pillar, Montana and had come to my house for a visit. I was expecting her to bring dessert, but she also brought along bad news.

"I have breast cancer," she told me, then started crying softly, almost immediately upon entering my house.

My mind was racing with questions but I didn't know what to say, so I just hugged her and told her I was sorry.

"It'll be OK. I'll have surgery and I'll be fine," she said, patting my back like I was the one who needed comforting. She stopped crying as suddenly as she had started.

"I brought a rhubarb pie—tastes like strawberry. What's for dinner?" she asked, changing the subject.

"Spicy pork tenderloin with mango salsa and roasted garlic mashed potatoes. Where's Dad?"

"He's in the pickup, drunk," she said, sounding apologetic. She took the plates out of my hands and began setting the table.

I called to Savannah to tell her to go out and tell her grandpa that it was time to come in for dinner. I heard her go out the door and then I heard the pickup start up.

"He'd better not be driving anywhere if he's drunk," I said to Mom. We both went to the window and looked out to see the pickup pulling out of the driveway. *He* wasn't driving—my eight-year-old daughter was!

"Oh, that's just great," I said. "He's letting Savannah drive." In my mind, I was trying to figure out who was the most capable person to be behind the wheel—my daughter or my drunken father. I decided that my money was on Savannah.

"Damn him," I said, feeling my insides getting hot.

"She'll be fine. He won't let anything happen to her," Mom said, defending him but sounding a bit panicked.

"Mom, he's drunk! She's eight, and last time I checked she couldn't even spell driver's license, much less have one. What don't you get?" I asked, noticing the panic in my own voice.

I saw the hurt in her eyes and immediately apologized and lowered my voice. "It's just really stupid of him," I told her, shaking my head in disgust. Once again, Dad had managed to turn something that should have been about her into something all about him.

Twenty minutes later, Savannah came jumping and skipping into the house with Dad staggering in behind her.

"Grandpa let me drive," she proudly announced.

"Really?" I asked, trying to act surprised, "How'd you do?" I shot Dad a dirty look.

"Good! Grandpa said I did good and that I could drive him next time too!" She gave me a big, triumphant smile. He gave me a shit-eating grin.

"We'll see," I said to her, not making eye contact because I knew I was lying.

"You're an asshole," I said to him, under my breath, as I turned my back.

Ten

I vaguely remember the first time. I was about twelve, so Val was around ten. I don't recall the actual details or being told anything specific by either one of my parents, but I know that Mom had a very large "spot" on her forehead. I learned the word "melanoma" years later. I knew that it was serious because my parents talked in whispers, and Mom confirmed that with the way she hugged us when she left for the hospital. She came home a week later looking like a mummy, her big, brown, glazed-over eyes peeking out from beneath tons of gauze. She must have been on a lot of drugs because she didn't act like herself. She talked crazy, which scared us and made us avoid her—and she didn't wait on Dad hand and foot.

Dad must have been scared to death for her too. He stayed drunk for three or four days, then got on an airplane for the first time ever and disappeared for two weeks.

When her drug haze wore off, Mom was sick with worry. That rubbed off on Val and I, so all three of us chewed our fingernails and were despondent together, not knowing if he was dead or alive. I was so concerned about Dad that I forgot to worry about Mom.

A couple of years later, when Mom was about thirty-two, she had a complete hysterectomy. She was hemorrhaging and the doctor said she had uterine cancer. After the surgery, the doctor said, "I don't know what to tell you, DiAnne. There was no cancer. Somebody bigger than me must have stepped in."

In the next twenty-some-odd years, my mother had her share of cancer scares; there were spots and lumps and then there were biopsies, lumpectomies, or other procedures. Somehow everything had always turned out fine, so when she stood in my kitchen in 1995 and told me that she had breast cancer, I thought that it would all be OK again. We just had to jump through the hoops first. Surgery would be a mastectomy and the removal of some lymph nodes, along with my respect for my father.

Dad and I were standing next to Mom's bed, just before she went into surgery.

"Mom," I pleaded, "Will you please use this time to your advantage and quit smoking? You are going to be in the hospital for at least a week, so this is the perfect time to quit." I qualified my point, just in case she didn't see it that way. Talking about quitting smoking was always a touchy subject around Dad.

"Her cancer isn't from smoking," he pointed out to me. He was rubbing her arm in a random, uneven rhythm.

"Still, it would be a good time to quit." I offered my rebuttal on a silver platter, like it was a fancy canapé at a cocktail party.

"I asked the doctor if he could make me a little tobacco pouch out of your ma's tit," Dad said, patting her arm and waving away my offer.

I had no comeback for that, so I just shut up and continued to hold Mom's other hand, trying not to squeeze too hard in my attempt to avoid screaming. Mom was ignoring both of us, but Dad's statement sure ended the smoking discussion. She came through the surgery like an emotional workhorse. Other than that first time that she told me, I never saw her cry. She had absolutely no follow-up treatment. No chemo, no radiation, no reconstruction—just a little pill called Tamoxifen.

"All cured; go home," we were told.

"Your father has just been a saint," Mom told me one morning while looking at me in the bathroom mirror as I fixed her hair. It was a few days after she had come home from the hospital and I was staying with her so I could help. "He has been so loving and concerned and so worried about me," she gushed, while her arm was strapped tightly to her side and I was trying to get her short, coarse, thick hair to bend into a curl.

Looking someone in the eye in the mirror and looking someone in the eye dead-on are two different things. I fixed Mom's hair all the time—at least three to five times a week when we lived next door to each other—and I realized that a lot of our conversations took place in the mirror. Dad was always sweeter and more loving in the mirror. He said nicer things in the mirror and he didn't drink as much in the mirror. Mom looked happier in the mirror. The truth was that the mirror wasn't always a good reflection of reality.

Ten minutes later I was standing at the sink washing dishes while Mom sat at the kitchen table watching Dad nurse a hangover. He was sitting with his head down and with the palm of his right hand stuck to his forehead, while a cigarette dangled between his first two fingers, making him look like his forehead was smoking. The index finger of his left hand was hooked into a coffee cup. Mom was keeping his cup full and every few minutes she would put the ashtray up by his head and tap the ash off his cigarette, all while her left arm was in a sling, close to her chest.

From the kitchen sink, I looked over my shoulder at the two of them and wondered which was worse, having breast cancer or having my drunken father for a husband. Mom smiled back at me, unaware of my thoughts, as if to thank me for being there and to apologize for Dad, whose drinking was getting so out of control that he was drunk more often that he was sober. She nursed Dad back to health and came through the whole ordeal rather quickly, with little or no emotional scarring—at least, none that showed.

So when she phoned me with this latest announce-ment, I was worried, but not in a life or death kind of way. I was more worried about my sauce's lumps than my mother's.

Eleven

The official diagnosis was metastasized breast cancer—metastasized in the lungs. Mom and I talked every day, and every day I begged her to quit smoking. She defended herself by pointing out that her cancer was "metastasized breast cancer," *not* lung cancer and that it had nothing to do with her smoking.

In early December we learned that the cancer was also in her liver. One day, while Dad and I were talking on the phone, he admitted that he was worried too, but he was trying to sound positive and encouraging, like a coach rallying his losing team. My first clue to the fact that he was sober was that he called me "honey," as in, "It doesn't look good, honey." I was scared and he was trying to comfort me—that was my second clue that he was sober.

The next time I talked to him, I could tell that he was shit-faced. He was being a smart-ass, saying things like, "Well, you can't expect to live forever," and something about "another nail in the coffin." It felt like Mom and I both were both on opposing, losing teams.

At the time, my parents were living in Deming, New Mexico, in a thirty-two-foot camper. Mom cried when she had to move out of her sixteen-by-eighty-five-foot dream trailer house in Montana and into that little camper. Dad ignored her tears and her sulky mood. To him, it was just another move. He didn't care that her plate collection and her grandmother's dishes would forever be in storage or that her forty-five houseplants would be left behind. As long as the good cast-iron skillet, the Crock-Pot, and his tack, guns, dog, and bottle of Black Velvet got packed, he was good to go. The trailer house that they were leaving behind was the first and only home my parents had ever owned and certainly the only new house my mother had ever moved into.

Val and I talked each day about Mom's diagnosis and we were very worried about her, but we were also busy planning our trip to the Bahamas. Seven days of fun and sun—no drunken father, no sick mother. It was just what the doctor ordered, I thought.

Looking back now, I realize that we had no idea of the gravity of Mom's situation. I know that Val and I were both loving and caring daughters, but we were also stupid daughters. Stupid for believing that everything would turn out all right just because it always had in the past, and stupid for not realizing that mom may have been downplaying the severity of her condition. If I could do one thing over in my life, spending that Christmas with her would be at the top of the list.

Nevertheless, I either didn't hear the voice that nagged at me or I ignored it. By this point, Guilt felt like family to me and she was sticking her nose into our business more and more. She finally won out and convinced us to cancel our Bahamas trip, be dutiful daughters, and drag our families to the armpit of the Southwest. We tried not to dwell on the fact that this meant that we would be spending seven days sitting in our parents' smoke-infested camper, while our nights would be spent in a run-down motel.

"You do know that this means we will be trading fine dining, good wine, and casinos for frozen burritos, Budweiser, and bingo, don't you?" I asked Val.

"It will be a good test of character," she pointed out.

"I know, I know. It's the right thing to do," I admitted, feeling like Guilt was holding a gun to my head.

So the next day I told Mom that we were canceling our trip and we would spend the holidays with her and Dad. Bless her heart, she insisted that we not cancel our trip, saying she and Dad "needed this time" to "discuss her options." She said that she would begin radiation immediately, but noted that this would give her and Dad the chance to decide on other treatment options, such as chemo, which she always said she would never do. I let her persuade me because it was what I wanted to hear. She didn't have to twist our arms. We should have known that "treatment options" was code for "Screw the Bahamas and get your asses to Deming, New Mexico."

We went to the Bahamas and God punished us by making the Bahamas cold and rainy—and by giving me a kidney stone. I toughed it out for a few days, sleeping in a hot bathtub and popping valium, pain pills, and old antibiotics, before I finally went to the hospital, doubled over in pain, and told the girl at the desk to get me a bed and some drugs because I had a kidney stone.

Larry and our American Express card went another direction. I got a dose of Demerol and lapsed into La-La Land. A black Doogie Howser, all of about fifteen years old, playing dress-up with a doctor's coat and a stethoscope, took me for an ultrasound and an X-ray, then high-fived an intern after both tests concurred with my previous diagnosis. My husband held my hair as I puked; my sister asked if she could have my tennis bracelet and Fendi bag if I didn't pull through.

Larry and Val got familiar with the Nassau bus schedule as they made their way back and forth between the hotel and the hospital a few times each day to see me. A couple of days later, I passed the stone and we were able to have one fine dining experience at Greycliff, Nassau's best restaurant. Val, Saul, Larry, and I celebrated my stone's passing with a ridiculously expensive bottle of wine and an even more ridiculously expensive (but fabulous) dinner. Then we lingered after with desserts, cognac, and cigars, not one of us daring to mention Mom, Dad, or treatment options.

We pretty much abandoned the kids for the entire week, but they couldn't have really cared less. They had been having their own fun, spending their days freezing to death on the beach and their nights dancing in the bar of the hotel. On our last night there, we coaxed them away from the bar and pizza to go out for a nice dinner with us. They only agreed to go because the name of the restaurant we had chosen was The Poop Deck.

"Who wouldn't want to eat at a place called The Poop Deck?" I asked them.

"What if the food's crappy?" Sierra cracked, trying not to laugh at her own joke.

"Yeah, and what if they have shitty service?" Dustin jumped in.

"Probably will be expensive and wipe us out," Sierra continued.

"That'd be a pisser." Dustin and Sierra continued trading poop jokes until we threatened to give them swirlies if they didn't knock it off.

We spent our last day on the beach, wearing our coats and using beach towels as blankets. With the exception of The Poop Deck, the kids ate Sbarro pizza for seven straight days and never complained once. They just put their coats on every morning and went to the beach to work on their farmer tans. They found out that it *is* possible to jet-ski while wearing a coat. I decided that getting a kidney stone for Christmas in the Bahamas was still better than being in Deming with my drunken father. Val agreed. I reminded her that the next time it would be her turn to take one for the team. I survived and the skinny bitch had to wear her own clothes and jewelry home.

Twelve

On New Year's Eve, Mom was deathly ill and Dad was dead drunk. We hadn't even made it home— only to the airport in Atlanta—when we called Mom and found out that Dad had locked her out of the camper. She was staying with Les and Dixie, who were their friends and partners in the RV park. They go way back. Dad and Les had cowboyed together at a few ranches and they had all been friends for over thirty years, so they knew how Dad could be when he was on a bender.

Dad refused even to talk to Les or let him in the camper. Mom was worried about Dad, afraid that he would do something crazy like shoot himself. We worried about that too, but honestly, sometimes I just wished he would pull the trigger and get it over with so she could get back into her house. I would have been willing to lend him my gun at that point.

Besides, shooting a gun off in the house was nothing new to me. It was usually fired into the ceiling, where Mom would then hang a plant to disguise the hole. The first time Dad shot a hole in the ceiling was in the bathroom of their trailer house. The shot scared Mom half to death. She thought he had killed himself and she was afraid to go look, so she had called me, shaking with fright, whispering her worst fears.

"Well, go look," I said.

"I'm afraid. What if he's killed himself?" she asked, near tears.

"What if he kills you?"

"God, Tammi, don't say that. He would never do that." She sounded disgusted that I would even think such a thing, when I had actually been worried about that very thing for some time. I was afraid of having to read about my parents in the newspaper. "Murder-Suicide" and "Drunken Rage—Man Kills Wife, Then Self" were the headlines I imagined.

"I don't know, Mom. You can use a gun or a bottle; go look and call me back."

She didn't call back, so I knew he was OK, but I was still uneasy. Later that night, when my baby monitor went off and I got up to check on Sierra, I snuck across the road, into their house, and into their bedroom to check on them. They were both sound asleep, Dad flat on his back, his belly rising and falling, a deep, uneven snore with a little "pffff" at the end, breaking the silence of the still night. Mom was on her side, curled into the fetal position, silent—facing, but not touching him.

The next morning, Mom told me that Dad had emerged several minutes after firing the shot, as if he had just been in there taking a crap. I went into her bathroom to survey the crime scene and found that she had hung a plant in the hole and a person would have to duck around it to get to the toilet. There were lots of plants, calendars, and other things covering up the holes in their trailer house. I was worried about both of them and I made a lot of middle-of-the-night visits that they never knew about. Dad was always passed out and Mom was either sleeping or pretending to be.

Now, with her so far away, I felt completely helpless and Guilt announced her arrival by bringing out her big guns.

"How could you have been so stupid as to have gone to the Bahamas when our mother was sick?" she kept badgering me, over and over again.

"I didn't know she was *that* sick," I kept answering myself.

"What were you thinking?" she replied, passing more blame. "For Christ's sake, she has cancer! You are such a dumbass!"

"Goddamn it! I just didn't know!" I screamed back at myself. My mind was raging at me, firing questions and answers and blame all at once.

I talked to Valli and found that Guilt had paid her the same visit. I asked God to forgive me for going on vacation, or to at least let me off the hook for being a dumbass. For all the praying that I was doing, I was getting a lot of static back in my head and I wasn't sure if it was Guilt or God talking to me. I started getting their voices confused. For some reason, they sounded a lot alike to me, even though they usually made me feel differently. I was, more often than not, in touch with that, but now I was confused. It should have been black and white, good and evil, ying and yang, but now everything felt the same—gray, like Guilt and God were double-teaming me.

No doubt about it, I thought to myself, *God is still punishing me.* Passing the kidney stone now seemed like about as big a deal as passing gas.

Thirteen

I had only been back at work for a couple of days when my secretary put the call through to me.

"Tammi, your dad is on line four."

I picked up, thinking she had misunderstood. My dad didn't call me; my mom made the calls. It gave her the chance to put Dad's words into a much nicer format, editing out anything mean or anything that she wouldn't have wanted him to say.

"Tam, this is Dad," he said. I felt my stomach do the flip it always does when I hear his voice on the phone.

"Dad, what's wrong?" I asked.

"I'm just calling to tell you that if you want to see your ma, you better get your globe-trotting ass down here."

"OK, Dad. What's going on?" I asked, trying to sound like the boss I was, sitting behind my big, important desk.

"I mean, has Mom gotten worse? I talked to her yesterday. I thought she was doing a little better." I hoped that if I kept talking I could hold back the tears. I inhaled deeply and then dove head-first into what I hoped was the deep end of a pool of courage.

"Dad," I said, "We need to talk about your drinking. I know that you got drunk and locked mom out of the house for a whole day. I want you to think about getting into treatment." I was still using my best boss voice but trying not to sound accusatory. It was about then that I realized I had just dived into a pool of contempt.

"I didn't call to talk about me," he hissed, sending flames through the phone. "I called to tell you that if you want to see your mother, you better get your sister and get your jet-setting asses down here."

Ouch! He had bitch-slapped me through the phone, just before I quit treading hope and hit the bottom.

"OK, Dad," I said, shaking it off and stepping up to take another beating. "We'll be right there." I didn't hang up the phone. I just pushed the button to another line and called my sister.

I always drive. Val won't drive on the highway and she's a paranoid passenger. Saul drove her to my home in Wyoming and we left Friday, January 5, at about five in the afternoon. We hit the road in my diesel pickup, loaded with three John Grisham books on tape, a couple of bottles of red wine, freshly ground coffee, and half-and-half. One might have thought that we were just two girlfriends on a road trip, but we were really driving straight to hell and laughing all the way there.

The day we left home, Mom told us that Dad had not had a drink in five days. She said that he was so worried about her that he had quit. She made a point of telling us how good he had been since January 1, when he quit drinking and she got back into the house. It had only been six days since he had locked her out, so needless to say, we were suspicious.

It is 1,125 miles from Dayton to Deming. We laughed for the first one thousand miles, cried for about fifty miles, and were scared shitless for the rest. Not knowing what we were about to face put the fear of God in us like only our father can. The closer we got, the more I could feel my breathing speeding up. The last town before Deming is Hatch, New Mexico, so we stopped there to get dinner and build up the courage to drive the last fifty miles.

A chalkboard menu in the little dive we stopped at read "Bean and Cheese Burrito—$2.75," so we each ordered one.

"You want guacamole and sour cream?" the little Mexican girl behind the counter asked us.

We did and told the girl, to which she replied, "$18.70."

We looked at each other and then at the menu. "It says the bean burrito is $2.75," my sister pointed out.

The girl responded in Spanish. Now, I don't speak Spanish but I can do easy math in my head and I figured out that she charged us twelve dollars for sour cream and guacamole. I am also smart enough to know that two people can't argue in two different languages—but I tried anyway. She pretended not to speak English but she found a way to communicate.

"You have avocado and sour cream?"

"Yeah, how much is that?" Valerie asked, still suspicious of this Mexican math.

"Three dollars," the girl said, sounding sure of herself.

"*Tres dineros*?" I piped up, rolling my *r*s and using my best Spanish accent.

I could tell that she was not impressed. I did the math, adding six bucks to each of our $2.75 burritos, which suddenly made them nine-dollar burritos, so I raised an eyebrow.

She read my mind and said, "Plus tax."

I scowled at her and forked over a twenty. Valerie blamed me.

"She saw you coming with your diamonds and Fendi bag," Val accused as we walked to my pickup.

"Shut up, open the wine, and eat your ten-dollar burrito," I told her.

It was eight o' clock on Saturday night when we pulled into the Ol' West RV Park. I instantly felt sick, and though I'd like to blame the burrito for my immediate urge to hurl, I knew it wasn't the cause. Regardless, I felt shiny little beads of sweat popping up on my forehead and my upper lip.

"Buck up and let's go in," Val said as we parked at our parents' camper. She looked at me like I was glowing in the dark. I knelt down briefly at the front tire, debating between praying and puking; since I could only muster some spit and a gagging noise, I offered up a quick prayer.

"Please God, let this just be a bad dream. I am not in Deming. My mom is not sick, and I didn't just pay ten bucks for a burrito that I am about to spew."

I was walking, still bent over at the waist, trying not to get spit on my shoes when Dad threw open the door of the camper, having heard my diesel pickup pull up. I swallowed big and snapped upright, to attention, looking him directly in the eye. He gave me a warm, genuine smile and held the door open as we climbed the two metal steps into their camper. Mom was still up, waiting for us, looking anxious but tired and hollow. Dad looked surprisingly good.

Maybe he really isn't drinking, I thought to myself. Mom was skinny and looked like hell, but I had thought that she looked like that for the last couple of years—at least she had since she started living in a camper and cutting her own hair.

Dad was happy to see us, but it was getting late so we didn't talk much.

"We cleaned the clubhouse for you to stay in," he told us, which really meant that Mom and Dixie cleaned the clubhouse. "No sense paying for a motel."

He ushered us to an old building on the grounds, which they referred to as "the clubhouse." It was an old house that had been converted into a secondhand store and was filled with all the junk that the people of the Ol' West RV Park had accumulated—the type of junk that people who live in campers don't have room for. The secondhand store also consisted of a few tables and chairs and was used by the residents of the RV park for holiday dinners.

With Dad as our bell captain, we were led to our accommodations for the week. They had even put a small TV on the floor next to the bed, knowing that we both like to fall asleep with the TV on. Dad tucked us in; he seemed really proud, really sober, and really glad to have us there.

We poured ourselves glasses of wine and climbed into bed. There we sat—two spoiled bitches who are used to crawling into feather beds with 800-thread count sheets and down pillows. We were propped up, heads against the wall, drinking wine out of coffee cups, staring blankly at the pictures on the wall, which all had little white stickers that stated their prices.

"Can you fucking believe that we are sleeping in a secondhand store?" Valerie asked me.

"I can't fucking believe that we are sleeping in a store and I'm not shopping," I said.

"OK, then go shopping. It's freezing in here," she complained. "Go find us some blankets."

"It's January. There should be a white sale," I reminded her as I crawled out of bed and browsed through the four rooms of the clubhouse/store until I found some blankets. We remade the bed, doing our best to make it resemble the fluffy beds that we were used to sleeping in at home.

"Still doesn't feel right," I grumbled, crawling back under the covers.

"Get used to it, Sugar," Val told me. "You think these sheets are rough, just wait until tomorrow."

We propped up in bed, silent and trying to relax. Both of us were still in shock and lost in thought. One reason for that was how Mom looked—and how she didn't look. Another was that Dad was being so nice after having put us all through the wringer for the past few weeks. We didn't discuss it. We didn't have to. Our thoughts were so loud that we could hear them reverberating throughout the room. We turned on the TV, and although we couldn't see it while laying down, we could hear it. The ten o'clock news told us about some escaped convicts dubbed "The Texas Seven," who were supposed to be in the area.

"Oh, great," Val said, "You do realize that we are staying in the perfect hideout for a bunch of killers? They will probably break in here and knife us."

"Don't worry. I brought my gun," I told her.

"Oh, good," she said sarcastically. "They can use that to kill us."

"We could let Dad torture us to death," I pointed out. "Besides, they can't break in. The door's not locked." Neither of us had the energy to get up, so it remained unlocked.

"If there is a God," Val assured me, "He will have them take us out before morning."

"Shut up and put your eye mask on," I told her. "That way you won't see them coming."

I shared my Valium with her and we washed it down with wine. Then I laid my .38 on the floor next to the bed and killed the lights.

"I cocked it for them," I told her, as I nestled into the bed and pulled down my own eye mask. "And stop spooning me."

Fourteen

The Texas Seven didn't shop at the Ol' West RV Park Store that night, so we woke up to a freezing New Mexico morning. I got up and kicked the thermostat up and an old furnace breathed to life. It was the kind that has the big, square grate on the floor, so I could see the fire below. I stood on top of the grate, waiting for heat, taking in the odors of d-CON, mouse shit, and cigarette smoke. It reminded me of some of the places we lived in as kids.

"Make the coffee while you're up," the wench in the other room demanded, interrupting my thoughts. My sister's feet won't hit the floor until she's had her quarter-cup of grounds in eight ounces of hot water. "And see if you can find something sweet to bring me with my coffee."

I checked the cupboards for food, but found only a few staples—sugar, flour (full of bugs), Sweet'N Low, Coffee-mate, d-CON, and salt and pepper.

"I can put sugar on some d-CON if you'd like," I told her.

"I'll check on the Texas Seven," she said, ignoring my offer and turning on the TV. "Hey, they're still in the area. Maybe tonight they'll come for us."

"We can leave a trail of beer and tacos for them," I joked as I brought our coffee back to bed. "We're out of half-and-half. I had to use Coffee-mate." I broke the bad news to her as I handed over a big, ceramic mug with imitation-colored coffee inside and fake cream clinging to its edge.

"Well, today might just be a good day to make a life-changing decision," she announced, sounding way too upbeat for this early in the morning. "Maybe like switching from half-and-half to non-dairy creamer," she continued, acting as though she had decided to do something really big, like, say, get a divorce.

"Oh, that big, huh?" I said, trying not to sound confused. "Good luck with that. I hope you will be very happy and successful."

She shrugged her shoulders like it was no big deal. I crawled back into bed with my own mug of coffee and fake cream, thinking that I wasn't sure if switching from half-and-half to non-dairy creamer qualified as life-changing, but I did know that it was a big deal. We are loyal half-and-half drinkers and we'd rather fight than switch!

We propped up in bed, drank our coffee, and went over some rules:

1. No matter what, don't get into an argument with Dad.
2. Do whatever Dad wants us to do.
3. Keep telling ourselves that it's only for one week and Mom needs us here.
4. The code word for "Shut the fuck up" is "guacamole."

We walked the short distance from the clubhouse to the camper and found our parents both up and looking chipper. Dad was happy to see us and had breakfast made. He was fussing over Mom and she was lapping up the attention like a kitten in front of a bowl of warm milk. We had seen our parents do this dance before: It meant that Dad knew he had been a real jackass and was feeling guilty so he waited on her and talked sweetly to her. Mom liked the role reversal, when she got to be stubborn and demanding for a day or two, depending on the severity of Dad's misbehavior.

Of course, the whole New Year's Eve episode of him locking her out of the camper was not mentioned, other than when Dad said, "Your ma got pissed off at me the other day and locked me *in* the camper for the whole day."

Dad had our day mapped out for us. He wanted Val to clean the camper and me to pay some bills, balance the checkbook, and fill out disability forms. After giving us our orders, he disappeared for the day.

We did our chores and spent an enjoyable day with Mom, laughing and joking. Val cracked a joke about mom's cactus plant looking like a penis and Mom was right in there with a prick joke. We let her in on our rules and the "guacamole" secret. We didn't talk about her sickness or Dad's drinking. It felt like a normal day—just a mother having a good time with her daughters.

The chores were done by mid-afternoon, so we surveyed the grocery situation and made a list. If we were going to be there for a week, we knew we would need some produce—especially fruit—and real cheese. From the looks of the refrigerator, Mom had been living on Ensure and Dad on eggs, Kraft Singles, and lunch meat.

Mom's clothing situation needed even more attention. After going through her closet, we found that nearly nothing she had fit her. Her clothes hung from her feeble frame like she was a Barbie doll dressed in Cabbage Patch clothes.

"Mom, you live like white trash," I told her, tossing a pair of shoes, which had been laying by the door, into the garbage. "I wore these in high school."

"Don't throw those out," she protested. "I still wear them."

"Mom, they're from 1978. They're older than the grandkids! We'll get you some new shoes."

"But I like those, and they are still perfectly good."

"They are worn out, they are old, and they are out of style," I pointed out. "I'll buy you new shoes."

She was mad but she knew it wouldn't do any good to argue with me; after all, I am my father's daughter.

The kiddie section at Kmart was the only place to find clothes for Mom because she was so tiny. It wasn't easy to pick out clothes for a fifty-nine-year-old woman in the kids' department. In fact, it was damn near impossible. We finally got four pairs of pants, six tops, and two pairs of shoes. When we got home with the goods, she was as happy as if she had just gotten new clothes from Neiman's. Beaming and strutting her way across the camper, Mom modeled all of her new outfits. The clothes fit pretty well and even Dad looked happy with our choices. He said something nice, like that she looked good or that we did a good job, which made all of us light up like the Fourth of July—fake and brief.

It broke my heart to see my mother wearing those kid-sized clothes as if she was playing some kind of reverse dress-up—but her smile told me that she was sincerely thrilled to have new clothes, regardless of the reason.

I outdid myself that night, whipping up a gourmet dinner on the camper's little eighteen-inch, three-burner stove. Cumin-rubbed New York steaks, served on a pinto bean and wild mushroom ragoût and topped with red chili onion rings and pico de gallo, were on the menu that night. The aroma of garlic and optimism hung in the air as I tried to cover the smell of sickness with southwest spices. Val, the vegetarian, just ate the ragoût and onion rings; Mom said how good it was, but she just picked at her meal; Dad went at his like a ravenous coyote on a deer carcass, which I was pretty sure was a sign that he was tired of the Kraft Singles and bologna he'd been living on. He was still on the wagon, but Valli and I sure were dying for a good red wine to go with dinner. We cleaned up and excused ourselves early to retire to our secondhand store, where we climbed into bed—numb—with our coffee cups of Merlot.

Fifteen

On day two, laundry was on the agenda. From the looks of it, the laundry had been piling up for a while. Dad loaded us up with several baskets of dirty clothes and laundry products, along with directions to a Laundromat. What he forgot to give us was a Laundromat essential—quarters. We looked like complete dumbasses as we sorted and loaded the machines, then realized that we didn't have the quarters necessary to make them actually wash the clothes. A roomful of Mexican women snickered at us two dumb broads, as we stood over our non-washing machines, looking dumbfounded.

I left Valli to guard the dirty clothes while I went in search of a roll of quarters and some margaritas. I returned with both and we parked ourselves on top of a washing machine and threw back the margaritas. The women were no longer scoffing—we were obviously onto something. They spoke in Spanish and watched us out of the corners of their eyes. We smiled at them and tried to appear friendly, acting like washing clothes and drinking margaritas at a Laundromat was something we did every day. In my imagination, they wondered how we could be having so much fun doing laundry. As the spin cycle went off under my butt, I wondered how many of their mothers were dying of cancer.

The next day was the first day of Mom's chemo treatment, so Val and I drove her the sixty-five miles to the doctor in Las Cruces. The three of us were sitting at the doctor's office, waiting nervously, when I broke the silence.

"Mom, is there any place in the world that you have ever wanted to go?"

She thought for a second and then, as if a light went off, she said, "You know, I've always wanted to go to the Lewis and Clark Cavern."

I said, "Mom, not Paris? Cancun? The Caribbean? The Lewis and Clark Cavern is in Montana."

"I know," she said. "We've driven by it a million times. I always begged your Dad to stop but he never would." She dropped the thought, like she knew she would never go there.

Over the years, my mother collected a lot of things— things that most people would consider junk. Things like old bottles she found in dumps, turned various colors from years in the sun. Things like rocks, knickknacks, brass figurines, old jewelry, miniature china dishes, plates from every state, and ashtrays. These "things" were all stored in big rubber tubs in the back of an old semi-trailer that my parents owned. Mom loved her "things" and from time to time, she would go out there and sort through them. She had to start her collections over many times because Dad would get drunk or pissed off and throw them all out or we would be moving and not have room for all of them.

Mom started talking about her things. Her brown eyes filled up with tears and she said, "I just want you girls to know that if there is anything of mine that you want, anything at all, you need to speak up now. Anything. Just ask."

I thought for a minute, then reached down and pulled the shoes, which I have just bought for her, off of her feet.

We were all laughing hysterically when the doctor came into the room. In fact, we had tears running down our cheeks—a bit from the emotion, but mostly from the laughter. I'm sure it did not look like a roomful of people who were about to experience their first chemo treatment, but it only took an instant for Dr. Downer to change the atmospheric pressure in the room. That man was so serious he could make a monk look like Ronald McDonald. I was sure that dealing with terminally ill patients all day could have that effect on a person, but thus far, it had only made card-carrying comedians out of me and my sister. Mom was trying to stop laughing when she introduced us. Unamused, the doctor flipped his "Instant Fun-Killer" switch and went immediately into Mom's diagnosis and prognosis.

"Metastasized breast cancer, in her liver and lungs. Chemo and radiation. Six to twelve months with no treatment. About two years with treatment."

We listened intently but in disbelief. I couldn't look him, Mom, or Valli in the eyes, so I just stared at Mom's new shoes. That was the first time since she told me last October that it seemed all too real. Dr. Downer asked Val and me to step out of the room.

As we were leaving, I stopped and looked back at Mom and said, "Mom, you did say the Lewis and Clark *Tavern*, didn't you?" All three of us cracked up again.

She got her treatment and we left Dr. Downer's office in a much more somber mood than the one we were in when we arrived. When we pulled back into the Ol' West RV Park, Dad ran through the door of the camper like it was on fire. His eyes were full of questions and he was looking at Mom like he expected her to look different after one treatment. He jerked the door of the pickup open before I could even come to a complete stop.

"Are you OK?" he asked Mom as he helped her out of the pickup. He was being very gentle and cautious with her. Then, at me, he snapped, "Why are you late?"

"We stopped for lunch," I answered.

"I was worried," he said, with real concern.

"I tried to call you," I offered, shrugging. He said nothing. He just went back to helping Mom out of the pickup and into the camper, asking her how she felt, if she wanted some water, and if she wanted to lie down.

It had not yet occurred to us that our father was a completely different man when he didn't have alcohol running through his veins. From the way that Val's mouth was hanging open, I could read her mind. I knew that she was about to ask, "Who the hell are you and what have you done with Gary?"

"Guacamole," I reminded her.

Sixteen

The following day I drove Mom back to the treatment center in Las Cruces for radiation. I instantly felt sick as I walked through the doors and saw all the cancer victims in the waiting room. They were easy to pick out and it wasn't hard to tell which stage each person was in. The fact that they called my mother by name and told her how good she looked did nothing to soothe my churning stomach. Mom chatted with these people like they were all close friends. Several of them smiled at us and said, "These must be your daughters."

Mom always had a knack for making friends in strange places, such as grocery store checkout lines and truck stop bathrooms. She could turn a gang of Hell's Angels into lifelong friends. She introduced us to her doctors and nurses as if we were all at a dinner party.

I was amazed at how upbeat the nurses were around all of those deteriorating people while I was on the verge of hysterics. Mom was taken into a big, bright room and helped onto a table by a nurse named Sandy. She removed her top and bra with no concern for modesty or shame. I turned and left the room. I had never been able to bring myself to look at my mom's mastectomy scar, though she had offered to show it to me a number of times. I always declined—even to the point that I think it hurt her feelings that I wouldn't look at her chest. I faked a cough, claimed that I need a drink of water, and made a beeline for a place where I could put my head between my knees.

Val, seemingly unaffected by our mother's near-naked appearance and the fact that she was about to receive enough radiation to cause cancer in lab animals, came to find me and ask what was wrong. She seemed oblivious to all of the women around us, about the same age as our own mother, wearing terrycloth turbans and ill-fitting wigs. I knew that she had to be just as bothered as I was, though, so I gave her credit for her act.

"Come on, Tammi," she said, "I told Sandy we both have some unwanted facial hair and she said we could stay in the room while Mom gets her treatment."

I laughed but told her that I had been working on my moustache for a few years now—at least since I turned forty—and I wasn't quite ready to give it up. She shrugged and walked off, leaving me and my moustache to ponder the power of radiation. I stayed in the waiting room, flipped through *Bon Appétit*, and mentally planned dinner. I could hear Mom, Val, and Sandy laughing the entire time, like women at a naughty-nightie party.

The chemo had been in Mom's system for about three days and she was feeling extremely ill when we went back to Dr. Downer's.

"Can't you give her something for this nausea?" I begged of him.

He wrote a prescription and we headed to Wal-Mart, hoping to get a miracle pill. I was trying to focus on finding Wal-Mart and Mom was trying to give me directions while puking violently into a Ziploc baggie. Val, who was sitting in the backseat of my pickup, was leaning between the seats, patting Mom's back and telling her that it was OK. I was doing my best not to fill the spare bag that, thankfully, we had the foresight to bring. Finally, in the Wal-Mart parking lot, exhausted from hours of vomiting, Mom was quiet. She slumped back in her seat, zipped the baggie shut, handed it over her shoulder to Val, and mumbled breathlessly, "Here, throw this away, would you?"

I got out, knelt next to the front tire, and let go of my own stomach. Then Val and I headed into Wal-Mart, leaving Mom reclined in the front seat. Valli dropped the baggie of toxic puke into the garbage like she was throwing away a candy wrapper.

I laid the prescription on the counter in front of the pharmacist. He studied it carefully, then looked me in the eye and said, "You'll have to come back tomorrow for this. We don't stock it."

"Why not?" I asked.

"Because it's about thirty dollars per pill," he replied, still looking me in the eye. This meant that the prescription would be about a thousand dollars.

"I'll have to go ask my mom," I said, breaking eye contact and feeling like I was twelve years old.

Mom was resting and barely opened her eyes when we got back to the pickup. "Did you get rid of it?" she asked, dead serious.

"No, Mom. We asked everyone we saw and no one wanted a bag of puke," I deadpanned.

"Couldn't give the stuff away," Val jumped in. "Even offered cash." Mom was too sick to laugh but tried anyway. Then I delivered the news about the prescription.

"Bullshit!" she snapped. "We can't afford that. You didn't get it, did you?"

"No, Mom. You have to order it."

"Well, we can't pay for that."

"You know that I would be willing to buy it for you, don't you Mom?"

"Yes, but you're not going to. That's ridiculous. Your father would just shit."

"I know, Mom. Let's go back to Dr. Downer's and ask him for something less expensive."

Seventeen

After a week of making the radiation and chemo rounds, it was time for Val and me to move out of the clubhouse. We should have been glad, but we both knew that our days with Mom were numbered and we were not as anxious to leave as we had thought we would be. Those several days brought the four of us closer together. Val and I bonded because we were the only two people on Earth who could relate to and commiserate over the past that we have endured and the future that lay before us. Val had the chance to care for Mom, to be her nurturing, sensitive self: to sympathize, to wipe up the puke, to clip Mom's toenails, and to help her in the shower—all the things I couldn't do. I was used to being the authoritative figure in my relationship with my mom, but for one week I stopped being her boss and acted like her mother. I fixed her hair; doled out pills; prepared her food and coaxed her to eat by bribing her with dessert; urged her to nap, lying down with her and pretending to be asleep when I knew she was awake, then silently slipping out of the room when I was certain she had drifted off—the easy stuff.

Val and I grew closer to Dad because we spent a week together with no fights, no mean comments, and no drunken rants. Dad didn't crack any fag jokes when Val's gay friends called to see how Mom was doing. He didn't pooh-pooh her vegetarianism. He didn't even make one Martha Stewart crack. He didn't call me spoiled or rich and he didn't pick on our husbands or our kids. Not once were we told that we had shit for brains. He complimented our cooking and thanked us for cleaning the house and doing laundry. He was *nice* to us. There was a part of me that felt like we needed to leave—that Dad deserved this. It was his turn to take care of Mom—to worry about her, to be there for her. I secretly feared that it would be more than he could handle. Fifteen days of sobriety and good behavior were not reason enough to let him off the hook. It was about damn time that her needs were put before his, we told each other.

Saying goodbye to Mom was the most difficult and painful thing I had endured since back labor. The reality of the outcome of her disease was finally setting in and not only was Mom upset about *us* leaving, I was also taking Captain, her beloved border collie, to live with me. Captain was eleven years old and had been in the family since he was a puppy. Mom loved him like she loved us, but she was no longer able to take him for walks so he had spent most of his days chained to the old storage trailer. Captain was thrilled to be off the chain and willingly jumped into the back of my pickup, anxious to go anywhere. Mom was openly sobbing like a child who had just had her blanket taken away when she told us good-bye.

Sober, Dad had been a stranger—a pleasant, caring, loving stranger. He wasn't mean, critical, or judgmental, and I knew that he needed Mom and was just as scared and unsure about the future as we were. He had been trying to be strong as we were getting ready to leave, but I could tell that he was torn up. As he walked us outside to the pickup, he hugged us and thanked us for coming. We knew that he was sincere so we both let our guards down and told him that we loved him when we hugged him back. He stuttered, "Ahh . . . yeah . . . ahh . . . me too."

Because we didn't know what else to say at a time like that, we told Dad to take care of Mom, but we didn't make eye contact in case one of us cried. Mom gave us a half-hearted wave from the camper door, still crying and looking so sad that I feared she would dissolve into a tiny pile that resembled a stick of butter that had been left in a skillet long after the burner has been turned off. At this most abnormal time, I felt that we were a normal family.

We drove out of Deming and Val and I didn't say a word. I learned that I can hold my breath for thirty miles. When I finally stopped holding it, I felt the tears come. The 1,125-mile drive home was a lot different than the one we had made seven days earlier.

At the time, I had no way of knowing that the glow-in-the-dark stars that Val and I had put on Mom and Dad's bedroom ceiling before we left would be the brightest thing that they had to look forward to at the end of the day.

Eighteen

By March, desperation had not only taken over our lives, it had taken on a life of its own. Valerie had heard about a new hotshot cancer doctor in Idaho Falls who was supposedly saving other people's mothers' lives right and left, so she made an appointment for Mom. We were willing to cling to any thread of hope that was dangled in front of us.

Next came the task of talking Dad into taking Mom to Idaho Falls, which we anticipated would be met with much opposition. Dad is generally against anything that isn't his idea, but Mom was going downhill pretty quickly, so he was not only ready to try something new, he was willing to let someone else make a decision. We knew that the daily drive to Las Cruces was taking its toll, so having Mom near her doctor would be a welcome reprieve. Fortunately, Dad was still on the wagon, which surely contributed to him allowing Val and Saul to go to Deming to pack them up and help them make the drive to Idaho.

It was around this time that despair turned me into a loan shark in my pleadings with God. In all of my prayers, I was trading something for my mom's life.

"Please, God, let Mom be OK and I'll start going to church."

"Please, God, let Mom live and I'll go to church and quit cussing."

"Please, God, get rid of the cancer and I'll go to church, quit cussing, and go on a mission to a third world country to hand out Bibles."

I upped the ante with every prayer.

Val and Saul took advantage of Dad's desperation and made the trip before he could call bullshit and change his mind. When they arrived in Deming, they found Dad tipsy and Mom looking like hell. Her hair was patchy and graying and she was very thin—except for her stomach, which was swollen enough to make her look six months pregnant. Val cut off what was left of Mom's hair and Mom was sick enough that she really didn't care. I was just glad that Val was there to do it because I knew I couldn't have. I sobbed uncontrollably when Valli told me about it. Saul helped Dad pack up the items they wanted to bring and they hit the road. Since Dad drives like an old fart (about fifty miles per hour) and he was drinking, the trip was torturous and slow-going. By the time they hit the Utah line,

Mom looked like an overdue mother and she was just as miserable.

Valerie and Saul's house sits on a big corner lot on Maple Street, framed by two ancient pine trees that have crippled the sidewalk with their enormous roots. It's three steps up to the inviting front porch, which hosts a white wrought iron bench and chair that Valli has decorated with her plush, homemade pillows. Blooming flowers and seasonal plants take turns accentuating the decor. Above, a funky, octagonal window peers out from the attic, overlooking a small terrace that resembles a widow's walk, without the walk. In the summers, we have been known to eat dinner on the roof. We have even spread out blankets and slept on it.

Stepping through the front door is like stepping into a grand mini-mansion. The front staircase, with its old, carved oak banister, leads the way to the second-story bedrooms. In the first room on the main level, an old sectional couch with pink- and cream-colored upholstery cozies up to Saul's baby grand piano. Both look as though there should be a diva with a bouffant, wearing a long, sparkly dress and gloves that reach beyond her elbows, draped over them. They are complemented by three chairs that were rescued from either an estate sale or a secondhand store, like puppies from a pound. My sister took them in and recovered them with vintage fabrics. Now big, fat, happy pillows are curled up and napping in their seats.

In the next room, a shabby chic cabinet containing old, mismatched china offsets a dining room table that sits upon a beautiful wool rug. Two more mismatched chairs frame the doorway that leads into what was once the family room, but became Mom and Dad's new bedroom.

Valli had moved the couch out of the room and moved in a double bed. The TV, armoire, end table, and recliner remained, giving the room an old, European hotel-like feel. Bookcases overflowed with a wide variety of topics to tempt my mother, an avid reader, while fresh flowers and candles conspired to make the room smell like vanilla beans and lavender were throwing a dinner party. Soft, plush rugs warmed the wood floor and the bed had been covered with beautiful, new, flowery sheets and pillows deep enough to get lost in. A comforter worthy of the Ritz-Carlton added the finishing touch, inviting Mom in for a Zen-like experience after the long trip.

The setting, with all of its accoutrements, was more reminiscent of a peaceful retreat than a sick room. Mom looked pleased as she stood in the middle of it all, turned in a slow circle, and oohed and ahhed at the transformation. She could tell that Valli had put in a considerable amount of work. As she kicked off her shoes and prepared to relax in her very own luxury suite, Dad stuck his head in the door.

"See there, Di? That's the dead bed." He used his fist to point in the general direction of the bed, since his hand was wrapped around a beer.

Mom ignored his remark, but Val shot him a look that let him know he was a son of a bitch. She was enraged and appalled, and she hated him. Mom was too sick and bloated to care. After the long trip, all she wanted to do was climb into that bed—dead or not.

Nineteen

I made the eight-hour drive from Dayton shortly after Mom and Dad got there. I knew that Val had cut off Mom's hair, leaving it about a half-inch long all over, and I knew that Mom was bloated to the point that she looked pregnant. I felt myself holding my breath as I prepared to greet her. A tiny, gray-haired woman with a crew cut, impersonating my mother, came towards me. Years that I had not noticed before had been hung on her face like heavy, velvet drapes. I knew the smile though, so I managed to smile back and tried not to squeeze too hard when I hugged her. If the shock was showing on my face, she did a good job of not letting me see that she noticed it. I claimed that I had to pee and went into the bathroom, sat on the floor in front of the toilet with my head in my hands, and cried without making a sound. Then I stuck my head in the toilet and dry heaved. I splashed a little water on my face, looked in the mirror, told myself to "suck it up," then gathered up my courage to face whatever it was that was coming next.

Captain had made the trip with me and he and Mom were getting reacquainted like two long-lost friends. They sat, heads together, in what looked like a deep conversation. Captain's head was on her lap and Mom was bent over him, talking into his ear, one hand on his head, the other under his chin. They looked like they could have stayed that way forever.

By now we knew there was no such thing as forever, but our hopes were as high as a junkie on crack. We all went with Mom to that first appointment with Dr. Hotshot, as we were excited about the new treatment and meeting our new messiah. He pumped us full of hope at the same time that he was pumping Mom's veins full of a new kind of chemo. Mom sat in a bright, happy-face-yellow, leather recliner, which was positioned in a semi-circle with seven other bright, happy-face-yellow, leather recliners, which were all filled with women in various stages of treatment—women who were young, old, had hair, had no hair, wore turbans, and one with a beautiful head of red hair. Mom, with her fresh crew cut, couldn't help but notice. The woman couldn't help but notice that the new kid in treatment was staring, so she admitted that her beautiful head of red hair was a wig. After the treatment, Mom seemed perky and went on and on about how "natural" and "real" that woman's hair looked.

Later that day I asked Mom if she wanted a wig. She shrugged and acted like it really didn't matter. I realized that it was probably because I had asked the question in front of Dad and he had said, "She doesn't need a wig. Her hair looks fine." So I took her aside and told her that I would take her to get a wig if she wanted one. I explained that it didn't matter what Dad wanted because this was about what she wanted.

The next afternoon, Mom and I walked into Cochran Beauty Supply. A tired, pink, terrycloth turban that definitely had "cancer victim" written all over it was covering her head. The salon was packed with women who were getting cuts and colors from young, hip-looking hairdressers. Scissors stopped in mid-snip, blow dryers clicked off, and all heads turned in our direction, as if everyone in the entire salon was part of a synchronized styling team. I knew that my mother looked like a train wreck, so it shouldn't have been a surprise to me when people couldn't help but look, be it out of compassion or curiosity, but still I felt myself bristle. I put my arm protectively around Mom and steered her toward the counter.

"We would like to look at some wigs," I told the girl with the halo of blonde hair who was standing behind the counter—Stephanie, her nametag read. I saw her swallow what I presumed to be shock, then gather up her composure and professionalism.

"What would you like to see?" Stephanie asked, looking directly at Mom. Mom's big brown eyes, full of uncertainty and almost hidden by that god-awful turban, peered back at Stephanie like she didn't know the answer to the million-dollar question. She looked to me for help, like she had already forgotten what her own hair looked like.

I was still hanging onto her, shielding her, trying to keep from screaming, "What? Have none of you bitches ever seen a cancer patient before? Turn around and stop staring! It could be your mother!" Instead, I took a deep breath and said, "Something in red, with short hair, maybe shag-like."

"Let's go in here," Stephanie said, leading us through a maze of women with suddenly downcast eyes. I kept my hand on Mom's elbow, stuck my chin in the air, and glared at anyone who dared to make eye contact with me. Stephanie led us to a small, private room with a caution-yellow-colored, over-stuffed recliner. It looked a lot like the chemo room, except it had mirrors. She laid a big hand mirror in Mom's lap and put a nylon stocking on her head, explaining that she had to wear it while trying on wigs.

"For health reasons," she said.

Whose health? I wondered. Mom didn't have any.

Stephanie brought in wig after wig and she was so gentle with mom each time she tried one on her. I thanked God for giving us Stephanie. I liked that she was tender and caring, yet treated Mom like she would have treated any woman wanting a new do—no sympathy, just a genuine concern for giving a woman a new look. Mom must have tried on twenty wigs. Her tiny face was lost in most of them.

"We can always cut the hair if you find one you like," Stephanie told her.

As each wig was placed on Mom's head, she would hold up the big mirror to look at herself and, without saying a word, lay the mirror back in her lap and slump down into the recliner. One made her look like she did in an old driver's license photo from the 1980s and we both laughed. She tried on a short, shag style and I saw her spirits perk up when she saw herself in the mirror. Stephanie and I gushed and told her how great she looked. Stephanie said she could style it and even trim it if Mom wanted it shorter. Mom seemed happy and wondered aloud if Dad would like it. I assured her that he would.

"It looks just like you . . . but having a good hair day," I told her.

Stephanie left to go write up the order, telling us that the wig would be in the next day.

Mom pulled the stocking from her head, happily chatting about how nice it would be to not have to fix her hair (though that was something she rarely did, even when she had her own hair). She was shaking the nylon cap, saying, "Look at this, Tammi." Little gray hairs were falling all over her lap.

"Jesus, what a mess," she said, still shaking the cap, hair still flying. I looked at Mom and saw that her head now resembled a baby's shiny, little butt. She was completely bald! The hairs flying around the room were the few she had left and, when she pulled the nylon off her head, they came off too.

"Come on, Mom. Just put on your turban and let's go," I said, kind of panicked that she was about to realize that all that hair had to have came from somewhere.

Whether it showed on my face or it just hit her, I don't know, but she suddenly picked up the mirror that was still in her lap and held it up. She stared at herself in disbelief for about five seconds and then fell backwards into the big caution-yellow chair. She put her hands to her face and wept. Not a sound came out of her, but her shoulders shook, almost violently. I knelt beside her, hugged her, and cried with her, making no sounds of my own. I had no idea what to say. Once again, there weren't any words. We stayed that way for a few minutes and then composed ourselves enough to leave the room. Mom managed to give Stephanie a genuine smile on our way out; mine was as fake as the hair on all those wigs.

Back at Valli's, Mom told Dad and Val about the wig and said she couldn't wait until the next day. She never mentioned the hair loss part, and the evidence was still hidden under the turban. The next morning, Mom was on pins and needles waiting for Stephanie to call. I sent up another quick prayer. "Please, God, let that damn wig be here today."

God answered my prayer. Stephanie called and Mom and I made our way back to Cochran Beauty Supply. Mom was wearing the same old pink turban, but this time she walked in with a big smile on her face. We went back into the same room and Stephanie gently fitted the wig to Mom's tiny head. She fussed with it, adjusted it, and trimmed it until we were both satisfied. Finally we held up the mirror. When my mother saw herself, she positively glowed and Stephanie and I both cried. I swear that Stephanie gave her a little more time. Maybe it was only minutes or hours, maybe days or weeks, but that day, my mother was a new woman when she walked out of Cochran Beauty Supply. Anyone who didn't know it would not be able to tell that she was dying of cancer.

The wig seemed to do more good for her than the chemo did and for the next couple of weeks, Mom continued her treatments, had good hair days, and looked pretty normal. Dad's drinking continued as if he was in a contest. He'd given up the hard stuff but was drinking cheap wine out of a box. When Val got home from work, she would usually find Dad cooking dinner, half-crocked.

Dinner never involved anything that her family might be tempted to eat. On the nights that she got home early enough to beat Dad to the stove, she cooked and he grumbled about it. Pesto pizza or pasta with Gorgonzola, roasted shallots, and asparagus was not his idea of a meal. If meat wasn't in the recipe, it wasn't dinner, as far as he was concerned. Val has no idea what to do with a piece of beef, but she would fry chicken or sauté shrimp for Mom and Dad. That would be OK for a meal or two, but Dad had to have his beef at least five nights a week.

Every evening, Valli and Mom snuggled into Mom's bed to watch *Wheel of Fortune* while Dad sat at the kitchen counter, drank his boxed wine, and glared at his beef as it simmered on the stove. Mom couldn't have cared less about either of their dinners. She faked it for both of them, being a vegetarian one day, a carnivore the next, while secretly spitting out both. It was just like her to say nothing and try to please them both while being pulled in opposite directions.

Twenty

I made another trip to Idaho shortly before Easter. In the evenings, I took up drinking the boxed wine with Dad and agreed with him when he carried on about gays in the military, same-sex marriage, unwed welfare mothers, Bill Clinton, and Martha Stewart. There wasn't an ethnic, political, or religious group that was safe from his narrow-minded rants. If I had learned anything in forty-one years, it was just to shut up and agree with him when he was drunk. No matter how absurd or off-the-wall he was, I would not argue or let him pick a fight with me. That became my mantra. *No matter what, I will not let him lead me down that road. No matter what, I will not let him pick a fight with me. No matter what, I will not let him lead me down that road.* I repeated it in my head, over and over, until it was so.

When Dad cracked fag, Jew, and nigger jokes, I laughed right along with him as if I was racist and homophobic too, when really I was nothing more than a phony—albeit one without a backbone. It didn't matter that Clinton wasn't even president anymore; Dad was still cussing him. And he showed even more hatred for Hillary, saying that looking at her was "like looking at a mud fence," and that he was sure that she "wouldn't even know how to make an egg sandwich." I cussed Bill, Hillary, and Martha with him, even though I didn't agree with what he said—well, OK, I did agree with the Clinton stuff, but frankly, I like Martha and I think most of us, including myself, could use a little help with style and sophistication.

Besides the Clintons, Dad hated war protestors—and since Valerie and Saul fell into that category, he had one more reason to pick on them. Val was smart enough to keep her political views to herself, but Dad would just shake his head and wonder how she turned out to be a vegetarian, a democrat, and a tree-hugger. At least Dad and I shared political views. Over boxes of wine, we solved the stray animal population problem and plugged the hole in the ozone. Then we cured attention deficit disorder and post-partum depression—neither of which Dad ever believed was real anyway. Whatever it took, I had decided, I would not argue with a drunken man—especially not when I was a drunken woman. I knew that when Dad was on one of his benders he could argue with a statue and piss off a painting, so I just gave in and bought my ticket to his Gallery of Bullshit Babble.

He did seem happy to have me there, which gave me mixed feelings. I'd spent my whole life wanting to have a relationship with him, and now, over boxed wine and radicalism, it almost felt like I was getting it—even if it was in more of a "drinkin' buddy who cooks" kind of way. It scared me to see my dad so cold and alienated because I knew that he desperately loved and needed my mother. Because of his detachment, I was driving myself crazy trying to be the glue that kept him and I connected to Mom and Val. I knew that my loyalty needed to lie with Mom and Valli, but I felt torn.

"Dad needs someone too," Guilt told me one day.

"Dad doesn't need anyone," I answered her. "He only needs an audience."

OK, so that was me. As long as he kept driving me down the road that led to I'm-proud-of-you-ville, I would find myself busting my butt to get on the bus. I knew that I could get a front-row seat, but being in the front of the bus meant that I was the copilot of radical, opinionated conversations—all served up with good food and cheap wine.

One night, I made flank steak with chimichurri sauce, roasted tomato ketchup, and white cheddar mashed potatoes. Dad loved it and as usual I was thrilled to have pleased him. Mom pretended to love it too, but I could tell that she could have been eating cardboard and not noticed the difference. Val, Saul, and the kids all seemed like dinner guests at their own table.

At one point, after agreeing with Dad about how good it was, Mom got up from the table, went into the bathroom, and threw up. She returned to the table quickly, as if she had just slipped away to grab the saltshaker. None of us let on that we had heard her puking. While the rest of us were holding our vintage linen napkins to our mouths to keep from joining her, Dad kept on eating, quizzing me about the ingredients of the chimichurri sauce. Valli and I exchanged a glance, but neither of us was sure if we should say anything. If we did say something—what? And to whom? Mom never said a word either. She just sat back down at the table, took a deep breath, and looked at her plate full of flank steak and green mystery sauce. I was still busy educating the table about the recipe and the origin of chimichurri when she let out a labored sigh, picked up her fork, and began eating again. Within a couple minutes, she went into the bathroom and threw up for a second time.

Valerie was trying hard to please everyone, too. With Easter approaching, she bought a turkey for the dinner. My Aunt Beth, Mom's sister, and her husband were coming for the holiday and Val was planning on making a nice dinner for everyone.

"She can't just buy a regular turkey," Dad told me one day over the phone. "It has to be a free-range, organic son of a bitch." He said "free-range, organic" in a mocking, condescending tone. I could just see him contorting his face as if he'd just been fed a spoonful of horse piss.

"It's just a turkey, Dad. I'm sure it will be good," I assured him.

"Probably cost twice as much," he said, still grumbling about it.

"Yeah, but it will probably be twice as good," I suggested.

Oops, I was wrong about that one. It probably *would* have been twice as good if he had let Val cook it, but the night before Easter he decided that he would cook the free-range, organic son of a bitch. He had been on a bender and was plowed when he made this decision so Val gave up on the idea of reasoning with him and went to bed, leaving him smoking and the turkey unsuspecting at the kitchen counter. As the clock ticked away that night Val lay awake, exhausted but unable to fall sleep. Reluctant to confront Dad, she forced Saul out of bed and sent him downstairs to check on Dad, where Saul became an unwilling accomplice as he watched Dad rub down the bird with spices and stuff it with my leftover chimichurri sauce. She lay awake listening while they banged around the kitchen before finally putting the bird to bed in the refrigerator. Once the house was quiet the only thing left to do was to lie awake and wait for the smell of smoke. Whenever Dad was in the house and was drinking, there was a chance that there could be a fire—or a gunshot.

The next morning, Dad greeted Val by saying, "look what I got" as he pushed a glass of wine under her nose. After a rough night, smugness and wine just aren't things you want served with a side of eggs. Instead she surveyed the tortured bird, which had a funky red color spread over the top of the chimichurri while Dad looked over her shoulder and asked, "Where we gonna bury this turkey?"

"In the same hole I'm going to bury you in," Val retorted.

Dad ignored the comment and instead turned to the one person that he knew he could count on for forgiveness—my shrinking mother.

"I love you, Di," he said, putting an arm around her. "I'm just used to loving more of you."

Twenty-One

Larry, the girls, and I went back to Idaho Falls in May for Mother's Day. Val and I bought Mom some huge, beautiful, hanging plants, which she normally would have loved. Val went all out, setting a beautiful table outside in her yard, complete with linens, candles, and fine antique china. Then we hung the big baskets of blooming plants in the trees around the table. It looked like a setting straight out of *Martha Stewart Living*. It was early afternoon, so it could have been brunch and we could have been serving a frittata, a smoked salmon tart, and chocolate-dipped strawberries, but Dad wanted chicken-fried steak and mashed potatoes. I complied. After the Easter fiasco, we weren't about to take the chance of letting him make dinner again. Mom was distant and completely uninvolved. To have all four of her grandkids together would normally have been enough to make her giddy and full of nonstop chatter.

The kids were equally as crazy about her. When they were with her, they got to do fun things, like roll out pie dough and bake their own concoctions. Sierra's always involved peanut butter and Savannah's were all about sugar. When Mom made stuffing at Thanksgiving, they got to put their hands in the gooey mess of soggy bread and eggs to mix it up. They played in it, squeezing it between their fingers until it was almost unsalvageable.

Mom always treated the kids like they were much older than they were and she gave them a lot of trust and respect—sometimes, maybe too much trust. She let them use big knives to cut up meat and vegetables, and when they helped her peel potatoes they used paring knives instead of potato peelers. She let them flick cigarette lighters until they were actually adept at lighting cigarettes on the first try. Armed with a roll of paper towels and a bottle of Windex, they would be occupied for hours, cleaning her mirrors, windows, floors, and whatever else they felt like spraying. No household chemicals, knives, or matches were off limits; she trusted them to be responsible and they wouldn't have dreamed of letting her down. And no matter how streaked the glass may have been, she always praised their work.

When Mom was away from the kids, she wrote letters to them at least once a week. Since Hannah and Savannah were the youngest, she always printed their letters. To Dustin and Sierra, she wrote in cursive.

Every letter that she ever wrote to Sierra ended with, "May you always walk in beauty and may a rainbow touch your shoulder." Sierra ended hers the same way when she wrote back.

Mom rode horses with the kids and played countless games of Candy Land and Yahtzee. She also read to them—not cutesy children's books, but stories like *My Friend Flicka, The Yearling,* and *Old Yeller.* They would gather around her and listen intently for hours as she read these wonderful old classics. When they were together, she and the grandkids were always touching. Someone would have an arm around her and she would be holding one kid's hand and rubbing another's back. Whether one, two, or all four of the kids with her, they always seemed to be intertwined. Now, suddenly, they were all keeping their distance.

Val said that Mom had been alienating herself for a couple of weeks, even failing to acknowledge Dustin's birthday in April. That wasn't like her, I had to agree. She worshipped the grandkids and had never failed to acknowledge any milestone or accomplishment, no matter how small. On this occasion, the gifts we gave her barely warranted a glance and cards were opened but quickly stuffed, unread, back into their envelopes. She also failed to notice the big blooming plants that we had hung in the trees over the table for her. Everyone— except for Dad, that is—seemed to be walking on eggshells.

Val and her family obviously weren't particularly thrilled with the menu. My meat eaters ate, but with

Mom being so distant, they weren't really enjoying it either. Dad seemed to be the only one in the mood for food and conversation, as he shoved chicken-fried steak and mashed potatoes down his piehole, all the while taking vegetarian pokes and Martha Stewart jabs at Valli. We all ignored him, but I knew that Martha would have been proud.

Twenty-Two

Sometime between Easter and Mother's Day, Dad decided to move them to an apartment of their own. Mom didn't want to leave Val's house, but she didn't have it in her to argue with Dad. Besides, she knew she wouldn't win. Valli didn't want Mom to move either; she liked taking care of her. Although she had to admit that it would be nice to live in her own house without worrying about Dad burning it down.

Dad found a small, furnished, two-bedroom apartment that was only about a five-minute drive from Valli and Saul's. Val helped them move the few belongings they had brought with them and she helped Mom furnish the place with some personal things, like pictures of the grandkids, and nice things from Val's store, like candles, pillows, and throws for the ratty couch that came with the place.

Then one day in early June, when Val took Mom to her doctor's appointment, Dr. Hotshot looked at Mom and her most recent tests results and told her to go home and call hospice. No apology, no sympathy, no goodbye—not one ounce of compassion. It was more like, "Next terminal patient, please." He did say, looking over his shoulder as he was walking out of the room, while Mom and Val were both crying, "Well, you do know that you have a terminal disease, don't you, DiAnne?"

Val and Mom left the clinic, both of them nauseous, numb, and speechless. When the silence became too loud to bear, Val blurted out the question that had been on all of our minds: "Who's going to take care of Dad?"

Mom just shrugged her shoulders and said, "I'm scared of dying."

"This isn't it, Mom," Val reassured her.

"Did you ever go talk to that Indian faith healer?" Mom asked Valli, like her immediate future hinged on that.

The answer was lost in the silence that followed them back to 240 Dale Street.

Twenty-Three

June 14, 2001.

Everyone knows that good news always sleeps until at least eight in the morning, so when Larry and I were awakened at three by the ringing of our phone, we knew there had to be bad news on the other end. Larry picked up, muttered a hello, then immediately passed the phone to me. It was Valerie and she was frantic.

"Saul and I just got back from Mom and Dad's. Dad called and said we needed to get over there. Oh my God, Tammi. It looked like a crime scene. There was blood everywhere—all over the floor, the walls, the bathroom. It looked like someone was murdered. She is throwing up blood everywhere."

Valli was crying and talking so fast that I could hardly process what she was saying. "You have to come. You have to come now. Oh my God, I think this may be it," she howled, sounding like a wounded animal.

Countless questions were racing through my mind: *How is Dad? How is Mom handling it? Is she scared? What is Dad doing? Why is there blood? How is Dad? What did you and Saul do? What is Dad doing?* My brain was processing these questions at warp speed, but my mouth couldn't get the words out in any form that resembled a sentence.

"It's bright red blood, not dark," she said. "That means she's bleeding internally. You need to come." I could hear Saul, who was just as frenzied, in the background but I couldn't tell if he was crying or vomiting.

"I'm on my way," I told her, as Larry and I got out of bed.

Two hours later, I called Dad from Billings and he said, "You need to hurry, honey." He had now called me "honey" twice in forty-one years. I barely recognized his voice. I had never heard him when he wasn't in control.

"I am, Dad," I said, sobbing. "I'll hurry. Tell Mom that I love her."

From Bozeman, I called my Aunt Beth. I'd forgotten that I had told her that the next time I made a trip to Idaho Falls, I would let her know so she could ride along if she wanted to.

"Beth, it's Tammi," I said. "I'm sorry, I forgot to call you. I'm on my way to Idaho Falls today. Mom's not doing well."

"Tammi, I heard. I know. I'm sorry. Do you know when you will have the funeral? Where will it be?"

"What? No! She's not doing good, but, you know, she could rally. She might—"

"Oh my God, I'm so sorry, Tammi. I thought you knew."

"Knew what? What are you saying, Aunt Beth? What do you know that I don't?"

It felt like I had just taken a bullet to my brain and that I was on the verge of consciousness. I couldn't see through the tears that immediately filled my eyes. Savannah was with me and she instantly burst into tears when she saw mine.

"I just talked to Valli," Beth said. "Your mom passed away about ten minutes ago."

I still had 150 miles to go, but I pulled over to the side of the road and Savannah and I held each other and cried. My precious little fourteen-year-old said that she could drive me the rest of the way if I was too upset. She never knew it, but it was her who kept me from falling over the edge.

The news barely had time to sink in when Guilt took her place in the backseat, directly behind me, and began whispering in my ear.

"You weren't there when she died," she said, "and you know that you are secretly relieved about that. You didn't want to see our mother in those final moments, did you? You didn't want to see her die."

My head was denying the allegations, "No! No! No! I wanted to be there. I was trying to be there."

Guilt was relentless. "You can deny it all you want, but I know that you are secretly relieved."

I argued with her for another two hours before Valli called to ask me where I was.

"Near Hamer, I think," I told her.

"Just hurry," is all she said.

"Valerie, I know," I said. "I know that Mom is already gone. I talked to Aunt Beth."

"She wasn't supposed to tell you!" I could tell that she was angry.

"She didn't mean to," I told her. "But I know that I'm too late."

"Well, don't tell Dad. He doesn't want you to know."

"We'll see you in a half hour or so," I told her, trying to keep it together for Savannah's sake. "I'm OK."

"Liar," Guilt replied.

Thirty minutes later, I pulled up to 240 Dale Street. As soon as I opened the door of my pickup, Guilt bailed out, leaving me alone with Relief and Sadness. I knew that Mom was gone and I had to admit, at least to myself, that I was grateful that I wouldn't have to see her. Valli met me at the door of my pickup.

"Dad doesn't know that you know," she whispered, "so don't tell him. He will only be pissed at Aunt Beth forever if you do, so act surprised. Mom is still here. He wouldn't let them take her until you got here." I didn't have to act surprised; that one knocked me for a loop.

Val linked her arm through mine and led me into their apartment. I needed the help; my feet felt heavy, like I was wearing iron boots and walking through wet cement. It was all I could do to lift them to take the next step.

Dad was at the kitchen table but got up immediately when he saw me. I buried my head in his shoulder and hugged him. He reeked of alcohol, cigarettes, and sweat, and I could feel him shaking. He tried to hug me back, but seemed unsure of what to do with his hands. He grabbed my wrists and pulled my arms from around his neck, took me by the hand, and started leading me down the hall toward the bedroom.

I dug my heels into the carpet and pressed my hands, face, and body up against the wall of the hallway as he dragged me along.

"No, Dad," I begged, sobbing. "Please don't make me."

The more I resisted, the more he tightened his grip and the more strength he used to pull me along.

"Please, Dad. I don't want to see Mom like this!" I could hear Val and Savannah crying in the other room, but neither was willing to come to my rescue.

Dad put his hand on the doorknob. "Nooooooo, Dad. Please, Dad, nooooooo!" I was wailing and clawing at invisible handholds along the hall wall.

"Ma, Tammi's here," he said as he opened the door.

I wasn't even on my feet, but he kept dragging me. I squeezed my eyes shut and turned my head away, refusing to look.

"See Ma, Tam made it," he said, pulling me to my feet, then immediately pushing me down on the bed next to her. I still had my eyes closed and my head turned away as I frantically tried to catch my breath. It was impossible. Death had sucked all of the air out of the room.

"It's OK now, Ma, Tam's here," he whispered, trembling. The voice didn't sound like his. He took my hand and I felt him put her hand in mine. It was cold, and I felt myself shiver in the ninety-degree heat. I opened my eyes and turned my head to look at my mother. Then I heard a noise that I didn't recognize, but I felt come from deep within me.

Twenty-Four

I had never realized how much space in the universe one tiny, five-foot, one-hundred-pound woman could take up. The void at 240 Dale Street on the afternoon of June 14 seemed like a black hole. I also couldn't believe how small Dad seemed without Mom. All our lives, Dad had been the one who was bigger than life—the strong one, the one we all needed, the one who rescued us when we needed to be rescued, straightened us out when we needed to be straightened, righted us when we wronged. He had so much control over us that our own thoughts and emotions had been programmed to mirror his. I was certain that he was the one from whom the sun asked permission to rise and set each day. Now Dad seemed like a stranger to me.

After a few more hours, he finally allowed the funeral home to come and get Mom. I stayed seated at the kitchen table but watched while Dad lovingly placed his hand under her chin and gently closed her mouth before walking her out to the car, as if he was sending her off on a trip, talking to her the whole time—telling her goodbye and that he'd see her soon. He was patting her arm and trying to keep her bare legs covered by the sheet that the funeral home guys had draped over her. Through the open front door, I saw him kiss her one last time and walk back to the house without looking back. His head was hung low, his chin on the sidewalk. It had the reverse effect of looking into a rearview mirror; the closer to the house and the farther away from Mom he got, the smaller Dad looked.

He came in and sat at the table with me, Val, and Savannah, crying and hurting like I had never seem him hurt before. In fact, in the past, I had only seen him in physical pain—like when he got bucked off of a horse and broke both of his wrists or when a bull got him up against a fence and stuck a horn in him. I had never known he was capable of such emotional pain and I felt so sorry for him.

I learned that day that when death takes one parent, it turns the other into a complete stranger.

Twenty-Five

On Friday, Dad, Val and I went to the funeral home to begin making arrangements. We sat on an over-stuffed leather couch and waited for the somber man in the dark suit to come and talk to us. I knew what he would look like before I saw him. Aren't all morticians somber men in dark suits? Dad was chewing gum, hard and fast, which he does when he's nervous and in a situation in which he can't smoke. His right leg was bouncing up and down—the toe of his cowboy boot wasn't leaving the floor, but everything from his heel to his hip was twitching fast, really fast—like he had to pee very badly. We didn't talk; we didn't know what to say to each other. We had never done this before.

Finally Mr. Tall-Dark-and-Somber approached us and offered some kind and sympathetic words, which were obviously rehearsed. He spoke the way cashiers and waiters do when they say "have a nice day" all day long. We nodded numbly to whatever he said. Since Mom had been cremated, he asked if we wanted to pick out an urn so it could be displayed during the memorial service. We nodded again.

He took us into a room full of urns of all shapes, sizes, colors, and designs. My shopping trance kicked in and I was prepared to browse when Dad walked in behind me, pointed, said, "I'll take that one," then turned to walk out.

I accidently blurted out, "Wait, Dad, what about this one?"

He didn't even look back. He just said no as he walked out with me and Val hot on his heels.

"The oak one with the rose?" Mr. Somber confirmed with Dad. "That's a lovely choice."

More pre-written rhetoric, I thought to myself.

We walked out of the dark funeral home and into the bright sunlight. Dad immediately spit his gum onto the green lawn and pulled a cigarette out of his shirt pocket. His lighter anxiously provided a flame before the cigarette even got to his lips.

"That's a nice one, Dad. I'm sure Mom would have liked it," I said, because I'm a dumbass and didn't know what else to say. Val glared at me, her eyes seconding the dumbass part, and sending me a clue just to shut the hell up. I got the message and we silently returned to 240 Dale Street.

I knew Mom's obituary was coming out on Saturday, two days after she had died, so I pulled into the Albertson's parking lot and willed myself inside to buy a newspaper. I stood in front of the stand, staring at the Idaho Falls *Post Register*, wondering if I could somehow make it so that if I just didn't get the paper, this hadn't happened.

Just get the damn thing and get the hell out, I told myself. I grabbed two copies and went to the checker with the shortest line. I could feel my breathing speeding up and I was sure that I was about to have a full-blown anxiety attack. All of the people in Albertson's were being way too cheerful, too friendly, and too smiley—like they knew something I didn't.

"And how are you doing today?" the happy checker asked me.

I just looked at her, stunned that she had the nerve to ask. Wasn't it obvious? Didn't my face give it away? I was certain it was freshly tattooed on my forehead: My Mother Is Dead!

Inside I was smoldering like a volcano barely able to withhold all the violence that was festering at my surface. I was on the verge of spewing, "How do you think I am? My mother's obituary is in this paper! I am not fine! I will never be fine! My mom is dead. Just ring me up, bitch, and stop smiling at me."

I wanted to roll those newspapers up and hit her with them, but I contained the eruption and slapped them down on her counter, maybe a little too hard. She either sensed my angst or saw horns sprouting from my head because her chipperness vanished with the smack of the papers and she forgot to tell me to have a nice day.

By the time I got to my pickup, I was beginning to hyperventilate. I ripped the paper open and flipped through the pages like an angry professor suspecting plagiarism, until I found it: there, staring back at me was Mom—*my* mom, *my* mother. It was a beautiful picture of her, actually from a driver's license from the mid-'90s. Mom had always taken good driver's license photos. I was not prepared for the feelings that seeing her obituary would bring. By then my breathing resembled that of a person who had just been pulled up from the bottom of a pool after five minutes under water. I was drowning in my own breath and no one was there to rescue me.

I took the papers back to Dad's house. For quite a while, they lay folded on the kitchen table, like yesterday's news. Finally Dad picked one up, opened it, and glanced at it, but not long enough to read it. He then folded the paper open to the obituary page and laid it over the back of Mom's recliner with her picture facing out. Sticking to my m.o., I avoided looking at it and I avoided asking him why.

That Saturday night, Saul and Val had plans to help a friend who was catering a big dinner for a wine auction. They invited me along to help, but we decided to cancel, knowing that, under the circumstances, their friend would understand. Dad insisted that we not cancel, saying he would be OK alone, so we then decided that we could use a little distraction—not to mention a lot of good wine. Then we did the second dumbest thing that we possibly could do (going to the Bahamas being the first), which was suggesting that Savannah and Hannah spend the night with him. We should have known better. With Dad, if there is no arm-twisting involved, it must not be the right thing to do.

We knew that Dad had been drinking heavily all day, but when we left the girls there at five o'clock, we figured he'd be passed out in no time. We figured wrong. The girls sat paralyzed on the couch, pretending to watch TV while he sat at the kitchen table, his sobriety deteriorating as his sadness escalated.

"Grandma is in the bedroom. I want you to go in and see her," he told them. "Go sleep in the dead bed. Grandma wants you to get in the dead bed with her."

He rocked her chair and told them that it was her ghost doing it.

Well, needless to say, this scared them half to death, as it would have any fourteen- and twelve-year-old kids. Savannah pleaded, "Grandpa, knock it off. You're scaring us," but he kept it up until they were so freaked out that Savannah picked up the phone to call me.

"What do you think you are doing?" Dad snapped at her.

"I'm calling my mom," Savannah said.

"Like hell you are," Dad said as he ripped the phone out of her hand.

There they sat, frozen on the couch like two little Barbie dolls, long forgotten, on a Barbie couch in the Barbie House of Horrors. When Dad's head was finally in his hands and he was no longer staring them down, they snuck into the spare bedroom and Savannah used her cell phone to call Dustin.

"Dustin, come get us. Grandpa is drunk and scaring us," she explained, whispering so that Dad couldn't hear her making the call.

The girls stayed in the spare bedroom until they heard Dustin pull up and honk the horn, and then they made a mad dash for the door and jumped into his waiting car. Running across the lawn to Dustin's car, they could hear Dad hollering at them, "Where do you think you're going? Get your asses back in this house!" When they looked back at the house, Dad was standing in the doorway, still hollering at them, but looking like he was wondering what had just happened.

Dustin brought the girls home and we got home a short time after. By then it was around one in the morning but Savannah and Hannah were both still shaken up, talking at the same time, trying to tell us about the dead bed and everything that Dad had said and done. They were still scared but they were also worried about their grandpa, who they had never known to be so sad.

We all knew that Dad was prone to doing some crazy things when he was hammered, but this topped a lot of them. Deciding that I was not going to let him off the hook for it, I grew a backbone and picked up the phone to call him. To my surprise, he answered on the first ring.

"Dad, what the hell are you doing scaring the girls like that?" I jumped him before he got a chance to jump me.

"Goddamned Dustin peeled out of here. He ought to have his ass kicked."

"Dad, you scared the girls with all your crazy talk. What's that all about?" I demanded.

"If that little son of a bitch comes back over here, I'll put knots on his head."

"Why are you saying that stuff, Dad? Do you want the girls to be afraid to stay with you?"

"And those girls are just big babies. I was just kidding with them."

"Well it's not funny, Dad. They're just kids and they don't want to go sleep in Mom's bed. Why would you tell them to do that?"

"Goddamn that Dustin. He roared up here honking the horn."

"And what's this talk about the dead bed, Dad? That's not funny. Why would you say something like that?"

"Then he squealed the tires when he left."

"And why were you rocking the chair and saying it was Mom's ghost doing it? That's mean, Dad. The girls will never want to stay with you again."

"He ought to have his ass kicked for driving like that, and those girls were . . ."

It went on and on and on. It was like listening to the radio and watching TV at the same time. There were two completely different programs playing. He was the TV show, doing a perfect imitation of a drunk. His words were slurred and slow, and in my mind, I could see his head swaying and bobbing. I was the radio. My song was fast, on pitch, and biting, like an angry rap song. I held the phone away from my ear to avoid hearing the rest of his ranting.

"This is not a conversation," I said to Val and Saul, shaking my head in disbelief. "This is a lounge act. We could take it on the road."

"Just hang up on him," Val said.

I put the phone back up to my ear to hear more about knots on Dustin's head, horn-honking, and spinning tires.

"I gotta go, Dad. Try to get some rest. We'll see you tomorrow." I hung up the phone while he was still beating up on Dustin.

Val and I spent most of the rest of the night parked across the street from his house, just watching it, waiting for a strange flash of light or something—for what, we didn't really know.

Twenty-Six

On Tuesday, June 19, which was Larry's forty-fifth birthday, we had Mom's memorial service. Valli and I stayed close to Dad and tried to make small talk with the arriving guests. Aunt Beth walked up to us and touched Dad on the arm, saying, "I'm so sorry for your loss, Gary."

"What the hell do you have to be sorry for?" he snapped, pushing her away so hard that she almost lost her balance as she stumbled backwards. Aunt Beth turned and slunk away, speechless, with hurt feelings to go along with her aching heart.

What Val and I had concluded over the past few days had just been confirmed: Dad selfishly thought that he was the only one who had lost someone and the only one whose heart was broken. It had never occurred to him that his daughters had lost their mother, his grandchildren their grandmother, and Aunt Beth her only sister. All of our grief and pain was there in the room in a big pile before us, and Dad called dibs on the whole thing. He stood over it, guarding it, and was not about to let any of us have our shares.

When it was time to enter the chapel, Dad grabbed me and Val by our hands and squeezed us a little too hard as we made our way to our seats. Larry sat on my right and Dad on my left, followed by Val, Sierra, Savannah, Dustin, Hannah, and Saul. Dad kept his head down, chewing gum, his jittery right leg hopping up and down again. Every so often, he dabbed at his eyes with a Kleenex and squirmed in his seat, obviously uncomfortable.

Hayden, the minister who performed the service, had known my mom well. He was the minister of the church in Billings that she had belonged to for several years. Hayden had officiated at the funeral services for all three of my grandmothers so he knew our family pretty well, although Mom, Aunt Beth, and Grandma Irene were the only faithful followers who regularly attended his church.

He had known Mom well enough to share a few funny stories and to know what a special person she was, but I wasn't listening a whole lot to what he was saying. I was distracted by Dad, plus I was thinking about how nice it would be to have a person of the cloth know me in a personal way if for no other reason than to be able to say nice things about me and share a couple of funny stories at my funeral. Dad and Valli and I didn't know any preachers well enough for them to give a rat's ass about us, let alone say two nice things.

Dad didn't know that Val was going to speak at Mom's service. She had decided not to tell him because she was afraid that he wouldn't let her. I was proud of her for doing it and I admired her courage. I wished that I would have been able to get up there and honor Mom like that, but I didn't trust myself to be able to hold it together.

When Valli got up to speak, Dad finally looked up—probably to see where she was going. He looked surprised to see her heading to the pulpit. Sierra slid over next to her grandpa and put her head on his shoulder. Valli's voice quivered as she began, but Hayden put an arm around her shoulder and said something encouraging to her so she wiped her nose a couple of times then read a beautiful and meaningful message that she had written for Mom, about Mom. Dad was visibly moved and looked down again, dabbing his eyes harder and more often. His leg jumped faster. I put my left arm around his shoulder and reached over and put my right hand on his leg. He stopped hopping it like my touch was that of a faith healer and his jitters had suddenly gone into remission. I felt his shoulders relax a bit and a quiet little sigh escaped from his lips. For a minute or two, he allowed me and Sierra to come into his space without pulling away.

Part Three

Dirt Roads

Twenty-Seven

Day One

"When did we live here? How long were we here? Why did we leave? Where did we go next?"

Val and I have asked Dad these questions at least twenty times in seven days, as we have gone from town to town, ranch to ranch. Sometimes he answers, but most of the time he just keeps looking for the answer in a cloud of Camel cigarette smoke and mumbles something I can't hear. Dad, my sister, and I are on a trip, traveling back to all of the places where we have ever lived.

Shortly after Mom died, Dad announced to us that he wanted to make this trek. Val and I agreed, saying, "Sure, Dad, just let us know when you want to go." We were both thinking, *Yeah, right, like that'll ever happen.*

We reminded each other that in our forty-some years he had never taken us on a trip or a vacation, or whatever you want to call it when you go somewhere just to go. We had once lived less than fifty miles from Yellowstone National Park and had never been to it. Whenever we asked to go there, he said, "Someday." It was kind of like Mom and the Lewis and Clark Caverns. We were pretty sure that this trip would never happen.

When Dad picked a date in August and it wasn't just "someday" anymore, we knew there was no getting out of it. Then just a few days before we were due to leave, he came down with a case of pneumonia that landed him in the hospital for a week. I was sure it was a sign from God; He was trying to save me from the torture chamber. Dad was miserable and cranky, which was not much different from how he was when he wasn't in the hospital. At first, we thought it was because they wouldn't let him smoke or have a drink in the hospital, but when he said, "Now I know we'll never go on our trip," we both understood how important it was to him. We promised that we would go and told him to pick a new date.

D-day comes and I am the designated driver of Dad's pickup; he's in the passenger seat. Val is squeezed in the small back seat, with Mom's ashes in a Harley-Davidson backpack next to her.

We start the trip in Billings, at Sunset Memorial Gardens where Grandma Irene and Great-Grandma are buried. Dad hands Val a Styrofoam cup and tells her to get some of Mom's ashes out. Now, I've been known to be able to unlock doors with a credit card and I am fairly talented in forgery, but I have no experience in breaking into urns and I have no intention of adding that to my list of petty crimes.

We are acting like two little kids. "You do it," one of us says.

"No, Dad told you to do it," the other replies.

"I'm not doing it, you do it."

Our squabble turns to laughter and Dad shoots us a stink eye—the one that says he's about to tear us a new asshole—so we shut up and take a joint crash course in Urn Breaking and Entering 101.

I'm creeped out, but I offer moral support while Val puts some of Mom's ashes into the cup. Then we join Dad. He spreads some of the ashes on Great-Grandma's grave ceremoniously, shaking the cup like he is a Catholic cardinal at a beatification. We are all looking down, as if in prayer, but we are really looking at our shoes, which the wind has dusted with a light covering of Mom's ashes.

It seems like one of us should say something. I wait for Dad, but he says nothing, making me wonder if he has taken a vow of silence. It becomes painfully obvious that none of us knows what to say, so we all just stand at the gravesite in our temporary vows, heads bowed. I'm thinking I'm probably the only one praying and I'm praying for lightning to strike me dead before I spend seven days in a row with my dad. With no eulogy whatsoever, we leave the cemetery and stay silent for a few more minutes. Dad seems sad for a moment, then starts us on a trip down memory lane. Some of it we know, some we don't, and a lot of it we have tried to forget.

Twenty-Eight

Molt, Montana, is a tiny ghost town about thirty miles outside of Billings. The buildings are so rundown that I'm sure even the ghosts have long since moved on. As newlyweds, this was Mom and Dad's first home. It was also my first home. We find the small shack, which is now beyond dilapidation.

"Now that's what I'd call a fixer-upper," I say to Val.

"I think I could do something with that," she says, trying to sound serious, and like Martha.

"There's the toilet," Dad says, pointing to a little, rectangular outhouse that's leaning at a forty-five degree angle.

"Owwww. I don't think I could do anything with that," Val says, still pretending to be serious, but cracking up at her own joke.

"Your ma hung curtains in there," he says, then tells

us that he tore them down because "what the hell you gonna do with curtains in an outhouse?"

"Stick 'em up your ass?" I suggest.

The fact that they actually called this little shack home is even more deplorable than the act of breaking into an urn, I decide. It's proof that Mom must have really loved her man, because I can't believe that a woman would voluntarily live in a shithole like this.

"Even forty-five years ago it had to be a shithole," I say to no one.

"Yep," Dad confirms, with no apologies. "Not much better than it is now." Everything seems to be in some form of deterioration and it doesn't take long to see all of Molt, Montana.

On our way back into Billings, we stop on the side of the road, along the rims, for a little picnic. Of course, we have a cooler that Dad has stocked with lunchmeat, cheese, mayo, and beer. I look into a grocery bag and find chips, bread, vodka, cranberry juice and cigarettes. Dad and I make sandwiches and he has a beer. Val eats cheese and chips.

From the rims, it's a straight shot down Twenty-seventh Street to the south side, where we'll do a few more drive-bys. Dad points out about half a dozen dumps that he and Mom lived in when I was a baby. This was all before I was old enough to remember, so none of it means anything to me, but I nod my head and ask those same four questions again. Leaving them unanswered—again—I drive out of Billings, heading east towards Forsyth.

Along the way, we stop in the little town of Pompey's Pillar and go to the bar, which everyone just calls "Lou's" (except for Dad, who has always referred to it as "Pimpy's Parlor"), even though the sign on the front of the building says "Lewis and Clark Tavern." This is the place that I joked with Mom about when she said that she wanted to go the Lewis and Clark *Cavern*.

Lou is behind the bar, as usual, and is surprised to see us. We don't discuss our trip or offer any explanations as to why we are passing through, and we don't stay long. Dad has a quick drink and then we drive the few miles to our old place.

In 1982 Dad and Mom and Larry and I moved to Pompey's Pillar. We each had our own little trailer homes and lived within shouting distance of each other. Dad had been trucking since 1977 and by then his little trucking company was doing pretty well. He and Larry were on the road, Mom was dispatching, and I was working for her as a bookkeeper—something that I had absolutely no qualifications for, other than that I was family.

Sierra was born in February of 1983 and in August of that same year Val, the agnostic, and Saul, the Jew, were married in the little Catholic church in Pompey's Pillar by Hayden, the Protestant minister. Shortly after their marriage they moved to Pullman, Washington, where Saul was getting his master's degree. They returned to Pompey's a couple of years later and lived just down the road for a little while, less than a quarter of a mile away. It seemed like a cozy, family setting—like a commune.

By 1984 Dad was tired of being on the road and had decided to quit trucking. There were enough guys working for them that he and Mom were making a nice living, so they could actually afford for him to be off the road. He spent his mornings hanging around the office and his afternoons in the arena with a half dozen young horses and some roping cattle.

About a year later, Dad got tired of putting up with the day-to-day tedium of the business and decided to quit. He gave us two choices: either Larry and I were each out of a job or we had to buy him out. We chose the latter and signed our names to a big, fat bank loan. Overnight, the boss's daughter and the boss's son-in-law became the bosses. I was twenty-five with a two-year-old devil-child, hiring and firing men who were twice my age. Dad retained a few shares of stock in the company—just enough to make me squirm.

Mom then began working for me as a dispatcher, her qualifications far exceeding my own. Larry was still on the road, sometimes staying away for several weeks at a time. Each morning, Mom and I jumped up and ran to our office (which was in the enclosed porch of her trailer house), while Dad had nowhere to go. No one cared if he even got out of bed. His horses only occupied so many hours each day and they only cared if he showed up to feed them and fill up their water tanks. It was about then that boredom and alcohol took over his days and nights.

At first, happy hour started at about five, when Dad would bring cocktails out to our desks. As time went by, it got earlier and earlier until we sometimes had drinks on our desks by two. By five, we were either tipsy or ready for our next round, depending on how busy our day had been. When we went from the office to the house, which consisted of stepping up one stair from the porch into the kitchen, Dad and a Crock-Pot full of beans were usually waiting for us. Even though I had my own house, Sierra and I usually ate dinner with Mom and Dad since Larry was never home.

Around that time, Dad started complaining about the office being in their house because the phone never stopped ringing, so Larry and I built a little log building just up the hill from our trailer houses. It was pretty basic and had no plumbing but it served its purpose.

Sierra came to the office with me every day and I tried to keep her occupied at her own little desk with pens, paper, markers, and a calculator. One day while she was mopping the office floor with her toy mop and I tracked through her pretend water, she glared and shook her mop at me and said, "Mom, just sit down and be constipated."

Besides learning to run a ten-key, she was learning a lot of very big words—some that shouldn't be repeated by a three-year-old. So when I overheard her talking on her play telephone and telling Frank, her pretend truck driver, to "get his ass down the road," I decided that the office might not be the best environment for her to grow up in and that she should go to a babysitter—I should have said "a *real* babysitter" because Dad said, "Bullshit, she can just hang out with me all day."

The one time Mom left Dad to babysit his own kids, he used a garden hose to clean off Valli's butt after she pooped her pants. I have a vague memory of him turning on the water and putting his thumb over the end of the hose to build up enough water pressure to squirt the diarrhea off her little white butt. He held on to her by one arm while she did a dance in a circle to get away from the cold water. Luckily for Valli, it was summertime.

Although I was aware of this fact, we were talking about a child who even the dogs didn't like, so I took him up on his offer. Besides, the office was within walking distance of our houses, so I could still kind of keep an eye on Sierra, I reasoned.

She loved being with her Grandpa and always came home with fistfuls of candy and a headful of stories. Dad would take her to Lou's, sit her on a bar stool, and feed her pop, pickled eggs, pork rinds, and candy all day long. If she got tired he laid her down on the pool table to nap.

This also coincided with the start of my relationship with the Poison Control Center. I was on a first-name basis with the staff there. After about the third time in as many months, all I had to do was say, "This is Tammi in Montana," and they would say, "What did Sierra get into now?" Then they would say, "Don't let her grandpa babysit her today." *They* even called *me* once—just to check up on us, I guess.

I am likely the only mother out there who has actually used more than three bottles of ipecac. I hate to admit that my daughter had her very own puke bucket (decorated with her name on it), but not to admit to it would just leave one more thing for me to be in denial about. Truth is, I used to chase her down with a spoon full of the stuff, saying, "Sierra get your butt and your bucket over here and take this! You need to puke." After the first few times, she just got her bucket and took her medicine.

Dad may not have been the best babysitter, but he was available. I called the PCC (Poison Control Center) early one morning after Sierra had gotten into a bottle of Aleve. She had woken me up around five, with the evidence of blue pills still sticking to her lips and tongue. The PCC told me not to let her eat or sleep for the next six to eight hours, so I relayed the instructions to Dad, only to find out later that she slept in the pickup while he was at Lou's. When she had woken up hungry, he had fed her a Milky Way, two Reese's, an orange soda, and a sack of pork rinds. She then promptly continued her sleep-fest on the pool table.

(FYI, a dose of four to six Aleve is not lethal to a three-year old, half of a bottle of Children's Tylenol does not cause permanent liver damage, sheetrock is not toxic when ingested, and pennies swallowed will end up being pennies pooped . . . I could go on).

From my office window, I could see Dad riding his horses with Sierra trotting along behind him, following him all over the pasture. If he wasn't on some bronc-y colt, he would eventually pick her up and give her a ride on his horse. She was as loyal to him as his dogs were; they all followed him everywhere. Sierra often went deer hunting with her grandpa and she once asked me to come with her out to the shed, where there were three dead deer hanging upside down. She then proudly pointed out which deer's head belonged to which decapitated carcass. It wasn't exactly the kind of matching game that most three-year-olds were playing, but I had to admit, she did know her heads and carcasses.

She helped her grandpa skin raccoons and rattle-snakes and trap coyotes. In the summer, they spent entire days on the Yellowstone River—camping, rafting, catching catfish, and picking asparagus and morel mushrooms. In the winter, they toughed it out in his tent, blowing on embers in his old wood stove to make the fire restart, then eating two- and three-day-old beans that had been heated and reheated with not much more than a farmer's match.

One wintery day, Dad shot a fox, put it in a running pose, and let it freeze solid before standing it up next to the front gate of their house. The dogs spent all winter barking at it while Sierra treated the frozen fox like a pet, talking to it and patting it on the head each morning and evening as she walked by it. It stood in its frozen race with time until spring came and it thawed out, then finally fell over and began to rot.

Sierra wasn't the only player though. Larry and I did our share—sometimes under silent protest and sometimes because we didn't want Dad on the prowl with a loaded rifle and a fifth of Black Velvet. We spent many evenings spotlighting. I would drive and Sierra would hold the spotlight, aiming it in the general direction that Dad directed her to while he and Larry aimed their .357s, .44 Mags, and AK-47s at deer, raccoons, coyotes, skunks, and anything else that moved.

Dad was even so ballsy as to poach a deer in the deputy sheriff's yard. After he shot it, he and Larry bailed out of the pickup and, with the stealth and precision of Navy SEALs, crawled on their bellies into the sheriff's yard, while Sierra and I idled by with the headlights and radio off, holding our breath. When they dragged the dead deer to the highway and signaled us with a quick flick of the flashlight, we coasted up with the engine and lights still off. Then we went home and let our adrenaline settle by the shed, alongside the deer guts, where we shared shots of whiskey and retold the story to each other. Needless to say, Sierra's bedtime was often very, very late (or very, very early, depending on how one looked at it).

Besides hunting, keeping hunting secrets, and camping on the river with her grandpa, Sierra did all the things that children of the late 1800s did. She drove Dad's mule wagon train, fetched wood for his fires, practiced her knife- and axe-throwing skills, skinned dead animals, and made his cocktails.

She and Dustin once spent two weeks on the wagon train camping with their grandpa and grandma. During the trip, Dad killed a five-foot-long rattlesnake, skinned it, poked it onto a piece of wire, and let the kids cook it over the fire. The kids each came home packing a piece of rattlesnake meat wrapped in saran wrap, which they carried around in the front pockets of their jeans. Several times a day, each of them would take the gray chunk of meat out and take a bite, telling us how good it was and offering bites to Val, me, and their grandparents (no takers).

This rite of passage earned them their Indian names: Sierra proudly announced that Grandpa had renamed her "Straight Arrow" and Dustin informed us that he was now to be called "Crooked Arrow." It took a few more months before Savannah earned her name, but she was bursting with pride when she declared that she would now be known as "Spills-A-Lot."

For the kids, spending the day with Dad was the equivalent of spending a day at the circus but like the rest of us, they were never quite sure what to expect from him. I have to believe that Sierra and Dustin ate two-week-old rattlesnake not because it was good, but because their grandpa liked watching them do it. One thing about it was for sure: the kids were having the times of their lives with the man they called "Grandpa Coyote."

Booze, mules, fires, and rattlesnakes didn't seem like that big of a deal. At least, they didn't seem like that big of a deal twenty years ago. Looking back, I have to ask myself, *What the hell were you thinking? Were you in a full-blown coma?*

The truth—about which I was most likely in denial—is that I was afraid that Dad was turning Sierra into me and I didn't know what to do about it. Letting my little girl hang out in a bar all day and ride around in a vehicle with a drunken man and a shotgun was against my better judgment, but I was busy busting my butt, trying to keep our little trucking company afloat. I figured that if I had survived my childhood, well . . . she would too.

I'm pretty sure that by pleading insanity, I would have gotten out of the Montana State Pen by now.

Twenty-Nine

During those years, Dad's only job seemed to be drinking. In fact, he was putting in overtime and was getting out of control. While he was busy corrupting my daughter, Larry, Mom, and I were all busy trying to pay the bills and keep the wolves away. Mom loved her job as a dispatcher and she was great at it. She oversaw about thirty truck drivers and each one of them adored and respected her as if she were their own mother. Nobody was a better listener than Mom and she was kind and compassionate to the men, often counseling them in love and money matters.

Mom was pretty much living two lives. There was the one that lasted from eight to five, where she had power, control, and respect. She was upbeat, laughing and singing her way through the workday. Then there was the life she went home to—the one in which she never knew what to expect. If she came home in a great mood and Dad was cranky and sulky then Mom's good mood evaporated like water in a hot skillet. If she had a rough day and came home to find Dad partying, she put on her party hat too. If he wanted a drinking buddy, she made cocktails. If he didn't want to talk, she shut up. If he wanted to argue, she picked the opposing side. If he wanted to eat rattlesnake, she put the salt and pepper on the table. Other than the fact that Dad prepared dinner every night, Mom's home life was pretty much a living hell.

Meanwhile, Valli and my emotions were being torn in two. The kids loved being with their grandpa; he gave them *carte blanche* and could keep them entertained for hours with games that would be guaranteed to be prohibited in school. Whenever he fell asleep and settled into a deep and rhythmic snore, they would unsnap the pearl snaps on his western shirt to get a clear shot at his belly button. Then they would play what they called "belly ball," which consisted of them making spitballs and trying to shoot them into his belly button. Once in a while, he would twitch or break-snore if a big wet one plugged him, but for the most part he slept through the attacks and the giggling. I won't even try to explain "butt darts."

It wasn't so much fun and games for us. Val and I stayed pissed off at Dad almost constantly. It had nothing to do with him feeding our kids old rattlesnake meat or teaching them to walk with a dollar worth of quarters pinched between their butt cheeks. It was because he was mean to Mom when he was drunk. We knew he loved her, but when the booze was flowing, it may as well have been gasoline. Dad was as unpredictable as a match and Mom as silent as a wood pile. Love can't put out a fire, so destruction was inevitable. We supported Mom, but only behind Dad's back, and we never dared to confront Dad about his drinking or his behavior. After all, we were only about thirty years old by then—not nearly old enough to stand up to our father. So we bitched at her for not standing up to him. We wanted her to have the courage that we didn't have—to be our backbone—even though we knew that we would have tucked our tails and run if she had stood up to him, leaving her alone to take on the monster. We questioned each other about why we were all putting up with his abuse. We didn't have the answer but we still put up with it. Eventually we started asking Mom why *she* was putting up with it.

"I love your father. I couldn't live without him," she had said. It was obvious that no matter how bad his behavior got, Mom was going to live with it. I knew that she could live with it, but I wondered if she could *survive* it.

We talked about trying to get Dad into treatment but Mom was scared to death to even broach the subject. She had once told him that she was going to go to an AA meeting and he told her, "If you do go, don't come back." Needless to say, she never went. It took a lot of persuading to get her to go along with us to one of the local treatment centers to inquire about enrollment and intervention. I spilled the beans to Dad a couple of days after that in the middle of one of our heated arguments when I smugly said, "Do you know where we went the other day, Dad? We went and talked to the Rimrock Foundation about getting you into treatment. We all think you need to go."

Then I watched Mom as she broke out in hives just from thinking about his reaction. He looked shocked; his eyes turned black and he aimed his verbal gun dead-on and shot me down with insults so quickly that I limped home like a pathetic has-been gunslinger. Not only was I unable to fire back, I couldn't even get my arsenal of reasons out of my holster. After that, we just plotted to have him committed—or killed.

Dad was drunk, but he wasn't stupid. He knew when he crossed a line, but he would never say that he was sorry for anything. We just learned to know when he was. Sometimes we held out and stayed mad for a while, but we usually accepted his apology when Mom told us that he was sorry.

Dustin was about eight years old when Val caught him and Dad on the farm tractor. Dustin was driving and Dad was drunk.

"Goddamn it, Dad. What are you doing letting Dustin drive? He doesn't know how to drive a tractor!" she ranted.

"Well, he's got to learn sometime," Dad shot back.

Valli stood her ground. "You've been drinking, Dad. I don't want Dustin on the tractor with you when you're drunk. He could get killed."

"You're overreacting. I'm not drunk."

"Yes, you are. Dustin, get off the tractor right now!" Val demanded.

"Besides," Dad said, "accidents happen. You got to expect to lose a kid every once in awhile."

That was it! Valli grabbed Dustin by an arm and jerked him off the tractor, then marched them both back to the house to tell Mom that she was not going to let Dustin stay with them. She began gathering up his belongings while Mom cried and begged her to let Dustin stay. Mom was apologizing for Dad, saying he didn't mean it and he was sorry.

Dad came staggering to the house and got pissed off when he saw that Valli was packing Dustin up. Mom was heartbroken and she was torn between being mad at Dad and making excuses for him. She loved spending time with the grandkids and she was devastated that Val was taking Dustin away, threatening never to let him stay over again.

Dad knew that he had screwed up big time and he was trying to make light of it, saying that he was just kidding about the "losing a kid" part, but Valli refused to be bullied. She stood up, looked him in the eye, and went toe-to-toe with him. She didn't know it at the time, but while she was chewing Dad out, she was also chewing through a piece of that imaginary cord that had kept her tethered to him.

By then my relationship with Dad had become pretty volatile. I had confronted him about his drinking, which made me public enemy number one, and for the first time in my life I was siding with Mom instead of him. Between the guns and the booze, we were living out an Ol' West show and all that we could expect from him was the unexpected. He would sometimes stay drunk for three or four days at a time and the more he drank, the more violent and unpredictable he became.

One day Dad came home from Lou's with a black eye and we all pretended that we didn't notice. Each of us turned a blind eye when he left in a rage, went to the home of the guy who had sucker punched him, and proceeded to shoot the shit out of the guy's pickup and tractor. We ignored the sound of gunfire when Dad came home and pumped a couple of rounds into the side of his own pickup to make the fight look less one-sided in case the sheriff was called.

We didn't call him on the carpet when he threw a hi-lift jack through the driver's side window of Larry's brand-new pickup just because it was locked when he wanted to borrow it. We watched silently when he got drunk and climbed onto a loose horse, then got bucked off and broke his collarbone and thumb. Mom just hauled him to the hospital and we all pretended not to notice when he came home with his arm in a sling and his thumb stuck in the air like a hitchhiker. We certainly never questioned him about it. He was the elephant in the room and we were all afraid of a stampede.

There were nights when our fighting escalated to barroom levels, like the night he busted out Larry's pickup window and then came home in a drunken tirade—ranting, but satisfied with himself for taking matters into his own hands. He cussed Larry, called him names, and threatened to kill him. I stood on my tiptoes and cussed back at him, defending my husband. He got in my face and poked his finger in my chest, punctuating his motives. I was shaking in my boots, but continued to lip off, trying to out-bully him. I called him an asshole. Dad snarled and looked rabid as his finger backed me out of his house, one word at a time, leaving a sore spot on my chest. My milquetoast mother looked helplessly on, afraid and reluctant to intervene on behalf of either one of us.

Thirty

Dad had me on an emotional rollercoaster. He would come into my office and sit in the chair across from my desk, telling me one day that I was a "piss-poor boss" and the next that I was doing a good job. If there was whiskey on his breath I tried to ignore him, but the truth was that I constantly felt like I was being dangled over the edge of a cliff by a string. Right after he pushed me over with an insult, he would pull me up with a compliment. When I asked him to sign papers pertaining to our trucking business (which he was still a minor shareholder in), he refused, saying that I was the "big shot," so I could figure it out on my own.

In 1994 Mom and Dad left Pompey's to take a ranch job in Idaho. Somehow Dad still managed to beat me up from four hundred miles away. The sleepless nights, the anxiety attacks, the hyperventilating, and the constant hot rock in the pit of my stomach finally got the best of me. I'd had enough, so that year I included a note with his Father's Day card that asked him to sign over his stock certificates. As incentive, I enclosed a check for thirty thousand dollars. He signed the note and cashed the check and not a word of it was ever mentioned between the two of us.

Then in May of 1998 the other proverbial shoe dropped: Dad was diagnosed with prostate cancer. Even though I spoke to my mother on the phone *every single day*, it was not until a few weeks after his diagnosis that I even found out about it. I'm ashamed to admit that even to this day, I actually know very few of the details. What I do know is that it was sometime between their move from Pompey's to Deming, so that would put the timeline *after* mom's mastectomy but *before* the shit really hit the fan.

On their way from Montana to New Mexico, they took a detour to Seattle so that Dad could receive some type of hormone shot or implant, I'm not sure which. My guess is that Mom was either forbidden to talk about it or had a gun to her head, which is why she never shared any fears or concerns with me. Dad totally blew off the whole thing, which is what I should have expected. I remember hearing about him not being a candidate for prostate surgery because his heart wasn't strong enough to be put under the knife. His heart may have been stressed and he did have high blood pressure, but the truth is that it was more likely due to his emphysema, which we were all still referring to as "Dad's breathing."

Finally in March of 1999, which was about six months after they moved to Deming and a good ten months after his diagnosis, Dad began radiation treatments in Las Cruces. His first treatment was one day before his fifty-ninth birthday. He then made the daily 120-mile drive by himself for the next four or five months. It was a rough year for him, but I never once heard him complain. He felt bad from the treatments and ended up drinking a good part of that year away. About a year after he finished his treatments, Mom's battle began. No wonder Dad was . . . well, like he was.

Looking back, I find it so sad that we never rallied around Dad like we did with Mom, but that's just the way things were. We weren't supposed to worry about him—and we certainly weren't allowed to tell him what to do. I only remember having one conversation with Dad that related to his cancer. He was talking in a high-pitched voice, being a smart-ass about the hormone thing, when I asked, "Are you growing boobs?"

"No," he said. "But I'm thinkin' I want some anklets and a canopy bed."

Although Mom and Dad lived in Pompey's longer than they lived in any other place, those had to have been some of the worst years of their lives. The happy days of cowboying were behind them and this was the place where Mom's breast cancer first reared its ugly head and where Dad's drinking sank him to new lows.

Being back in Pompey's and seeing their old trailer house makes me sad. The spot where Larry and my old trailer house used to sit is now a barren piece of dirt. A few old sewer and water pipes are poking up from the ground, along with an electric pole that is breathing no life into anyone. I can barely make out where our yard used to be, but the old shed that housed the deer carcasses is still standing, keeping our hunting secrets.

I can tell that it makes Dad sad too. He is fidgety but suddenly quiet, and he is chain-smoking. I know that it pains him to see their old trailer house—the house that Mom had loved and the only new house that she had ever moved into. She had put her heart and soul into that home and its yard and garden. The eighty-year-old iris bulbs that she had dug up from her aunt's house in Big Timber, Montana, are still standing tall, although the flowers went to seed a couple months or so ago.

We don't stay long. A quick look around and Dad seems ready to leave the ghosts of Pompey's Pillar behind, once and for all. I know that I am ready to split. I never left a damn thing in Pompey's Pillar.

Thirty-One

Forsyth is where we lived from the fall of 1966 until the spring of 1969, which was the longest that we stayed in one place during our vagabond childhood. I was six years old and Val was four when we moved here.

At Forsyth, I lost my first tooth and my second one—on the same day. Although it barely wiggled, I was so excited about finally having a loose tooth that I proudly made the announcement to Dad.

"Let me see," he said.

I pointed out my bottom center baby tooth to him, and he wiggled it back and forth with his thumb, barely moving it.

"We better get that thing out of there," he said. "Go get my pliers—the needle nose ones."

I brought back his pliers and then opened wide while he hooked on to my miniature tooth and began twisting it.

"I don't think it's ready to come out, Dad," I tried to tell him, but since the pliers were still in my mouth, it sounded more like, "Rye ron't rink rit's ready ro rome rout."

"Shit-o-dear, that thing must have a helluva root on it," Dad said to himself as he pulled and pried. Finally I heard the roots give up their hold. I felt the tooth rip free and the blood gush into my mouth.

"Got it!" Dad said triumphantly. "Better go rinse your mouth out."

I went into the bathroom and stuck my head under the faucet, swished and spit out a mouthful of bloody water, then stuck my tongue in the deep, fleshy hole where the tooth had been.

"Come here, Tam. Let me see," Dad called to me. I opened up and he grabbed my chin and tilted my head in different directions to examine his work.

"Shit," he said, "we better get that one next to it out so it can come in straight."

"But that one's not loose, Dad."

"Don't matter. You don't want your new tooth to come in crooked, do you?" He had a point.

I thought about it for a second, then said no and opened up my mouth. Mom tried to come to my defense by saying, "Gary, don't pull it if it's not loose."

"It needs to come out," he said, still mostly talking to himself. "Hang on to the table, Tam. This one may hurt a little," he said.

Valli watched the whole procedure, but kept her hand over her mouth and shook her head when Dad asked her if she had any loose teeth before he put the pliers away.

Thinking about it now, I glance in the rearview mirror and flash myself a big phony smile—the same one I use at the dentist's office during a teeth whitening procedure. *Damned if my teeth aren't perfect. Maybe Dad was right about pulling that second one*, I think. While checking out my cheesy grin, I swear I notice a few new lines on my face—probably laugh lines . . . or bad lighting, I lie to myself.

As we drive on the gravel road to our old place, I feel like I know the way, but when we come to the house, I don't recognize it. We bounce across the railroad tracks where the school bus used to pick us up, and I glance out my window for a petrified piece of frog-bacon. The little white house with faded green trim sits next to a big, empty pasture.

We used to have so much fun here in the winter. Valli and I would sit on an old car hood that had been turned upside down and Dad would pull us through the snow on his horse, riding at breakneck speed. Val and I would squeal with delight and hang on for dear life as we tried not to fall off when Dad slung us around corners. As long as there was snow, he gave us a ride almost every day before turning his horse out for the evening.

But for as much fun as we had in Forsyth, we also got in more trouble here than almost anywhere else we lived. While living here, I think we got spankings from Mom almost every day, due to our nonstop fighting and name-calling. Usually sometime after breakfast she began hollering; by lunchtime she was threatening us. Our fights would escalate to hitting, biting, Barbie-bashing, pinching, hair-pulling, and kicking. Mom usually picked a random moment to snatch us each by an arm and whip the hell out of us. Valli promptly cried and apologized while dancing in a circle (doing what we called the "Valli stomp"). I stood still and laughed while Mom whaled on my butt, which made her all the more mad and would cause her to hit me even harder, which caused me to laugh harder. I wasn't about to cry during the whipping, having decided that if anyone was going to, it would be her. I could tell that she was killing her hand with each hit from the way that she talked in broken sentences: "If—" smack me, shake hand, "—you—" smack me, shake hand, "—don't—" smack me, shake hand, "—stop—" smack me, shake hand, —[insert whatever it was that I needed to stop doing immediately].

If you asked my dad, he would say that he has only given Valli two whippings in her entire life. One came was when she was about five years old, when she let the tomcat into the house and it got into a fight with the house cat. They got underneath the refrigerator and nearly shredded every bit of wiring that was under there. Dad poked a broom under the fridge and snagged one of them, but when he reached down to grab it, it opened up a can of whoop-ass on his arm. In one swoop, he threw that old tom plumb over the telephone wires and then grabbed Valli, who had been standing there, wide-eyed, watching the fight, and whaled her little butt.

He would also say that he has given me about twice that many. The truth is that he is probably right. I don't want to insinuate that Dad beat us, because that's simply not true. He rarely spanked us, but he did kick us in the butt, thunk us on the head with a spring-loaded middle finger fired off his thumb, smack us with a rope, and knock our heads together. Whichever method he chose, it was over in one swift, stinging motion.

As we pull into the driveway, we can tell that the house is abandoned so Val and I jump out of the pickup, anxious to go inside. Dad snaps at us, "No, you can't go inside."

It only stops us for a second. Together, we have the strength to gang up on him and say, "No one's here, Dad. We're going in."

The weeds are waist-high. The door is stubborn but it gives way with a good, swift hip thrust. Whoever lived here last left without taking a thing. The house is full of junk, but I assume none of it is ours. The walls are nicotine-colored and there are still curtains hanging over the living room windows. I search my memory to see if they are the ones that Mom made. I remember her dyeing old bed sheets and sewing them into curtains for this room, but for the life of me I can't remember what color they were. I tell myself that these can't be them, although these curtains *could* pass for old sheets.

There is a beautiful leaded glass window in the living room and Valerie wants to steal it. We hatch a plan, but decide that there is no way to sneak it out without Dad noticing, especially since we can see him through it, sitting in the pickup, smoking a cigarette, sipping a cocktail, anxiously waiting for us to come out. There are several religious pictures (not ours) on the walls which have multiple colors of paint peeling off of them, and the house reeks of mouse shit.

I poke my head into the bathroom and notice that the floor still slopes away, leaving a big enough gap that snakes and salamanders can still crawl in between the toilet and the tiny tin shower.

Whenever we had the croup (which was often in this freezing cold house), Mom would turn the shower on full-blast, sit us girls on the toilet, and make us breathe the hot steam. It was in this bathroom that I started to suspect that my mother smoked, although I never saw her actually inhale that first puff that gave life to a cigarette. I would classify her as a wannabe smoker—not a pro like my dad, who could roll his own with one hand and light a match off of his jeans with the other.

Mom only came out of the closet when one of us got a head cold. She would then diagnose us with an ear infection, which prompted her to prescribe a sip of whiskey, light up a cigarette, and blow smoke into the afflicted ear. I had my suspicions that this treatment was not an actual medical procedure, but an after-dinner smoke to go along with a nightcap.

While we sipped a shot of whiskey, she casually puffed a whole Camel into our ears. If one of us managed to stay sick for more than a day, she would usually produce a pack of something menthol, like Salems. Truth is, I liked the feeling of the cool mint going into my ear. This ritual was always done very late at night, in the quiet of the steamy bathroom. It had a secret feel to it—like I wasn't supposed to be sipping whiskey and Mom wasn't supposed to be puffing cigarettes.

We make our way up a staircase that is much narrower and steeper than I remember and find our way into our old bedrooms, which are also much smaller than I recall. I stick my head into the closet and the memory of old brown beer bottles, broken but with the tops still in place, seeps into my mind. Mom and Dad had gotten on a beer brewing kick and put the beer bottles in my closet to age. Most of them had exploded for no apparent reason. Not only was I awakened many nights by the sound of bottles shattering, but my room reeked of beer for about a year.

Valli sticks her head into what used to be my room and surveys the junk scattered all over the floor. "You always were a bad housekeeper," she tells me, interrupting my thoughts.

"That's why I have a maid now," I remind her.

"We're here, Mom," she says. She is holding the cup that carries Mom's ashes. "Just one thing missing." I see tears instantly fill her eyes.

"Come on, let's go downstairs," I say, "before we both start boobing."

Back downstairs, I walk into the kitchen and instantly feel sick, just like I still do to this day when I see Almond Bark.

I ask Val, "Do you remember that New Year's Eve when Mom and Dad went out partying and Aunt Beth stayed at home with us?"

I don't wait for her answer. "Mom and Dad got into a huge fight," I continue. "I remember her begging, 'Gary, no! Gary, please! I'm sorry!'"

Val just listens, with her back to me, not offering any of her own recollections of the incident.

I go on, the scene clear in my mind.

"And I remember getting up the next morning and seeing one of Mom's shoes lying on the kitchen table with the heel broken off."

I imagine that the other one was probably left along the highway somewhere between here and the Century Club. I picture a fight between them—Dad driving off, Mom running after him, losing a shoe like a white trash Cinderella, and breaking the heel off of the other because she was running as fast as the pickup, or maybe because she was hanging on to the door handle and he was dragging her.

"There was also a handful of red hair," I tell Val, "and then there was that little plastic container of white chocolate Almond Bark." I feel sick just from dredging up the memory.

For the next twenty years of my life, I claimed to hate almonds without having ever actually eaten one. And to this day, I would rather chew tinfoil than eat white chocolate. Even thinking about it makes my stomach do a flip—and seeing Almond Bark brings on a mild anxiety attack.

Val finally turns to face me and she looks shocked.

"I don't remember that!" she snaps, referring to the shoe and the handful of hair. "I remember crawling into bed with Mom the next morning, and she had a black eye, a bloody lip, and a hangover," she tells me.

"I don't remember that," I bark back at her. "They fought that night, but he never hit her."

Val rolls her eyes at me, as if to say, "whatever," obviously still irritated that I always stick up for Dad. She knows that I am in denial, even though I would deny that.

I roll mine back at her, shrug my shoulders, and search my mind for a reason that could explain my selective memory.

"Come on," she says, "let's get out of here before he comes looking for us."

When we get back outside, he gives us the third degree about what we have seen in there, so we invite him to come in, like we own the place. He looks at us like we have two heads each and snaps, "Let's get the hell out of here before someone sees us." I notice his eyes are damp.

As we back out of the drive, Val points out the leaded glass window and asks Dad if we can steal it. He ignores her.

We leave the house and the window in our rearview mirror and Dad points me in a direction that takes us into the hills of Rosebud County.

Something about big pastures dotted with black cows with no fences in sight brings out a side of Dad that I like—and that I'm not used to seeing. It's like these open pastures and dirt roads calm him down and give him peace of mind, taking him to a higher spiritual place.

Is it just him or is it the memory of Mom in these hills? I wonder. I don't know the answer, but it doesn't matter—I feel it too. With our windows rolled down, the lukewarm September air calmly wraps itself around us as it makes its way through the cab of the pickup, allowing the scents it carries with it to linger over us for a moment. The faint aromas of sagebrush, dust, and Mom pass over us and with them Dad's edginess dissipates and is carried out of our air space in the arms of the slight breeze. For an instant, Dad seems to have found his Nirvana and I find it relaxing to see this sad, unpredictable man at peace. Driving down this dusty road, he does more reminiscing and storytelling than I have heard him do in my entire life.

He reminds me that this is the place we lived when I got my first horse. As I recall, that was the best day of my young life!

Mighty Mite was a young, unbroken, spooky, high-spirited horse. I was eight years old the first time Dad threw me up on his back. Mite immediately bolted with me—the first of many times. When I got him shut down and turned around, I came loping back into the yard with a huge smile on my face, asking, "Can I have him, Dad? Can I have him?"

Dad spent two hundred dollars and made me the happiest kid in the world. Putting a kid on that crazy animal would probably constitute child abuse today. Over the years, plenty of people warned my parents, "That crazy horse is going to kill that kid." Mom kind of worried about it, too, but Dad just ignored them. Mite was the love of my life for the next several years.

Dad changes the subject to he and Mom riding, moving cows, and fixing fence in these pastures. He has me driving on an old cow trail, looking for a cave. He seems disappointed when we can't find it, but he tells us about our parents taking cover in the cave during a rainstorm. Although he doesn't come right out and say that they had sex in the cave, he does mention something about their "batwing chaps slapping together." I raise an eyebrow, cock my head, and give him my that's-more-information-than-I-need-to-know look. I glance over my shoulder at Val and she gives me the shut-the-fuck-up-Dad look.

While they were happily riding through these hills, we were left alone in a truck all day with Barbie dolls, peanut butter sandwiches, and instructions not to get out of the truck unless we had to pee. To think that they were worried about us getting bit by a rattlesnake now seems absurd compared to the fact that we were two little kids left alone for eight or more hours, on the side of the road, in a truck with keys. But it never occurred to us to disobey Dad's orders. Oh, sometimes we would turn the key on and off, or push in the clutch to make the truck roll a little, or step on the big, round, silver dimmer button on the floorboard, but if Dad had specifically *said, "Do not turn the key on and off, push in the clutch a little, or step on the dimmer switch," we wouldn't have dreamed of doing so. I spent many hours— many days—alongside a road in that old truck with Barbie, Val, and only one pee break.*

At certain places, Dad has Val put some of Mom's ashes in the cup and hand it to him, and then he hangs his hand out the window. The roads are all dirt, so I drive slowly. From time to time, he wipes his eyes with the back of his hand. I can't tell if there are tears or ashes in his eyes, since some of them are blowing back into the open pickup window. I genuinely feel sorry for him. I miss Mom; I can't even begin to imagine how much he must miss her. Dad leaves his peaceful, happy place as soon the dirt turns to pavement.

In Forsyth, we find a motel, and while I'm moving the cooler and suitcases into the rooms, Dad makes himself a drink and tells Val to look in the phone book for fast-food joints. She flips through the few yellow pages, pretending to look, but all the while is making fun of me, saying that this must be the first time in at least ten years that I have stayed in a place without a bellman, valet parking, room service, and a minibar. I'm not apologizing—and I'm thinking she could be right.

Thirty-Two

Day Two

Dad has us up early. He wants coffee and he knows that Val and I are packing our own. I've brought the Gevalia and the half-and-half and she has the French press. Dad makes fun of her for that, asking, "What the hell is that thing?"

Val explains, to which he replies, "Oh, for Christ's sake, can't you just drink coffee from a pot like everyone else?"

"Back off, Dad, or I won't make you any. I'll make you get your coffee from crappy motel lobbies in the mornings," she tells him.

"Well, at least it probably won't have grounds in it." They bicker until he has the last word.

We drive back into the countryside around Forsyth, to some more of the places where Mom and Dad used to spend their days on horseback. Dad points out the place where he caught Bucky, the pet antelope that we had for almost two years.

Bucky was about two days old when Dad roped him and brought him home. We bottle-fed him out of an old pint-sized Rainier beer bottle.

He was free to wander wherever he wanted to, sometimes staying gone for a few days at a time. It never failed: During hunting season, men from the east would get permits to hunt in Montana and they would come west with their guns drawn, wearing their brand-new, neon-orange gear. Mom would counter their attacks by tying an old red sweater around Bucky's neck as a sign that he was a pet.

One time Bucky came racing back to the safety of the house at a dead run with a pickup full of hunters, rifles drawn, hot on his trail. He ran straight up to Mom, who happened to be outside. They were ready to shoot our pet right in our own yard, but Mom stood her ground, hollering at them at the top of her lungs, calling them "dumb sons a bitches," and placing herself between Bucky and the hunters. When she got done with them, they tucked their tails and headed back east. Anyone who hunts knows that red always trumps orange.

After that, we tried to keep Bucky close to home during hunting season. He survived two of them, but then started spending more and more time away. He also got a bit mean and started knocking people over, so Dad decided that it was time to get rid of him. Val cried when Dad got out his big knife because she thought that he was going to slit his throat right then and there. Instead, he put a long slit in each one of his ears and hauled him back out to the hills to turn him loose. About a year after that, Mom and Dad were out riding and they saw him. They called to him and they said that there was some sort of recognition, but he was no longer a pet.

Forsyth also holds most of my Christmas memories since most of my Santa-Claus-believing years were spent there.

Mom loved Christmas and she did her best to go all out. She decorated the house, baked cookies and candies, and played Christmas songs. At night, after we had all gone to bed, she would drag out the fabrics that she had saved up all year. Then she would sew dresses for us girls and a western shirt for Dad. She had two dress patterns, so all of our dresses looked the same, only in different two-tone colors.

When we were finally allowed to wear pants to school, Mom would take our jeans and make long slits up the outside seams then sew in different fabrics, making them into big, colorful bell-bottoms. She would sew through the night, singing Christmas carols, and then hide whatever dresses, shirts, or jeans she was working on in her bedroom closet. The only store-bought presents we got were from Santa, with the exception of some items that Mom would get by cashing in S&H Green Stamps, which she collected and pasted into books.

Usually, about a week before Christmas, we would go to Billings and Mom would give us each a few dollars to buy something for her, Dad, and each other. Dad would hang out at Uncle Bart's and partake in the Christmas spirits. When I got older, Dad would give me five or ten bucks and tell me to get Mom "something nice." Then we'd go home, wrap the presents up, put them under the tree, and wait anxiously for Christmas morning and Santa's arrival.

I gotta be honest, I was never very impressed with Santa. I tried to make the old guy think that I was a good kid, and every year I left him milk and cookies and hay for his reindeer, but every year he left me disenchanted.

We would get up at about three or four in the morning when we couldn't stand to lay in bed for one more minute. Then, in a flurry of paper, it was all over in a matter of seconds. Mom always managed to have a few small items individually wrapped for us, but Santa usually brought us only one present and it was something for us to share. Each year, I tried to outsmart Valli and convince her that the big part of the gift, which was whatever we first laid eyes on, was really for me. First it was the four-foot-tall, talking doll. I told Valli that the doll was mine and the little discs that slid into her back to make her talk were hers. The next year, we got a record player and some records. I exclaimed, as I made beeline for the tree, "Look, Santa brought me a phonograph and you got all these cute little books!" (which, upon closer examination, turned out to be records). The best shared present ever was the Easy-Bake Oven. I initially told Val that the oven was mine and those neat little envelopes that came with it were hers. As it turned out, those envelopes were packets of cake mix.

For the better part of each year, those items that I had so thoughtfully divvied up were useless, because we refused to share them. My doll didn't talk without Val's discs, my record player didn't play without her records, and I had no batter to put into my little cake pan. Valli mixed up her cake batter and put it in one of the two pans that I had unselfishly given her, but was unable to bake it, unless we were in the midst of one of our rare cease-fires. They might as well have given one of us (me) a car and the other (her) the key. They could have been assured that it would never have made its way out of the driveway.

In 1968 in Forsyth, Mom spent the three months before Christmas telling us how only "special-good kids" got little envelopes pinned to the Christmas tree with a picture inside, showing them what Santa had intended to bring for them. She said that Santa was very busy and knew that these special-good kids would understand that he was running behind and couldn't get all the presents to all the kids on time. Val and I spent the last few weeks before Christmas trying to be special-good kids, hoping to find an envelope pinned to our tree. As Christmas approached, we forgot about receiving any real presents. We got up early on Christmas morning and ran to the tree, hoping to see no presents underneath.

Yesssss! There were none—we really were special-good kids! Santa had left no presents but envelopes with our names on them were pinned to the Christmas tree. Inside Valli's envelope was a picture of a purple bicycle that had a banana seat and high handlebars. Inside my envelope was a picture of a saddle, fully-tooled, with a caramel-colored, padded seat.

I had never seen Santa's handwriting before that Christmas, but when I saw it there on the envelope, I thought that it looked a lot like my mom's. Still, I wasn't about to blow it by saying so!

One day about five months later, we came home from school to find a purple bike sitting in the kitchen. I promptly jumped on it and pedaled off, calling to Val over my shoulder, "If you can catch me, you can ride your new bike!" I should have said, "If Dad catches me riding your new bike, he's gonna tear me a new asshole," because that's pretty much exactly what happened. I pedaled as fast as I could up the hill towards the railroad tracks, my skinny little butt sticking up in the air over the banana seat, bobbing up and down and side to side. Valli was chasing me, crying and yelling at me to let her ride her new bike. At the tracks, I turned around and headed back down the hill, meeting Valli about halfway up the hill. Still pedaling as frantically as a circus clown on a unicycle, I swerved to avoid a head-on collision, then lost control on the loose gravel and wrecked her new bike within the first two minutes of her owning it. The wreck twisted the handlebars and skinned up the vinyl seat, along with my knees. Then Dad skinned up my seat.

We came home from school a couple of months after that to find my new saddle in the kitchen. Valli wasn't even tempted to try to ride it. That is my best Christmas memory.

My worst goes like this: It was 1971. I was eleven and we had just moved again, this time to Winnett. Christmas was approaching; we had a tree up, but had yet to buy any presents. We kept asking Mom when we were going to go Christmas shopping, but all she would say was that she didn't know. What she should have said was, "We're not. We don't have any money this year." We never had any money immediately after a move.

Dad had been hitting the tequila pretty hard a couple days before Christmas and got tired of hearing us badger Mom about shopping, so he picked up the Christmas tree, cussed at its flickering lights, and threw it out the door—decorations and all. I didn't want to believe that there was not going to be Christmas at our house. I already knew that Santa was a fake, but I still held hope that Christmas wasn't. On the night of December 24, Dad broke the two days of silence by announcing that we were going to Billings. I watched the clock and silently hated Dad and Christmas for one hundred miles as I imagined all the stores at Rimrock Mall closing their doors on our holiday. We went to Grandma Wanda's house and, with no ceremony, surprise, or even gift wrap, she gave each of us girls a parka that had fake fur around the hood. Mine was brown and Val's was green. Those were our only presents and everyone was pretty quiet that Christmas. I quit hating Dad and started to feel sorry for him. I knew that it must have been hard on him not to be able to give us Christmas that year. When we got home the next day, our fully decorated tree was lying on its side just a few feet away from the front door. It was a cruel reminder that even traditions are disposable.

Thirty-Three

One of the back roads from Forsyth leads to Angela, Montana, which, thirty years ago, consisted of nothing more than a small store along the side of the road. Today, the building is there but it is boarded up like it's waiting for a hurricane to come to the dry, dusty plains of eastern Montana. At Angela, we hang a left and head toward the little town of Cohagen.

We pull into what was called the Nickels Ranch when we worked there. A knock on the door of the house goes unanswered, and since we would have to drive through the main ranch yard and then another four miles on a dirt road, we decide to wait until we can get permission.

"I guess we could come back," Dad says, clearly disappointed. "We might as well head to Miles City."

I remind him that we aren't on any schedule, so we will take as much time as we need to make this trip. He doesn't say anything back to me, but he seems relieved to know that we can come back.

Like we did with our trip to New Mexico, Val and I have preemptively set some ground rules:

1. No bitching; we'll do whatever Dad wants to do.
2. No bitching; we'll go wherever he wants to go.
3. No bitching; we'll eat fast food if that's what he wants.
4. No bitching; if we have to kill him, we shoot, shovel, and shut up.
5. "Guacamole" is still code for, "Shut the fuck up."

When we get to Miles City, Dad perks up and insists that we stay at the Olive Hotel, which is a place that he and Mom stayed several years ago. I remind him that the Olive is a *hotel*, not a *motel*, which means that we will violate his rule about parking at the door to avoid walking through a lobby. It doesn't matter; it's where he and Mom stayed, so the Olive Hotel it is. Dad also won't go out to eat, so we bring some fast food to him and tuck him in with some vodka and cranberry juice, then head out in search of some real food.

Miles City is Montana's original cowtown. It is full of cowboys, cowboy bars, and steakhouses. It's OK to wear your spurs to town and it's not necessary to remove your cowboy hat at the table. Many of the pickups that are parked at the bars have gun racks with rifles in their back windows. Each one has the driver's side window down and the keys are likely to be in the ignition. Border collies or blue heelers ride shotgun and have been known to drive their owners home if they stay at the bar too long. At least, that's what the cowboys will claim—and their dogs will back them up.

Across the street from the Olive Hotel is a bar that serves dinner, so we head there. It's a lot more of a meat-and-potatoes kind of joint than we would prefer, but after all, this is beef country. I've traveled and eaten out enough to know that you do not order seafood in an Argentine steakhouse. I did it once and lived to regret it, so since I'm in cow country, I figure that I better eat some cow. I order the filet mignon, medium.

"You want soup or salad?" the waitress asks me.

"Salad. Do you make a house dressing?"

"Nope. Ranch, thousand or bleu cheese."

"Um . . . how about a lemon?"

"OK. Fried, baked, or mashed potatoes?" she asks next, never looking up from her pad.

"Baked—loaded."

She doesn't even look at Val; she keeps her pen poised over her pad, but shifts from her right leg to her left, indicating that she is done with me.

Val orders a baked potato with butter, sour cream, and chives—no bacon—and a salad.

"You want a steak or chicken with that?" the waitress asks, as if Val is ordering backwards.

I crack up. "Lucy, you got some splainin' to do," I say in my best Ricky Ricardo voice. The waitress obviously doesn't get it, because she gives me a what-the-hell-you-talkin'-'bout look.

Val ignores me. "I'm just not very hungry," she lies.

"But can you make that a *really big* potato?" I ask, in my best snobby-restaurant-critic voice.

"Bitch," Val says, laughing along as the waitress walks off.

Thirty-Four

Day Three

The next morning, we all have our French-pressed coffee without any guff from Dad, then leave the Olive Hotel and head east toward Sidney. Dad has been anxious to go to Sidney so he is talkative all the way there. He and Mom moved there in the fall of 1961, when I was a little over a year old. On February 14, 1962, Valerie was born. At the time, my parents were living in a boxcar, Val's first home.

Being the firstborn of ten grandchildren, Dad claims to have been the favorite. His granddad was a savvy, serious-minded, Christian man who owned quite a lot of land and, at one time, several hundred head of horses. It was his dream that each one of his grandchildren would have a college education, a relationship with the Lord, and a horse. However, not long after he had helped Dad slip out of his sentence to the "bad boy" school, he died of a sudden heart attack. Shortly after that, Grandma married Granddad's brother, a fun-loving, happy-go-lucky alcoholic who squandered any chance of any of her grandchildren getting a horse, much less a college education.

I drive while Dad directs me to his grandparents' farm—the closest thing to a home that he has ever known. Seeing it again, after all these years, makes him act like a kid recalling his first trip to the circus. He can't seem to take in everything fast enough. Things have no doubt changed over the years, but they still take him right back to when he lived here. He points out the barn where he used to milk cows and the shed where he got caught smoking—and consequently, got a big-time ass-whooping from granddad. He shows us the old dented tractor that once tipped over and nearly killed one of his cousins and the big, old oak tree that he broke his ankle jumping out of. Everywhere he looks, some memory comes flooding back. It's a new experience for Val and me to see some excitement in his eyes and hear him talk so much. He's still a little melancholy, but I can't recall ever seeing him so thrilled about anything—certainly not since we lost Mom.

I have never felt like I have had a place to call home, but this little farm gives me a sense of my roots—of having come from somewhere. I want to claim it as my own, to be able to say that it was my home, too. I just wish that I could remember my great-grandma and the time I spent here. Maybe then I could figure out what the feeling of going home is like. Instead, I feel nothing.

We check into a local motel for the night and the three of us sit in Dad's room, making a dinner plan for the evening. According to the Yellow Pages, we will be eating at either McDonald's or McDonald's.

"This is the last time I'm letting you plan a trip," Val says, as she looks into the filthy bathroom sink.

"Oh, come on. This is fun," I tell her.

"There have been lots of words to describe this, but 'fun' has never once entered my mind." She's dead serious and she looks pissed.

"Fun-hater," I say, ignoring her bad mood.

"Fun-hater," she mocks, sticking her tongue out at me like we are little kids again. "I think we could get the hantavirus in this place," she scoffs.

Dad looks at her and scowls, "What? It's not that bad."

"He's right," I point out. "It isn't as bad as a lot of the places that we've lived in, but it *is* the worst place we have ever paid money to stay in." Dad turns his scowl on me.

I do have to admit that this is my idea of roughing it. Three nights in a row without HBO, room service, or a hot tub is a stretch for me.

After the quarter-pounder lands in my stomach like a gut bomb, I crawl into bed and slide my eye mask down over my eyes, blocking out Val's bad mood and the flashes of light from *Letterman*. I'm glad I've brought my own pillow—and my gun. I'm thinking I may need them both.

Thirty-Five

Day Four

On our way out of Sidney, we make a stop at the Newlen cemetery to visit our grandparents' graves. Then we head to Richey, which is where we moved after Forsyth, sometime around 1970. We wander around the hills for hours, trying to find the old place. It is so far out in the sticks that even Dad can't remember how to get there. We drive until roads end, then backtrack and try other dusty trails. All of the roads look the same— red dirt leading over the next hill and never ending.

Dad used to allow Valli and I to ride down these dusty red roads in the horse trailer. We had an ongoing competition to see who could stand up for the longest time without touching the sides of the trailer. Dad would keep it interesting by occasionally swerving, hitting a big bump, or tapping the brakes. If one of us fell or touched the sides of the trailer, the other was declared the winner. It was the most fun we had at Richey.

Finally we come upon a house and talk Dad into stopping to ask for directions. He sits in the pickup while Val and I go to the door. A young, heavyset woman answers the door of the small trailer house. She is nice and seems glad to see other women. She sticks a bare foot in the door to hold it open, while her right hand reaches up to push aside hair that doesn't look like its been brushed yet today. Her left hand imitates an iron, making a pass over the front of her wrinkled T-shirt, which states that she thinks my tractor's sexy.

She talks nonstop while carefully studying me and Val. My sister's chic hairstyle, Chacos, and Nike running skirt indicate that she is not from these hills, while my hand-painted, pointy-toed cowboy boots, straw hat, and Versace shades don't help me blend in either. The woman has heard of the old Macaulay place but can't help us much, other than by saying that she thinks we are on the right road. I'm sure that we lived here before she was even born. We thank her and continue down the road.

Back in the pickup, I say, "Dad, did I ever thank you for moving us again and getting us out of them there hills?"

"What are you talking about?" he asks.

"I just want to thank you for moving us. I could have ended up stuck here, married to a dirt farmer, living in that little trailer house."

"What's wrong with that?" he asks. "That wasn't a bad little trailer. She probably has a pretty good life."

"Well, in case I never thanked you for uprooting me and dragging my ass all over the country, let me just tell you 'thank you,' now."

He just shakes his head—he doesn't get it.

We finally find the place and discover that barely anything remains but a collapsed barn and a little shack. This ranch looks as unfamiliar today as it did the first time we drove up to it thirty-two years ago.

Mom had gotten mad and cried when she had seen where she would be living—and what she would be living in. The tiny, run-down trailer house—which was only about ten feet wide and in horrible condition—hadn't done anything to brighten this grim location. Dad had gotten pissed about her being pissed and they had fought about it.

Mom did not like it here from day one. She liked it even less on day two, when the stray dog (a dumb dog, not a cow dog) that she had dragged home a few months prior got into a fight with the boss lady's lapdog. Our new pet killed the lapdog, so Dad told Mom that since she was the one who had brought it home, she had to take our dog out and shoot it. She begged Dad not to make her do it. We kids briefly took her side and begged Dad too, but from the look in his eyes, we could tell it was a hopeless cause. We didn't tell our pet goodbye or even give him a pat. We just kind of accidentally touched him as we brushed by and went quietly into our dumpy trailer house as Dad, looking pissed, Mom, looking terrified, and the dog, looking hopelessly clueless, drove off in the pickup. When Mom and Dad returned about a half hour later, Mom's eyes were red and puffy and she looked like she was going to be sick. Dad was still pissed off and Valli and I were still silent. We stayed mad at Dad for a long time and we hated this place.

Things only seemed to get worse after that. Dad's boss was always yelling at him, which did not sit well with Dad. I saw his teeth clinch and his jaw tighten as he tried to contain the combustion that was building inside him. Macaulay knew just how far he could push Dad and then he would walk off before Dad exploded, leaving him to yell at me.

Dad was much harder on me than Val because I was the oldest, I guess, and I spent the most time with him. I may have been his flunky, who didn't know my ass from a hole in the ground, but I worked right alongside him, doing the shit detail while also doing everything I could to get promoted to right-hand man. When Dad snubbed a calf up to a post, flanked it, and told me to hold the hind legs so he could brand it, I knew better than to turn loose. The calf could outweigh me by two hundred pounds and be kicking and dragging my butt all around the corral, but I had been forewarned. If I turned loose, Dad would stomp a mud hole in my ass. I was way more afraid of my dad than I was of any calf, so no matter what, I held on like a pit bull on a pork chop.

The same applied to horses. Being stubborn is not just a habit of Shetland ponies, it's in their DNA. While we were living in Richey, someone gave us a cute, little, brown and white pony, which meant that Valli finally had a horse she could call her own.

Kelly came with a couple of bad habits though. One was that he would rear up, sometimes so high that he would tip himself over backwards. Another was that he kicked like a miniature mule. From the get-go, Val was scared to death of him and wanted nothing to do with the devil pony.

Dad had a plan to break Kelly of his bad habits, which naturally involved me. First, he found a club that was about the size of a French baguette. Then he made me get on Kelly and gave me instructions to smack the hell out of him, right between the ears, every time he reared up.

"Kick him! Keep him moving!" Dad coached from the sidelines as I tried to keep the hell-horse in a trot around the pen that we were locked into. Kelly would rear up and I would bring the club down, as hard as I could, between his ears. With each rear, he would get higher and higher in the air until finally, I would slide right off of his butt.

"Get out of the way!" Dad hollered at me as Kelly's two hind feet backfired over the top of my head. "Get back on him and knock the shit out of him if he does that again, Tam," Dad instructed me.

After the third or fourth time sliding off of him, I asked Dad if we could put a saddle on him so I wouldn't keep falling off.

"Better not," Dad concluded, shaking his head. "If he goes over backwards on you, the saddle horn could go through your chest and kill ya. Just keep smacking the shit out of him. He'll quit sooner or later."

It was pretty much later. I spent a few hours a day cracking Kelly between the ears with the club and then tucking and rolling to get out of the way of his rapidly-firing hind feet. After a week or so, he finally quit rearing up and I escaped the round pen without a collapsed lung or a ruptured spleen.

Not counting the time we spent with Kelly, I always loved working beside Dad and I tried my hardest to do a good job to make him proud of me. He was so mean and miserable at this place, though, that sometimes I wished I was a city kid.

My horse, Mite, was just as afraid of Dad as I was. One day, Dad had a calf roped and wanted me to dally the rope to my saddle horn so he could doctor it. I was supposed to ride my horse close enough to his that he could hand me the rope, but Mite was not only afraid of Dad, he was afraid of ropes. He wanted no part of this angry, screaming man with a rope in his hand.

It took so long that the calf got itself choked down and Dad got so pissed off that he got off his horse, walked down the rope, doctored the calf, took the rope off its neck, and gut-kicked it as he walked back to his horse. The calf sucked up its breath in much the same way that I did when Dad kicked me in the butt. It got to its feet, shaking its head, and staggered off. I was thinking, Whew, I'm glad he didn't make me hold the calf since Mite was so afraid of the rope.

Dad never said a word. He just coiled up his rope, got back on his horse, built a loop, and began beating Mite on the butt with it. Of course, Mite spooked and began running away with me, hell-bent for leather. Dad kept chasing us, hitting me and my horse with the rope. I was screaming, which didn't help me in my attempts to stop my runaway horse. We could run faster scared than Dad could mad, so he chased us until we outran him. When he quit chasing and hitting us, I quit screaming and got my horse under control. I was mad at Dad, but I was even madder at myself. I was also embarrassed that Mite and I had been scared and that I had screamed like a girl.

I waited until almost dark to come home. By then, I had put Mom through hell worrying about me. She thought that my crazy horse had probably run away, jumped off a cliff, and killed me, fulfilling the prophecies of all the people who had said Mite would kill me. She was angry with Dad and wouldn't talk to him other than to say, "Gary, she's only ten."

We drive down to the old horse barn and Dad finally gets out of the pickup to walk in with me and Val. The barn used to be bright red but now only a small amount of red paint is even visible. Inside, the old horse stalls are still standing and the gates hang open on rusted hinges. Under the dust, I know the planks are shiny; worn smooth from the rumps of the circling horses that have rubbed up against them. The top rail of the wood has been eaten away and the planks randomly dip into *U*s shaped by the bored, cribbing horses. You can tell where their necks have chafed against the hay manger, wearing it down, slick and uneven, and I see the rectangle wooden feed boxes that I used to dump oats into, dished in from years of the horse's soft muzzles trying to get every last bite of grain.

"This used to be a nice barn," I say.

"Mac was a son of a bitch," Dad says, referring to his old boss. He must be remembering all the screaming fits that took place in this barnyard.

"Mom hated it here," I say to no one in particular.

"It wasn't that bad," Dad says.

"We all hated it here," Val reminds us.

We leave the barn and drive back up to where Dad thinks our trailer house used to sit. Val and I wander over the ruins of some old building, trying to recall what it was. "I remember that I got the worst beating of my life at this place," I tell Val. "But so did you."

Dad had been down at the barn when he had heard us fighting and hollering, so he had come up to the house to see what the ruckus was about. As he got closer to the house, he could hear us arguing and name-calling. It was just our luck that right by the door there was a big stick, which he picked up before quietly opening the door and catching us by surprise. My back was turned to him so I didn't see him come into the house. I only saw the shock register on my sister's face when she saw him.

Dad kicked me in the butt so hard that I was sure he had pierced my kidney. When he pulled the toe of his cowboy boot out of my rectum, it sucked the air right out of me and I heard myself make a high-pitched squeal as I sucked in through my mouth. Then he beat the hell out of me with the stick. Valli got it next. Not only was I bruised for a week, it hurt to sit down and I bled when I pooped.

"He beat the hell out of us with a stick," she reminds me.

"Yeah, I remember. What were we fighting about anyway?" I ask.

"Who could ride a horse better," she refreshes my memory.

"Oh yeah," I say, shrugging it off.

"I'm thirty-nine years old and now I'm reliving a past that I've spent thirty-nine years trying to forget," Val says. Even though she's laughing, I know she is dead serious about that.

Dad hollers something at us but we can't hear him. We look over and find him leaning across the hood of the pickup, smoking a cigarette and looking at where the old house used to be. He is pointing at something in the distance with his first two fingers because he has a cigarette pinched between them. We look in the direction that the cigarette is pointing but have no idea what he's trying to bring to our attention. He is just out of earshot.

"You got your gun?" Val asks. "We could off him and leave him here. It would be months before anyone finds him," she points out (Rule #4).

We laugh because that's what we've been doing for this entire trip. I think that as long as we keep laughing, we can survive it.

Dad hears us and looks our way, no doubt wondering what we are laughing about.

"I've had enough of this place. Let's get out of here before we remember something else," I say.

As we walk back to the pickup, I remind Valli that I can still ride a horse better than her. She reminds me that it's still not too late to take the old guy out.

Thirty-Six

We leave the red hills of Richey in our dust and drive to Jordan, where it will be necessary to set our watches back a few years upon arrival. Jordan is a one-horse town in Garfield County, which is spread out over 4800 square miles in the most remote part of northeastern Montana. It's a huge ranching and farming community and nearly everyone who lives there is somehow related to everyone else.

When we moved there in 1972, Dad was working as an independent fence contractor instead of a cowboy, which meant that I got my wish: we got to be city kids.

Living in town was fun! For the first time in our lives, we had friends to play with. We kept our horses in our yard and we rode for the sheer fun of it instead of having to move cows, ride fence, or do ranch work. A lot of the kids we played with also had horses, so most days during that idyllic summer were spent on horseback, from the moment we got up until our mothers called us home at dark.

We rarely saddled our horses. We usually just jumped on them bareback and ran wild in the streets of Jordan. We did everything on horseback—played hide-and-seek and tag, had water balloon fights, ran errands, and even went to the grocery store for our mothers. One of our favorite things to do was run our horses through sprinklers until people hollered at us for leaving hoofprints or horse turds in their yards. We'd giggle like crazy and then move on to another yard.

This was where I picked up the habit of chewing tobacco. A couple of the girls I ran around with chewed Skoal, so I began chewing too. Valli tried chewing a little Beechnut but usually ended up puking, so she gave it up after a few attempts. Mom and Dad never seemed to care—at least, they never said anything one way or the other about it—so I didn't have to hide it from them. I asked Mom for money to buy a can of chew once and she wouldn't give it to me, so Dad gave me the forty-five cents. He understood the tobacco habit. Most of my jeans had the telltale sign of a Skoal ring in the right rear pocket.

Fencing proved to be less lucrative than Dad expected so toward the end of summer he told us to pack up because we would be moving again. I cried and begged him not to make us move. He didn't say we were out of money, but I knew we were because when we went to the grocery store with Mom, she wouldn't let us get a piece of candy.

When we had any extra money, she would tell me and Valli that we could each get a piece of gum or candy. We never asked for anything; we just knew the routine. We waited patiently by the checkout while Mom unloaded the groceries, mentally adding them up and matching the coupons to the items as she put them on the sliding belt. When the cart was almost empty, she would either say, "You girls can each get a piece of candy," or she would say nothing and avoid making eye contact with us.

I loved Jordan and I loved being a carefree kid. Going back to the ranch meant that I would still be on horseback every day, but I would be working. It wouldn't matter if it was blazing hot, raining, or blowing snow. It also meant that I would have to ride in a saddle, move cows, wrestle calves and barbed wire, and have Dad hollering at me every day. Summer was about over and so was my life—or so I thought at the time.

We moved back to Jordan in March of 1975, late in my freshman year. Dad took a job at the Nickels Ranch near Cohagen, where he, Mom, and Val lived. Valli attended seventh grade in a one-room country school that was about ten miles away from the ranch. Since I was in high school, I lived in a dorm some forty miles away and only went home on weekends.

The dorm was a three-story building that housed around fifty kids. The girls lived on the top floor, the boys had the middle one, and the kitchen, dining room, and rec room occupied the lower level. Dorm life was usually pretty fun, even though our dorm mother, Mrs. Daniels, a heavyset woman with a permanent glare, was so hard-nosed that she could have brought a drill sergeant to tears. She barely ever bothered to give any of us the time of day unless she was chewing one of our asses. Making eye contact with her was the equivalent of taking a lie detector test, but we all respected her like soldiers respect their country. The first time that two of my giggling girlfriends and I came in drunk, she gave us just enough time to crawl into our beds before she thundered up the stairs and marched us back down the two flights to the kitchen. She then handed a toothbrush to each of us and made us clean the kitchen and dining room ceilings all night while she sat at the table, drinking coffee, flipping through a magazine, and smoking cigarettes while she watched us. By the time the wake-up bell went off at six, we were no longer giggling. My friends and I still came in drunk on many nights after that—we just learned to stand upright, salute at the door, and leave our giggles in the car of whichever boy had dropped us off.

Dad didn't stay at the Nickels Ranch very long. Nickels hollered a lot, like Macaulay did, and that didn't go over well with Dad. By the start of my sophomore year, they had moved into town and Dad had taken a job in construction. He didn't seem very happy to be spending his days on a yellow piece of iron instead of a horse, but the money was twice as good. Cowboying may have put beef on the table, but it didn't put shoes on our feet or prom dresses on our backs. Val and I had grown up, and as teenagers we wanted to wear something other than shit-kickers and jeans.

I traded one tobacco habit for another and gave up chew in favor of cigarettes, which I stole from Mom when I could find her stash. She was still in the closet with her smoking, only doing so in front of Valli. Dad's cigs weren't hidden, but he either rolled his own or smoked Camels with no filters, so I preferred to steal Mom's menthols. She had to have known that I knew she was smoking, but for whatever reason, she pretended not to.

Not only was I stealing cigarettes from her, I also did my best to sneak in and catch her with one as often as I could. She could pinch out a cigarette and stuff it down her blouse so fast that the smoke didn't even have a chance to clear the air. Dad never knew that Mom was smoking, but by then, she and I and Val were all hiding our cigs from him and stealing from each other. There were a lot of things that we were keeping from Dad and a lot of secrets that Mom was keeping for us.

When Dad's construction job moved out of town, Mom moved with him and left us home alone. When we weren't in school, I waitressed at the Ranchers Café and Val worked at the Tastee-Freez. And we partied—a lot. The Rolling Stones had nothing on us.

During my junior year, Dad continued to work construction but made a point of being home most nights. Mom went to work at the local motel, cleaning rooms during the day and cooking at the Ranchers in the evening. We were in a small town, so word probably got back to them that we girls had been having a few too many parties and staying out a little too late while they were gone. As far as Dad was concerned, we were corrupted because we were city kids. He and I still had a good relationship in the arena since we were team-roping partners, but other than that he was largely uninvolved in my day-to-day life. Mom did the disciplining and her usual means of punishment was "grounding," which was pointless. It just meant that I had to enter and exit through my bedroom window instead of the back door.

Dad only stepped in for the real biggies, like when I snuck out of the house to be with a guy I was forbidden to date and we tipped a pickup over while spinning cookies at the stockyards. Mom heard about it from gossip at the café and she ratted me out to Dad. When he heard about it, he let me know that being sixteen didn't mean I was too old to have my ass kicked up between my shoulder blades.

Dad may still have had some sort of control over me but my teachers certainly didn't. I was disrespectful and talked back to most of them. I hated school with a passion and I was a horrible student. I rarely did homework—usually just enough to earn a D. It didn't help that I was also hungover a lot.

When the teachers finally had enough of my mouth or they had grown frustrated with my utter lack of participation, they would kick me out of their classes for the remainder of the year. As a freshman, I flunked home ec because I refused to wear a dress once a week. When I was a sophomore, I took math with the freshmen, and in my junior year I had to retake sophomore biology. I got kicked out of English too, but I talked the principal into letting the journalism teacher, who was also the librarian, teach me English for the *remainder of the year. I usually spent the hour hanging out in the library, drinking Tab and acting like I seriously cared about learning. I furrowed my brow, hit my forehead with the palm of my hand, and claimed that I just didn't get it until she inadvertently fed me most of the answers. I passed English III with a B that year, but I flunked band. I used to show up every day and blow into a saxophone, though I was actually a drummer. When the teacher finally caught on, I got kicked out.*

I spent the majority of that year skipping school with my best friend, Dayna. We snuck out nearly every morning at 10:45 and went to her house to watch the Don Ho Show, *which came on at 11:00. If her parents happened to come home, I would hide under her bed and she would pretend that she was home for lunch.*

All of our skipping was big fun until the day my mom went into the hospital. It was unexpected, so she called the school to let me know that she was checking in to have surgery. That very morning, I had forged her signature and turned in a note explaining that I was allowed to go to Miles City with her for the day. Actually I was under Dayna's bed at about the time that the call came through. Since Dayna was AWOL that day too, having turned in her own forged note, the principal had called Dayna's mom.

I heard the footsteps. She threw open the bedroom door, then hesitated just long enough to glance around the room. I saw her sensible shoes at the side of the bed, and then her upside-down face looking back at me. I was so busted!

When we weren't skipping school for Don Ho, *we were doing it so we could smoke cigarettes. We smoked behind the* stage in the auditorium and we even had the audacity to crawl into the backseats of teachers' cars and crouch on their floors to smoke our cigs.

I'm not sure if the principal liked me or if he just didn't know what to do with me. I spent so much time in his office that I became like an assistant to him. I would answer his phone and take messages if he wasn't in the office, and I could tell the teachers where he was when they poked their heads in. Sometimes I also ran errands for him. He once told me that I was the most stubborn person that he had ever met. I don't think that he intended it to be a compliment, but since a chip on my shoulder was something that I never had, I took it as one and simply said, "Thank you." That year, I think I spent more time in his office than he did, but I somehow managed to pass eleventh grade.

Thirty-Seven

*R*ight before the end of my junior year, when I was seventeen, Dad bought me my first car. Mom told me, like it was top secret, that he paid two hundred dollars for it—coincidentally, that was the same amount that he had paid for Mite. I could tell you all about a horse, but all I knew about this car was that it was green and I think it was a 1960-something.

That summer, Mom and Dad moved somewhere else—wherever Dad's construction job took him—so Val and I took the old green car and drove the 178 miles to Billings. We were supposed to be living with Great-Grandma and Grandma Irene, but Grandma Irene went crazy, locked us out of the house, and nailed all the windows shut, so we moved in with Grandma Wanda. She worked from two in the afternoon until nearly midnight, finally went to bed around three or four in the morning, and slept until about *eleven, so our paths rarely crossed.*

Val immediately got a job at Dairy Queen and I mostly partied at the Spur Bar. At that time, the drinking age was eighteen, but I was still a year away. So the first time I walked into the Spur, I had an ounce of courage and a bar glass full of Coke. I walked right up to the bouncer and chatted him up, pretending like I had just walked across the street from the 17 Club with a cocktail in my hand. He never carded me; we became buddies, and after that I didn't have to bring my own Coke from home. I drank, danced, played the drums, and partied with all my new friends until around midnight, when it was time to pick Val up from the Dairy Queen.

I was usually half-crocked when I drove across town to get her. Sometimes I would go back to the bar and make her wait in the car while I continued partying. To keep her from complaining too much, I would sneak an occasional drink out to her, along with a promise to call it a night . . . soon.

Val financially supported me for most of that summer. I did finally get a job as a waitress at the Woolworth counter, but by then it was August and about time to move back to Jordan for my senior year of high school. I always thought it was ironic that I ended up back at the Spur Bar and Woolworth's as a teenager, more than ten years after sneaking over there with Grandma Irene when I was just a toddler.

A couple of months later, Great-Grandma, who was then eighty-four, took a fall—a sign that she shouldn't be living alone, as she had been since mid-summer. The grandmas had been living separately ever since Grandma Irene went off the deep end and nailed the windows shut. That, along with calling 911 to report phony fires and burglaries, was her ticket to the funny farm. Mom and Dad decided that Great-Grandma should live with them so that Mom could care for her, so they moved to Billings. That's when Dad got into the trucking business.

Valli loved the big city life and she was excited to begin her sophomore year at Billings Senior High. During her days at DQ, she had made friends with several of the Mexican kids who made up most of Billings' south side population. The good-looking Latino boys loved having a cute little blonde girlfriend, and it wasn't long before she started dating one of them. That put Mom in the position of having to lie and cover for her. If Dad found out that Val was dating a Mexican—especially one who had a ponytail—he would have killed the guy.

Mom was always this contradictive kind of mother. One minute she would be covering for us and the next she would threaten us with, "I'm telling your father. Just wait 'til he gets home! You're really gonna get it!" The good news was that the older we got, the better she got at covering for us. The more we screwed up, the less she told Dad.

While Valli was happy about the move, I not only protested, I put my foot down! I did not want to be uprooted in my senior year, so I convinced Mom and Dad that I could take care of myself and I talked them into letting me stay in Jordan—not that it took much talking. It was more like, "I don't want to move again, I want to stay here and finish high school," and Dad just said, "OK."

What the hell were they thinking? They put 178 miles of badly paved roads between them and me without so much as batting an eye. I was seventeen, living in a dorm during the week with about fifty other high school students. Then on Friday nights, I was checking into the motel, where I would spend the weekends working on my degree in intoxication.

The only classes I had that year were English, government, journalism, and the so-called work-study. I was the editor of the school newspaper for three years and, other than getting an A in that, I pretty much pulled Cs and Ds. Mom offered me fifty dollars to make the honor roll my senior year, so I did it the first semester. She paid up but didn't offer me the money for the second semester, so I went back to my Cs and Ds. It wasn't that I was dumb, I just didn't apply myself—that was my mother's explanation, anyway.

Besides, I was busy with what the school liked to call the "Work-Study Program," which I referred to as the "Job I Need to Have to Support Myself." I went to school from eight until ten in the morning, cooked in the restaurant of the Ranchers Café from ten until two in the afternoon, then bartended in the Ranchers Bar from two until midnight or two in the morning, depending on how busy the bar was.

I didn't have a car so every night after work I walked about a quarter of a mile down the highway to the dorm. Dad may not have left me with a set of car keys to put in my purse, but he did leave me with a .22 pistol to put in it.

Somehow I managed to graduate from high school—ranked twenty-something in a class of twenty-something.

College was not in my future. In fact, not once in my life did either of my parents ever mention that word to me. The thought of going on in school or having a career had never even occurred to me. It was just a given that after high school, I would go directly to work.

So after graduating from Garfield County High School with the class of 1978, I moved to Billings and got a job as a cocktail waitress at the Holiday Inn. A few months later, sometime around the end of August, I met Larry, a truck driver who was passing through town.

At closing time, I had held the door open and ordered everyone out. As the last of the drunks and stragglers stumbled and protested their way out of the bar, Larry stopped in front of me, pressed me up against the door, and planted a big kiss on me. I scribbled my phone number on a bar napkin and handed it to him, speechless, as he walked off. A few weeks later, he came back into the bar and we actually exchanged words. During the next two months, we saw each other about four or five times. Then, on October 31, I quit my job and took him up on his offer of a ride out of town.

The night before I was due to leave, I went to my father and said, "Dad, I'm leaving town tomorrow—with Larry, the truck driver. Do you have any last words for me?"

"Yeah, for five bucks you can marry him and own half of that truck," was all he said to me, only slightly opening one eye to look at me, since he was sleeping when I broke the news.

I whispered, "I'll remember that," and let out a big sigh of relief as I tiptoed out of the bedroom. I wasn't about to analyze his response—not even for a second. I couldn't wait to leave town.

I packed a suitcase full of clothes and Mom drove me to the truck stop. She hugged me goodbye and I could tell that she was trying not to cry as I crawled up into the Kenworth.

"What do I tell people?" she asked me, sounding kind of embarrassed.

"Tell 'em whatever you want, Mom. Tell 'em I ran away. You can say I joined the circus or became a carnie. I don't care."

"That's not what I mean. I mean, what do I tell people about you and Larry? And what do I call Larry? Your boyfriend? Your live-in? What will people think?"

"They'll think I got lucky, Mom." I smiled at her and shut the door of the semi. I could see that she was crying when she waved goodbye to me.

I didn't care what anyone thought. I was just thrilled to have a ticket out of town.

Fifty-two days later I became co-owner of that semi when Larry and I got married by a Justice of the Peace in the Yellowstone County Courthouse.

Thirty-Eight

Dad, Val, and I check into the same motel that I used to live in on the weekends, the same one that Mom used to clean. It's so full of flies that I wonder if it's been vacant, sitting empty like some kind of shrine to me since I left. The room doesn't have a remote control for the TV, but it does come equipped with a couple of flyswatters.

"Time for some redneck aerobics," Val tells me. "Grab a flyswatter. It'll be a good workout." Seconds later, we are jumping on the beds like two little kids, swatting at swarms of flies so thick that it looks as if we have just disturbed a beehive. We finish our workout while Dad washes down his chicken strips with a couple of nightcaps.

Val and I head downtown to the bar. I used to hang out and dance and play the drums at jam sessions here. I take a deep breath and silently pray that I won't know anyone, as I pull open the door to the Hell Creek Bar. All heads turn. We pause just long enough to see that we are the only two women in the bar, except for the bartender, who I recognize from high school. *Shit!* We belly up; I order whiskey and coke and cringe when Val wants to know what kind of Merlot they have.

"If they do serve wine, it's probably Boone's Farm," I whisper, giving her a heads-up before she looks like a complete dumbass.

"I'll have what she's having," she says, like she's suddenly changed her mind (and smartened up).

Cristina doesn't show any sign of recognition as she makes our drinks. The dozen or so men in the bar are all farmers, ranchers, truckers, and local drunks. I recognize some of the same guys, looking a little worse for wear, but holding down the same barstools that they were more than twenty years ago. A few of the guys gather around, no doubt curious about the new meat in town.

"What brings you ladies to town?" one asks.

Oh shit, I know him, I think to myself. *I'd recognize those two silver front teeth anywhere.*

"Just passing through," I tell him, trying to decide if I want to make eye contact or not.

"You look like ladies on a mission," he continues.

"Yeah, we are. You know of a good place to dispose of a body?" I look him directly in the eye, hoping he's still gullible.

"Hey, you look familiar. I think I know you," he says, like a light went off, which also prompts all of the other guys to stare even more than they already are.

I come clean and reintroduce myself and Valerie. Most of them remember us, as we do them. We are all about the same age, so this is kind of an impromptu class reunion.

"Well I'll be goddamned," says the rancher to my left as he slams his fist on the bar, right where my purse is sitting. His fist, which is about the size of a cantaloupe, slams through my cute little hard-sided purse and smashes the mirror inside. He fails to notice. He hugs me, roughs me up a little, then says, "Cristina, get us a round of drinks." We finish those and I follow up with another—and another.

Val is into what sounds like a deep religious conversation with another local, whom Dad would have referred to as a "full-blooded Catholic." There were more people in Jordan's Catholic congregation than there were flies in the motel. Many of them could be found at the bar on Saturday nights, drunk, flirting and sinning with women who weren't their wives, but by God, they would be in church on Sunday mornings, come hell or high water, hungover and full of repentance. I eavesdrop, thinking, *Uh-oh, this guy is going to have his hands full in a religious conversation with my sister.*

Instead, I find that Val is intrigued and she even appears to be somewhat moved. The man is very well-spoken and he seems nothing like the party boy I knew him to be twenty-five years ago. He may be in the bar on a Wednesday night, but he has me convinced that he and God are pretty tight. He says that he isn't afraid of dying and that he can't wait to meet his maker. He has recently lost his father and it seems to me that he is having a heck of a lot less trouble dealing with his father's death than we are with our mother's. I'm envious. I wish that I knew his secret.

Something about this night makes us feel as though he has been sent to minister to us, and I find some peace and comfort in his words. Maybe it's the alcohol, maybe it's not. I think that he could be at the pulpit of his own church and I could be a follower. For a while, I have faith that he is going to make a believer out of Val.

After a few hours and a few more rounds, we leave the bar, wasted and enlightened. And Val is almost born again.

Thirty-Nine

Day Five

Dad's up early and Val and I are the ones with the hangovers today. We tell him about our trip to the Hell Creek Bar and all of the old acquaintances we caught up with. He opens up the glove box and for some crazy reason he has a bumper sticker in there, which he pulls out. It reads, "Meet Me at the Hell Creek Bar— Jordan, Montana."

"Jeez, Dad, how long have you been packing that thing around?" I ask. I know it has to have been at least twenty years since he's been to Jordan.

"I don't know. I just remembered I saw it in there the other day when I was looking for something."

Val asks Dad if she can cut it up and rearrange it to say "Meet Me in Hell," and put it on the pickup.

"There's not an *I*," I point out.

"I'll make one out of the *B*," she says, studying the sticker.

Dad responds the way he usually does—by ignoring her. He puts the bumper sticker back in the glove box and says, "We better head to Cohagen."

"I still think 'Meet Me in Hell' is a good one," Val says.

"You both probably will," I crack. They both shoot me stink eyes.

So for the second time on this journey, we pull into the old Nickels Ranch. This time, someone is home and we get permission to drive back to where we lived.

"They've widened the road," Valli points out as we cross the creek and drive past the field that we used to spend hours picking rocks out of, no doubt remembering how Dad used to make her drive an old pickup down this road to the bus stop every day.

Even back then, Valli hated to drive. There was a narrow spot in the road which crossed over a small creek and she was scared to death to drive across it. From the house, Mom and Dad could watch her for the first couple of miles as she barely crawled along. When she got to the creek, she would slow down even more, turn the radio off, sit on the edge of the seat with her hands frozen on the wheel at ten and two, and idle across the narrow passage.

In the summer, Dad would drop us each off in that field with a five-gallon bucket, a thermos of water, and a sandwich, and he would pick us up about eight hours later. We would fill the buckets and dump them in another rock pile—one that we had made to avoid having to walk too far with the heavy buckets. It was hard work for two skinny kids like us. For our slave labor, Dad's boss paid us a dollar a day. By the end of summer, we had each earned about thirty-five dollars, which meant that we had picked rocks approximately three or four times a week, for eight hours a day, and made what figured to be a whopping twelve cents per hour, putting us in the same tax bracket as the kids from Thailand. We hated it, but no was not a word that we had ever learned to say to our father.

"God, I was fifteen when we lived here. I should be able to remember this place. Why doesn't it look familiar? How long did we live here?" I ask Dad.

"Well, you were only here on weekends," Val reminds me.

"House is gone," Dad points out, ignoring my questions. An unfamiliar trailer house stands in its place.

I dig through the miscellaneous files of my memory to see if I can pull out the one that says "Cohagen: 1975." Nope. I can't remember anything about the house or the barn. Then I see an old milking stanchion by the barn. "Oh yeah, I remember that thing," I tell Dad and Valli. "That's the site of the last cow I ever milked!"

Mom loved milking cows and we had one at almost every place we ever lived. She did all the milking until I got to be about ten or eleven years old, and then I did it if she was busy or couldn't do it for whatever reason. Let me just say that I did my share. Most of her milk cows weren't really milk cows at all, but old range cows that had lost their calves. Dad would have to rope them and tie them down, and Mom would milk them while they were lying on their sides. It's not always possible to get milk out of a cranky, old cow that's having its teats pulled on while tied down. Only if their bags were so big that they were about to burst would they give up the goods without much of a fight. Every day, Mom would coax them with cow cake and hay and eventually, after a few months and a lot of patience, she would get them tame enough to milk like normal cows.

This particular cow, at this site, started out as such. She always kicked me, slapped me with her shitty tail, or stuck a foot in my bucket and spilled my milk, so I always protested when Mom asked me to milk her. The last time I ever milked her, Mom persuaded me by saying, "She's a nice cow. You don't even have to tie her feet anymore," which really was code for, "Watch out, the old bitch is going to cut loose and kick the daylights out of you."

I had the bucket about half-full when the old bitty went apeshit and, yes, kicked the living daylights out of me. First she stuck her foot in the bucket, tipping it over, then she put her foot in my coat pocket and proceeded to finish me off by banging my head up against the fence until she'd succeeded in tearing the pocket clean off my coat. I was bruised, battered, and swollen when I got back to the house with an empty milk bucket. That day, I swore to Mom that I would never again milk another cow and I would never, ever ask her for milk. I told her that when I had babies I would walk to town, uphill both ways, in a blizzard, to get them milk if I had to, but I would never again ask her for a drop of milk, so she was not to ever ask me to milk her cow again. She agreed and we both kept our words.

We knock on the door of the trailer house and introduce ourselves to the lady who answers, explaining that we used to live here. She's pretty, appears to be close to fifty, is a little overweight, and the skin on her face seems to be in serious need of some sunscreen and moisturizer. From her handshake and the tanned and weathered appearance of her hands, I can tell that she is hardworking. Her nails are too short to have dirt under them, but there are signs of dirt around the edges, clinging to dry cuticles. I glance at my own hands, with my manicured nails and diamond rings marking wedding anniversaries, before I hide them behind my back, feeling a little guilty and a little sad for her.

I got out of here; she could too, I think to myself. She says that she remembers my name from high school. I don't remember hers, but I tell myself that if we are anywhere near the same age, I must look damn good and life must be tough in the sticks. I make a mental note to point that out to Val and Dad once we leave. The lady invites us to look around, although there really isn't much to see other than what is visible by turning in a circle.

Five minutes later, we leave and I get Val to agree with me on the age thing as we get back into the pickup. Dad just says, "What? She didn't look that rough to me."

I ignore what sounds like an insult—I'm still busy saying the "Thank-You-God-that-I-Moved-Again-and-Didn't-End-Up-Stuck-Here-Married-to-a-Dirt-Farmer" prayer.

Forty

The little town of Cohagen looks like a place where everything goes to die. The houses, the weeds, the antelope, the highway—nothing seems to be alive here. Were some kids' dreams discarded here, along with the swing sets, bicycles, and teeter-totters? So many windows are boarded up that it looks like a town full of secrets—a town that you could be stuck in forever, unable to untangle yourself from the choking weeds. Or maybe it's a place where you could be left behind by a broken-down car or an out-of-gas pickup that was abandoned wherever it stopped running. The only sure way to get out of town is to blink when you pass through. Then it's like you never even saw it, so you were never really there. Christmas and misery are the only things guaranteed to come to Cohagen every year.

The tiny, two-room country school that Val attended in the seventh grade still stands, but we can't tell if it is occupied or not. Only about a dozen kids attended, with one teacher, in 1975 when Val went there.

"Look at my school bus!" Val shouts, pointing at the little yellow bus that's parked by the school. It has all of about four rows of seats.

"You always did ride the short bus," I tease.

We leave the tumbleweeds and dying prairie of Cohagen behind (for what I hope is forever) and head to Mosby, where some dear friends live. Cole and Lynette Walker's ranch on the Musselshell River is where we lived for three weeks between—well, we don't remember exactly, but sometime between our first and second moves to Winnett. Though we were only here for a short time, this place holds some of my fondest memories. It always felt like Saturday when I walked through their door.

We pull off the county road onto a smaller gravel road and drive the last half mile to the house. For the first time on this trip, something looks familiar. The trees have grown and our friends have a new fence around their yard. I look for the old cream cans that used to stand on the back porch, holding water. Inside I recognize some new furniture, new carpeting, and a new kitchen table, but the old silver bucket with the big ladle is missing from the kitchen counter. I used to love walking into this kitchen, scooping up water, and drinking from the old alkaline-crusted ladle. Remembering the feel of that cool water floods my brain with warm memories.

Jessie Walker was my age and we were partners in crime as well as best friends. I would get to stay with her for a week or two each summer and we would roam all over the nearly twenty thousand acres that made up the Walker Ranch. We rode our horses backwards and swam them in the river, where we would slide off of their butts, hold onto their tails, and let them pull us across. We would tie a rope onto a little red wagon and then take turns pulling each other on horseback at a breakneck speed, trying to tip it over and spill the other. When we couldn't catch the horses, we rode the old milk cow across the river, tying a piece of cow cake to a string and dangling it from a stick in front of Old Bossy's nose.

Sometimes Valli and Jessie's brother, Joel, would ride with us. When they did, we always made them play our favorite game, which involved throwing horseshit at each other. Whenever one of our horses took a crap, we would all jockey for position to catch the hot, steaming pile of road apples in our hands. Sometimes we divided ourselves into teams; sometimes it was every man for himself. Mom and Lynette always griped about us playing this game, because most of our shirts and jeans got permanent shit stains from doing this. One time, Valli got hit in the side of the head with one of the big, hot piles of poop and went wailing back to the house, horseshit packed into her ear like gauze and a big green stain on her long blonde hair.

Jessie and I called ourselves "river rats" and spent most of our time on the river—or in it, is more like it. There were certain times of the year when we were forbidden to go in because of the fast current or high water, but we usually ignored that rule and went anyway.

One day after doing just that, we sent Val back to the house to get dry clothes for us. We waited and waited, not knowing that when Val was crawling in through Jessie's bedroom window, Cole had busted her. We finally gave up the wait and went sneaking back to the house in our soaking wet clothes only to find Val sitting at the kitchen table with her short little legs swinging back and forth, nervously chewing her fingernails and looking guilty for not coming through, but not saying a word. It should be noted here that Cole always had a soft spot for my sister. He was known to hug her and offer comforting words and a sympathetic ear, while we only saw her as the tattletale loser in the shit-throwing game, or the decoy from the river to the room. Cole saw her as our scapegoat and he had genuine compassion for her. That day, Cole whipped Jessie's butt while Valli and I looked on.

The crazy thing was that in the winter, when the river was frozen over, they would let us pack .22 rifles and walk up and down it, shooting holes in the ice. Then we would run downstream, chop a small hole in the ice, and scoop out handfuls of dead floating fish. We held contests to see who could get the most fish in a single shot. We lived kind of a cowboy-Huck-Finn existence and most of our days together were carefree and idyllic.

Well, not every day was like that. We did have real work to do. One summer Cole gave us the job of riding the sheep pasture to check on his ewes and lambs. Every day, we would come home and report that we had found a dead one. This went on for about a week.

"Do you think it's coyotes?" Cole finally asked us.

"Nope, they're just dead, not eaten," we told him, like

we were highly-paid ranch foremen rather than snot-nosed peons. At that time, we really didn't know why they were dying. It had Cole stumped too, until the day he snuck out to his sheep pasture and caught me and Jessie chasing an old ewe around, trying to rope her. We would chase her until she would quit running and lie down, panting with her tongue hanging out. Then we'd ride off and pick out another one to practice our roping on. We didn't mean to kill them and we didn't put two and two together until a few days later, when there were already four or five dead ewes. After that, we took up roping sagebrush. It wasn't as much fun, but it was sure a lot easier on our pride.

By the age of thirteen, Jessie and I had graduated from slinging shit and shooting fish to drinking beer and kissing. I still remember that our first night of necking followed a long day of branding and docking lambs. The neighboring ranchers would always get together to complete this chore, each bringing his wife and kids along to help. After a long day in the branding pen, the men would sit around a BBQ pit, swigging beer and watching the lamb chops turn black, while the women marched like ants, hauling bowls of their homemade salads to the big wooden picnic table.

On this occasion, Jessie and I skipped dinner, stole a six-pack of beer, grabbed two unsuspecting, pimply-faced, fourteen-year-old boys whom we had randomly chosen to initiate us, and headed to the river. We got our buzz on and then we made out. After about twenty minutes of sloppy kissing, we ditched the boys to go and talk about it. The conversation that followed went something like this:

"Are you going steady?"

"I think so."

"Did he try to feel your boob?"

"Sick! No!"

"Well, did you French kiss with him?"

"Yeah, did you?"

"It was wet."

"And gross."

"Did you spit out your chew?"

"Hell no!"

"Me neither."

By the next day, our make-out session was long forgotten and we were pretty sure that we were not going steady and we would not have to get married any time soon. Sure enough, we were still in love with our horses.

"I think I spent most of my time here hog-tied to a chair with a hankie stuffed in my mouth," Val says, snapping me back to reality. "I'm pretty sure you and Jessie should be in jail."

"We'd be out by now anyway," I point out.

"Well, it wouldn't be for good behavior," Val rebuts.

We visit for a while longer, Cole confirms that Val was an abused child, and then we say our good-byes and leave Cole and Lynette's full of good memories. Dad is the happiest that I've seen him on this trip. I can tell that he is really glad we made it. I have to admit that at this moment, I am too.

Forty-One

From the Walkers' we go about fifteen miles and turn onto a dirt road, then go another eleven miles back into the rough country known as the Missouri Breaks to a ranch called the Beckett Place.

We moved here in 1971 when I was in the fifth grade. The house was then an old log building with a dirt roof that predicted the seasons with eerie accuracy. The winter thaw caused a runoff of dripping mud that told us spring was approaching. Then flowers sprouted up on the roof, promising that summer was in our immediate future. When the blooms were sunburned beyond recognition and the pitiful stems begged to be put out of their misery, we knew that autumn was about to take its turn. The roof then wore the cracked, gray dirt like a heavy, shrunken coat as it braced for winter. Finally, snow blanketed the roof and warmed all of us who were fortunate enough to be under it.

Now the dirt has been replaced with tin and the house appears to be grieving the loss of its penchant for forecasting the seasons. The interior walls are still composed of the big, shiny logs and adorned with the same deer-head mounts that were there thirty years ago. In the old days, the house had been its own town, known as Ashley, Montana. The kitchen had been the store, complete with a flour grinder and an old cast-iron stove that had once burned coal or wood but had been updated to run on propane. The living room used to be the post office; the front door still holds a letter drop. On the wall near the door hang several small, square, wooden shelves that, back in the day, served as post office boxes. In the back of the house is a huge room that was used both as a dance hall and a funeral parlor.

When we lived here, we used the front part of the room as a bedroom, which Val and I shared, and the rear part to hold Mom's milk separator and Dad's roping dummy. There was no heat in that end of the house, so we froze our butts off in the winter, sleeping with our socks and layers of clothes on. Mom and Dad's bedroom and one small bathroom were off the living room. Having a funeral parlor in our house was spooky enough, but when the lights turned themselves off and on, we were pretty sure we weren't living there alone. Dad pooh-poohed the idea, but Mom always swore that the place was haunted.

Right after we moved into the Beckett place, Dad's father got into an accident that required him to be hospitalized for about a year so Dad's half brother, Troy (my Uncle Troy), came to live with us. He was only one year older than me and a city kid—which made him a sissy in my book. I didn't care if he was family, I had absolutely no use for him, and he wasn't exactly thrilled to be living with us either. I was not about to have some punk taking over my role as Dad's right-hand man, and the threat of a real boy taking my place was not something I was going to take lying down.

Troy and I clashed from the beginning and fought constantly. Mom refereed and tried to break up the fights. Dad just watched, egging us on by making fun of Troy if he was getting his butt whipped by a girl and shaming me if I was letting a city-slicker beat me up. It was a rocky relationship and neither of us had any desire to call a truce. We both thought of it as a fight to the death.

In the city, Troy was used to playing school sports and having friends, freedom, and fun. What he got at our house were two girls who thought that rolling a quart jar of cream across the floor (churning butter) was a game. To us, playing cowboys and Indians was a like an Olympic event. It involved riding horses—bareback at breakneck speeds—dodging arrows, climbing over rocks, and hiding behind pine trees. Troy didn't know how to ride a horse, shoot a gun, or throw a knife. He was foe, not friend, and we weren't interested in changing the status quo.

Troy threw a conniption fit when school started and he wasn't allowed to play basketball with the sixth-grade team.

My folks didn't have the extra fifteen dollars it would have taken for him to be able to buy shoes—not to mention the fact that we lived twenty-two miles from the school, with most of those miles made up of dirt road. Troy still tried to cry, pout, beg, threaten, and bargain his way onto the Winnett Rams basketball team. I could have told him that he was barking up the wrong tree, but I liked knowing that he was miserable and I enjoyed watching him squirm, so I never clued him in on a little secret that I knew—the one thing that Dad didn't do was change his mind. Troy hated being a country bumpkin and I hated having a stepbrother/uncle in our house.

While at the Beckett Place, Mom, Val, and I spent hours sorting through an old dump that was near the house, looking for old bottles and other antiques that might be of value. Besides hundreds of old purple and green bottles, we found an old crockery jar in which Mom ended up keeping her sourdough starter for the next several years. The rest of the treasures would just be more junk that Mom would be upset about leaving behind in the next move.

We all (except for Troy) liked living at the Beckett Place, surrounded by the rocky bluffs and pine trees, but I hated school in Winnett. Before Jessie and I became friends, we were mortal enemies. She was the "Boss of the Whole Fifth Grade Class," and every day she would pick a fight with me, then get some other girl to do her dirty work. For twenty-two miles every morning and twenty-two miles every night, I got picked on by the kids on the school bus, who were egged on by Jessie, who was unfortunately the first kid on and the last kid off the bus.

"Zit Pig," Jessie and her cronies called me. I'd go home and study my face for zits. I didn't have any, not one—only freckles. "Freckle Pig" just doesn't quite have the same ring to it though. That's probably why they called me Zit Pig, *I reasoned.*

Sooner or later, I had to fight just about every girl in the fifth grade class. I was pretty sure that Jessie could have whipped me, but lucky for me, my experience in the ring trumped her confidence, so she and I never got in the dirt.

After a few months, Jessie and her goons quit picking on me. I was leery about becoming her friend and wanted to resist her powers, but she had given me something that I needed. There was a new feeling inside of me. I think that she was the first person to ever respect me. Maybe eleven-year-old, prepubescent girls don't intentionally give respect to their peers, but I knew that when the fighting and name-calling stopped, I felt differently about myself. Pride was something I had already had an abundance of, but respect was a brand-new feeling for me. It felt good, I liked it, and I knew that I had earned it. In the end, Jessie and I became great friends, but by then we were ready to move again.

The house seemed huge back then, but now as we pull into the drive, it looks so small and rundown. The dirt roof has been replaced with tin, which would piss off Mom because she had loved this house for its dirt roof and spring flowers. We meet the current owner and she happily gives us a tour. The logs don't seem as big and shiny as they once were and the kitchen, which has been redone, looks even worse than it used to. *Another place bites the dust*, I think.

As we drive off, Dad tells Val to get some of Mom's ashes out, and passes the Styrofoam cup over his shoulder. By now, Val has the whole urn-breaking-and-entering routine down to an art. She is even packing her own screwdriver. Dad randomly scatters ashes and wipes his eyes as we drive the eleven miles of dirt road back to the highway.

Forty-Two

*J*ust *as we lived in Jordan two different times, we also
lived in Winnett twice, having moved back in the fall of
1973. That time, we lived in one of the nicest trailer houses
that we ever lived in and Dad and Mom really liked the
people they worked for. Dad's boss treated him with respect
and he didn't have a problem with Dad being a better
cowboy than him. He didn't work Dad to death and he even
let him have most weekends off. This place wasn't too far
out in the sticks, so we even had TV, which was rare. The
only problem with it was that the antenna was stuck in
a pole beside the house rather than mounted to the roof, so
whenever the wind blew, it spun around and messed up the
picture. It was pretty similar to* not *having TV.*

*On Sundays Dad wanted to watch football, so one of
us girls would have to go outside and turn the pole while he
coaxed coat hangers covered in tinfoil into showing him a*

snowy picture. When the wind blew, Val and I would take turns running outside to hold the pole so that Dad could watch the game.

Near the house was an old building that used to be a one-room schoolhouse. That spring, armed with a broom and an inkling of independence, I began the process of turning it into a bunkhouse. I spent my days sweeping the floor and moving the old, one-armed desks into the corners. Then, after I had freed the chalkboards from the years of dust that had accumulated on them and hauled out all of the old junk wood that had been stored in there, Mom helped me move my bed and dresser and some other belongings into my new home.

Doing nothing but pushing a broom for several days straight gave me a lot of time to think. It was then that I figured out that I was born eight months after Mom and Dad got married. I knew what that meant and I was shocked! I did the math over and over in my head, on my fingers, on the chalkboard, and in the dust, until I was sure that I had figured it right. Then I confronted Mom.

"Yeah, so what?" she had asked.

"Mom, it takes nine months to make a baby, so that means that you and Dad weren't married when you made me."

"You were born a month early. That's why you have bad knees," she said, shrugging, seeming to be telling the truth. I do have bad knees—and the surgery scars to prove it. She had me on that one.

After a couple more days of sweeping and thinking, I had asked her what Jesus's middle name was. "He doesn't have one," she said.

"Well, is Christ his last name?" I asked.

"He doesn't have a last name. Jesus Christ is just his whole name," she told me.

I argued with her. "He does have a middle name," I informed her. "It starts with H, but I don't know what it is."

"What makes you think Jesus has a middle name?" she asked me.

"Because Dad says 'Jesus H. Christ' when he's mad, and I just wondered what the H stands for."

"It doesn't stand for anything. Your dad's just making it up," she told me. I could tell that she wanted to end this conversation, but I had invested too much time in it to give up.

"So is he crippled?" I asked next.

"What? No, he's not crippled. Why would you ask that?" The expression on her face told me that she immediately regretted asking the question.

"Well, sometimes Dad says, 'Christ on a crutch,' and I just wondered why he was on a crutch. I always thought he was on a cross."

"He was on a cross, not a crutch," she confirmed. "And I'm pretty sure he doesn't have a middle name, but if he does, it's probably Hank or Henry or Harry or something," she said, obviously wanting me to drop it. Then she told me to quit doing so much thinking and sweeping.

Finally my brain and my broom took a time-out and I settled into my new bunkhouse—which, too bad I hadn't noticed before, had no electricity. That very first night, excited by the prospect of being on my own, I crawled into my twin bed while it was still light outside, pulled the chenille cover up under my chin, and waited for darkness. When the sun and moon finally traded places, the bats came out. The old school's attic was full of them and they circled over my head like a welcome wagon. A few of the windows were broken out, so by the light of the moon I could see the bats flying in and out, ignoring the new tenant as they went about their creepy, late-night business.

Piss on them! I'd done too much work to move in; I was not about to be run out by a few (hundred) bats. I just pulled the covers over my head and went to sleep. Valli was scared to death of my bat-infested bunkhouse and never got near it. At that time, she was pretty much afraid of her own shadow. Even at age ten, she was still occasionally crawling into bed with Mom and Dad in the middle of the night.

I stuck it out in the schoolhouse until fall came and it got too cold for me. Then I talked Mom into letting me move into an old camper trailer that in the summer was used by whichever Mexican had been hired to be the irrigator. It was close to our house so I was able to plug into a power pole to get lights and heat.

I woke up to the smell of smoke one night and found that my little electric heater was sitting too close to the plastic countertop and had caused a small fire, which had melted the counter. I caught it before a full-blown fire ensued, but when Mom and Dad saw the damage the next morning, that was the end of my emancipation.

I still spent a lot of time working with Dad, hauling hay to feed the cows in the winter and checking for "hot cows" during AI (artificial insemination) season. We were also pretty big into rodeos by then and Dad was teaching his boss to rope, so we were allowed to get away most weekends for rodeos. We also found time to practice a couple nights a week at the local rodeo grounds.

Mom occasionally roped with Dad but she was becoming more interested in running barrels. Valli and I were barrel racing too but I was growing increasingly frustrated and disgusted with it. No matter how much I practiced or how hard I rode, my ranch horse could never beat the boss's daughter's expensive, professionally-trained, high-powered horse. Dad didn't like barrel racing either. He said that it was a waste of good horse flesh, but he still tried to help me—even though I would have preferred to hate it without his help.

My horse probably liked it even less than I did. Dad had a young horse named Brandy, who I was trying to turn into a barrel horse. Brandy kept tipping over the first barrel, so Dad came up with a bright idea to break him of that habit: he would sit on top of the barrel with a stock whip in his hand and as I approached the first barrel at a dead run, he would begin hollering and swinging the whip, trying to keep Brandy away from it. I had to close my eyes because the whip would get dangerously close to my face. I took more of the beating than my horse did. I did have to admit, though, that it kind of worked for a while. Brandy didn't want to get too close to the barrel when there was a yelling, cussing man waving a whip around on top of it.

Brandy did run into the barrel once, which sent Dad and the barrel flying. After that, Dad would stand, rather than sit on it, and he hollered and cussed louder and waved the whip more frantically. We finally gave up on making a barrel horse out of Brandy, and Dad went back to roping off of him. I still had Mite, and by then I had grown up enough that I wasn't playing shit-throwing games, so I tried to run barrels on him.

Once again, Dad hatched a "plan" to help me. He made me a whip out of barbed wire, and wrapped an old sheet around the handle part of it. When I practiced my barrel racing, he would "help" by hollering at me. He told me that if I hung on to my saddle horn, he would saw it off, and that if I didn't use the barbed wire whip on Mite, he would use it on me. When I finished my runs, Mite's butt would be peppered with little blood spots and my right hand would be downright bloody. This was after the Richey days, but Mite had not forgotten and was still scared shitless of Dad. He would take off at a dead run whenever Dad entered the arena, and that had nothing to do with that damn barbed wire whip.

While living at Winnett, Valli took up running. She was eleven years old when she first took off for a jog down our gravel road. At the time, I never even gave it a second thought, but looking back, I have to wonder what it is that makes a kid start running at that young age. I can still see her with her long, blonde hair whipping back and forth and her small hands clenched into fists. Her chin was thrust forward and her short, stubby legs reached towards stability as gravel and ambiguity crunched under her little feet.

I didn't get it then and I still don't now, but I have never been any good at analyzing anything more important than whether or not I can pull off coral in the off season (I can, so say the ladies at Macy's). Honestly, the only good reason that I can think of for running is that someone is chasing me with a rope or a gun. So what was she doing? And why? I'm sure that's one for the therapists to figure out. God knows she already had plenty of discipline in her life. Looking back, the only answer I can come up with is that it was the one thing in her life that she had control over. She is still running to this day.

During this period, Mom was sick and bleeding all the time, which made her constantly exhausted. She then had a hysterectomy and was on different drugs while trying to work out the hormone thing. Sleepy, drugged, weak, and tired pretty much summed up Mom's life for that period of time.

On Wednesday evenings, we went to the local arena for practice ropings. One Wednesday Dad came home a little late, so he was in a hurry to get hooked up to the trailer and get the horses loaded. When he went to the barn, he found the corral empty and the gate open. We could hear him hollering all the way from the house.

"Who left the goddamned gate open?" he roared.

I was thankful that it wasn't me, but Val had no choice but to come clean.

"I'm sorry, Dad. I didn't mean to," she said, already crying in anticipation of the trouble that she knew she was about to be in.

We both scrambled to the pasture to get the horses in. Val and I ran with halters in our hands while Mom hooked up the trailer and Dad kept on ranting and raving. We caught his horses and handed the lead ropes over to him as he jumped them into the trailer. Mom was already in her spot, the gear-shift between her knees, when Dad jumped in behind the wheel and began driving off. Luckily, I was standing on the passenger side so when I heard the truck pull into first gear I made a run for the door and bailed in. Valli was standing on the driver's side of the pickup, looking amazed at all the hustle going on around her. As she saw us leaving, she ran to Dad's window, which was open, and grabbed onto the doorframe with one hand and the rearview mirror with the other.

"Please, Daddy, don't leave me," she begged. "Please, I'm scared to stay alone. I'm sorry, Dad. I didn't mean to let the horses out, I'm sorry."

Valli kept running, begging even more as she chased us. Dad formed a fist and used the side of it to pound her little fingers, which were clinging to the pickup. Mom and I looked straight ahead, both still thankful that we weren't the ones who had left the gate open. Val was still running alongside the pickup, begging and apologizing, but when Dad slipped into second gear, she finally turned loose. I looked in the passenger-side mirror and I could see her sitting in the road crying, our dust sticking to her tears, getting smaller and smaller as we drove off and left her.

One beautiful spring day, Dad and I were driving over to the boss's place to move some cows when a jackrabbit ran across the road in front of us. Like most rabbits do, it ran for a while, then froze in place next to a big sagebrush, surely thinking that if it didn't move, we wouldn't be able to see it. Dad hit the brakes, rolled down his window, and pulled the .22 rifle out of the rack in the back window. "Here ya go, Tam. Shoot that son of a bitch," he said.

He rested the rifle on the door and leaned back out of my way. I scooted across the seat, leaned over him in front of the steering wheel with the butt of the .22 against my shoulder, and took aim. I didn't really want to kill the rabbit but I knew that I could. I also knew that if I had a choice between pleasing the rabbit or Dad, well, I would rather make my dad happy. I decided that I would miss the first shot anyway, in the hope that the rabbit would run away. My shot kicked up dust in front of the rabbit, but the dumb thing only blinked; it didn't move. I felt the horses in trailer jump at the sound of the rifle.

"Shit-o-dear, can't you hit that son of a bitch?" Dad asked. I cocked the .22 again, telling myself (and the soon-to-be-dead rabbit) that this was his last chance for survival. I fired again, this time just over his head. I felt the horses jump a little again, but the dumb rabbit still didn't move.

"For Christ's sake, Tam," was barely out of Dad's mouth when I cocked the .22 again and fired the third shot, hitting the damned rabbit square in the head. It flopped on its side and kicked once. The horses didn't even flinch that time.

"'Bout damned time. I thought I was gonna have to do it for you," Dad said, dropping the pickup back into gear. He

eased out the clutch and gave me a smile and an atta-girl
pat on my back as I slid back across the front seat, feeling
sick inside.

"Tammi, what were those pills called that I used to make you take when we lived here?" Dad asks me, forcing the memory of the rabbit out of my mind.

"Are you talking about those big, butterscotch horse pills that you force-fed me?" I ask, although I know exactly what he's talking about. My stomach turns at the memory.

"Yeah, you were scrawny. They were to make you gain some weight."

"They were called 'Wate-On,' Dad. They tasted like shit. I can't believe you made me eat those things. I think they caused me permanent damage because I still don't like butterscotch."

"Well it looks like they worked," he says, feeding me a shit-eating grin.

"Thanks, Dad. That's just one more thing that I can blame you for," I say, feeding it right back to him.

Forty-Three

We leave Winnett with plenty of what I consider to be bittersweet, butterscotch memories, and Dad is chatty and in a good mood. He talks about the Beckett Place and working at the Burns Ranch nonstop, all the way to Roundup, Montana. As we pull into the town, he says, "Slow down, Tammi. I want to see if the old arena is still there."

I let off the gas and go where he points for me to go. No matter where we lived, it seemed like we always came to Roundup for the Fourth of July Rodeo.

"This is where you cracked your noggin wide open and 'bout spilled your brains," Dad says.

"That was a serious head injury. I think I got b-b-b-brain d-d-d-damage," I reply.

"Yeah, that's probably what's wrong with you," Val adds.

"Yeah, probably," Dad says, like I'm being serious.

I was twelve years old and we were there for the annual Fourth of July Rodeo. Dad was roping and Mite and I were entered in the barrel race. As we rounded the third barrel and ran for home, Mite saw an open gate and ducked out from under me. I flew off his back while he was at a dead run, hitting my back on an iron brace post in the arena fence and my head on the tailgate of a pickup that had been let down and backed up next to the fence. It knocked me cold.

When I regained consciousness, the first thing I heard was Mom frantically screaming, "Gary! Gary! Where are you?" He was already standing over me and he was the first person I saw when I opened my eyes, although he was out of focus. I couldn't move my legs or get my breath for a few minutes, and the dirt beneath my head was getting sticky and turning red. A crowd of men had gathered around me. I must have been gasping for air, because someone bent over me and unbuttoned my jeans, and then someone else yelled, "Give her air."

Then another voice hollered, "We need to call an ambulance!"

"Bullshit," I heard Dad say. "She's OK. Get up, Tam."

I tried to get to my feet and couldn't. My legs wouldn't move. Dad grabbed my arm and pulled me up, my knees still unable to hold all seventy pounds of me.

"I'm a nurse," a lady said as she pushed her way through the crowd. "Let me take her."

Dad forked me over like I wasn't his kid. The nurse, Mom, and I walked a short distance to a trailer house that was near the arena. Dad went back to the horse trailer to get ready for the roping.

We knocked on the door of the trailer and when the lady of the house saw the blood all over me, she didn't ask questions. She just immediately led us into her bathroom.

"The hospital is just across the highway. We really should take her there," the nurse told my mom.

"We don't have insurance," Mom said. "Are you OK, Tammi?"

"I have a headache. Did I win?" I asked while bent over the sink, watching the red water run down the drain.

"She really needs to go to the hospital. She needs stitches," the nurse tried one more time.

"We don't have the money and her dad said no," Mom said, standing her ground. She was good at doing that with anyone except Dad.

"Can I get some aspirin? I have a bad headache." My head was pounding as if someone was running a jackhammer on my brain.

After a few more minutes with cool water running on my head, Mom gently wrung out my hair and we went back to the arena with my hair dripping water and blood.

"You OK?" Dad asked when he saw me.

"I don't feel good, Dad. I have a bad headache," I said, trying not to whine.

"You won the barrel race!" he said, patting my leg and handing me a five-dollar bill (my winnings). He was smiling at me but not wanting to show too much pride.

I tried to smile back, but it hurt to smile.

"I'm OK, I guess," I said, not really convinced that I was.

"Atta girl; you really kicked their ass. Here," he said, handing me a can of 7UP. "You won three cans of pop, too."

A week later my head was still bleeding off and on, oozing nasty stuff, and my hair was so matted into my wound that Mom couldn't comb it out. She finally convinced Dad that I needed to see a doctor.

"This kid should have had stitches," the doctor told Mom. "She has a bad infection." My head was down, but looking through my hair, I could see that Mom looked embarrassed about not having taken me to the doctor sooner. He scolded her and she made excuses.

It hurt like hell as he pulled all the hair out of my wound, causing it to bleed again. My hair was so thick and sticky with dried blood that it was like trying to pull a wooden spoon out of a saucepan of hardened caramel.

"Damn near killed ya," Dad says, snapping me back into the moment. "Good thing you've got a hard head."

"Yeah, good thing," I say back to him.

"But you won the barrel race," he points out, still proud and still trying not to sound like it.

"Yeah, like that was really worth it," I say, thinking about how dumb it was to get almost killed for five bucks. Besides, I prefer Coke to 7UP.

"Yeah, Ma sure chewed my ass," Dad says, referring to Grandma Wanda. "When she heard about it, she said, 'I would have given that kid ten bucks and a six pack to stay off that crazy, goddamn horse.'"

Dad chuckles at the memory.

Another train wreck behind us, we head for Cody, Wyoming, where we will spend the night.

An old friend of ours owns a restaurant in Cody and since Dad is in a cheery mood, Val and I double-team him and bring up the subject of having dinner in a nice restaurant tonight, rather than having more fast food in our motel room. We are surprised when Dad consents. The fact that we have threatened to roll him up in a tarp and leave him in the back of the pickup if he makes us eat at one more fast food place may have something to do with it. He also knows that I'm packing heat and he's pushing his luck. There is only so much we have to take from him, now that we're over forty.

Once we get to the restaurant, the hostess seats us and the waitress comes over to take our bar order. I ask if Terry is in.

"Yessss . . ." she says, somewhat hesitantly.

"Could you ask him to come here? I'd like to talk to him."

I can tell she's still suspicious. "Can I tell him whoooo is asking for him?" she asks, just as hesitantly.

"Just tell him it's an old frieeeennnndddd," I say.

"OooooooK" she says, as she turns and walks off.

"She thinks I'm a food critic," I tell Dad and Valli, giggling. "I get that all the time."

I'm in the booth, facing the kitchen, as Terry comes walking towards me. I see a light go off in his head and I know that he recognizes me.

"DiAnne!" he says, smiling. "How are you?" He reaches our table and sees Dad and Val sitting in the booth, across the table from me.

"It's Tammi," I tell him.

"Oh my God! You look just like . . . I thought you were . . . oh, that's right . . . I'm so sorry . . . I heard about . . . my God . . . you look just like your mother!"

He finally finishes a sentence then grabs Dad's hand and begins pumping it up and down, staring at us in disbelief. I slide across the booth so he can sit down next to me. We visit for a little while, mostly talking about him. He doesn't mention Mom again and neither do we. He cooks us a wonderful meal and then picks up our check.

Forty-Four

Day Six

The area has developed a lot over the past several years, so we have a hard time finding the road that will lead us back to 1972. Dad finally recognizes a landmark and we start our jaunt into the past. We drive by the calving sheds, which look like they have been abandoned for many years, and from there the road turns into not much more than a cow trail. A small, red house sits in the middle of nowhere, surrounded by nothing. We park at the cattle guard and Val and I walk up to the house, leaving Dad in the pickup, smoking a cigarette.

It was late in my sixth-grade year when we moved to Cody. Not only was I the new kid again, I had a big cast on my arm, which was good for even more unwanted attention.

Between Jordan and Cody, we had spent a couple of months in Billings while Dad was looking for a new ranch job. Val and I had enrolled in Bitterroot school, and not long after that, I broke my arm on the playground. Rather than tell the teacher, I just went into the bathroom, sat down in a stall, and tried to ignore the pain and nausea. When recess ended and I didn't return to the classroom, the teacher came into the bathroom and found me propped up against a toilet, sick to my stomach, with my wrist dangling down and the bone protruding unnaturally upwards. She called an ambulance and then my mother.

Shortly after that, Dad got a job at a cow camp at the Hondo Ranch, several miles from town. My first memory of Cody, Wyoming, is a neon sign that read "Cassie's Supper Club." Famished from a day of packing up, moving, and not eating, we had pulled into Cody late on a spring night in 1972. Cassie's Supper Club was the only restaurant we could find that was open, so we steered our Beverly Hillbillies-*looking rig into the big parking lot. The four of us—dirty, bedraggled, and tired—walked into what turned out to be a "fine dining establishment." Looking like dirty, homeless people (which we technically were), we were led by the hostess past the staring fine-diners to a table draped with freshly starched linens, accented with a cloth napkin and two forks at each setting—not the type of place at which we normally ate. One look at the big, leather-bound menu was all I needed to determine that this was not a place where we could afford to be dining. The expression on Mom's face confirmed that. I immediately equated "Please Wait to Be Seated" with "expensive."*

As hungry as we were, we still suddenly lost our appetites when we saw the prices. We just wanted simple hamburgers, which were nowhere to be found on the fancy menu. Like loyal cow dogs, we waited for Dad's command to see if we were eating or leaving. Probably because his family looked like a nest full of baby birds waiting for big worms to be dropped into their open mouths, Dad placed his order. Pretending not to be ravished, the rest of us followed suit. I learned the meaning of à la carte.

When the bill came, Dad shuffled his BankAmericard and MasterCard one on top of the other, unsure of which card could pay for dinner without being declined. Finally he folded, put them both away, and fished for cash while Mom did the same. I pretended not to notice but made sure to say what a great meal it had been.

Most of my days in Cody were spent learning to rope and to drive. I threw at least a hundred loops each night, in what Dad and I called "roping contests," so I got pretty good at roping the dummy. Roping live, running animals while on horseback turned out to be another story.

"Tam, jump out there and rope that cow," Dad said to me one day. His roll-your-own pointed at a black, baldy heifer.

I built a loop and kicked Mite into a lope, pointing him in the direction of the designated cow. As soon as she realized that she had been singled out, the heifer immediately took off at a dead run, Mite and I hot on her heels. My legs were kicking hard and my arm was swinging a frantic loop, which got bigger and bigger with each swing. Finally I took a shot; my loop fell short, not even touching her.

"Goddamn it, rope her!" I heard Dad holler.

I coiled my rope and built another loop. Over and over, the same scenario played out until finally the cow that had drawn the short straw no longer had the energy to run from me. By then, I had thrown about twenty-five loops. Some had hit her on the butt, some on the head, but none of them had made the figure eight that was necessary to circle her neck. My scrawny, twelve-year-old arm was hanging from my shoulder like an overdone noodle that's barely connected to a pasta fork.

Dad continued to holler and cuss at me. "Jesus H. Christ! I thought you could rope! Shit-o-dear, you're about to run her to death! You better rope her this time!"

A "Goddamn!" an "Ahhh, shit!" or a "For Christ's sake!" followed each loop I threw. She finally got tired of running and lay down in front of me. Mite stopped next to her, his head hanging, his nose at her hip with his nostrils flared, and his body dripping with sweat. We all three just sat there, breathing hard and looking ashamed at our individual failures.

"Well, we might as well head for home," Dad said, obviously disappointed in me. Relieved that the humiliation was over, I bit the inside of my cheek to keep from crying and used what energy I had left to coil up my rope. I rode the rest of the way home a horse-length behind Dad.

My driving was not so good either. A few days later, while driving through a pasture, we came across a cow that needed to be doctored. Dad had a plan and at the time it sounded like a pretty good one. Maybe he left out a few of the details.

The plan was that I was to drive the pickup as close to the cow as possible and Dad would be in the right front corner of the box, standing on the headache rack. When I got close enough to give him a shot, he would rope the sick cow. He forewarned me that the cow would constantly be going to the right, since I would be hazing her that way. Dad's rope was tied on hard and fast, so the idea was that when he caught her she would hit the end of the rope and fall down. Dad would bail out of the pickup before she could get to her feet, and he would doctor her. This was all a lot harder than it sounds.

First I had to get close enough to the cow to give him a shot. "Closer, Tammi, closer!" I could hear Dad hollering. I mashed on the gas pedal and the closer I got the harder right she went. I cranked the wheel and kept going hard right.

"Ya gotta get closer!" I heard above the roar of second gear. I got closer—too close, you could say. I hit the old gal, knocked her down, and sent her rolling.

"Whoa!" Dad bellowed. Both of my feet instantly slammed on the pedals and raced each other to the floorboard, my brake foot beating my clutch foot, killing the engine. I heard a thump on the roof and then I saw my dad's upside-down face staring through the windshield at me, his rope still in his hand and his cowboy hat smashed into an unusual shape with the brim pinned against the wipers. His black eyes glared at me and he snarled, "I said, 'Whoa,' Goddamn it!" as he unfolded himself and slid off the hood. He walked around to the box to grab his vet bag, continued over to the *still-downed cow, filled a syringe full of medicine, and stuck the needle into her hip, adding insult to injury.*

Sure that my driving days were over, I pried my hands off the wheel and slid over to the passenger side just as Dad jerked open the door. I thought it meant a blistering.

"You better drive. Looks like you need some practice," he said, grinning. "You damn near killed me."

I breathed a sigh of relief and laughed as Dad tried to reshape his hat. I told him how funny he had looked with his upside-down face against the windshield and his hat squished into something that resembled a Sunday School bonnet, and we laughed about it all the way home.

At Cody, we finally had a bit of a social life. Dad would enter the Cody Night Rodeo a few times a week, and while he was competing I would hang out with a gang of little boys who were a couple years younger than I was. We would cruise the rodeo grounds, talking tough and picking fights with other kids. We chewed tobacco, cussed, and threw rocks and punches at our rivals. God, I loved Cody!

Val and I make our way to the little red shack. Years of neglect and cold weather have turned it into something resembling a festering sore. The red has faded to the color of an infection and loose boards hang on it like scabs on an old wound. The door is partially open, swollen by years of soaking rain. It's permanently frozen in its position, too fat to open or close completely. We squeeze through it into a house that neither of us recognizes. It's empty except for several big piles of animal shit—fresh animal shit. The smell is overwhelming and the piles are big enough to be bear shit—from big bears.

"I have to get out of here," Val says, covering her nose with her hand. "I'm going to ralph." We are only in the kitchen, about five steps in to a four-room house. She turns for the door.

I cover my own nose and hold my breath, hoping that whatever animals live here are at work today. The shit is fresh and there is a lot of it. Still covering my nose and holding my breath, I walk into a bedroom, half-expecting to see three beds for the three bears in the Goldilocks story; no—just more big animal shit. I take a quick look around to see if anything looks familiar. It doesn't. I don't even know which room was Mom and Dad's or which one was Val's, but I'm about at the end of my maximum breath-holding capabilities, so I make a beeline for fresh air.

I do know that when we moved here my independent streak was in full swing so instead of living in the little, two-bedroom dump with my family, I moved into the little shack across the road. I spent a week cleaning it out, and then, once again, Mom helped me move my bed out of the house. There was no water or electricity, but there was an old red velvet couch and a chair that matched it. I didn't know that they were red until I beat them with a broom for about two days and got most of the dust out of them. Then, in the barn, I found an old can of paint, called "Chyna Red," which was exactly the same color as the couch and chair. I fished three old vegetable cans out of the garbage, painted them, and used them as spittoons. Using the cast on my arm as a hammer, I hung pictures on the walls. That was my first attempt at interior decorating and I was happy as a clam in my little bunkhouse.

A few weeks later, Mom took me back to Billings to see the doctor about my broken arm. It was a wasted trip. We returned to Cody with me still wearing the cast after the doctor said that my arm still wasn't healed.

"That's bullshit," Dad said when he heard the news.

"Come here, Tammi. Give me your arm," he demanded. Then, with a pair of wire cutters, he began cutting the cast off of me.

"Goddamned doctors don't know what the hell they're talking about," Dad said as he pulled the cast apart.

"Dumb bastards," he continued, cussing the doctors as the cast ripped apart in dusty pieces. When my arm was set free from its plaster prison, it emerged shriveled, hairy, and shrunken, but it sure felt good to be out in the fresh air! However, my bone was still protruding unnaturally upwards.

While living in Cody, Mom worked in town at a western store, and she also had thirty-six bum calves to feed. Twice a day, we lugged four five-gallon buckets of calf supplement down to the barn to feed them. Mom also had a milk cow *and I was doing most of the milking because she was always fixed up in the mornings to go to work.*

One morning, Dad saw her milking the cow while she was in her good work clothes.

"Why are you milking? Where's Tam?" he asked.

"Must be still sleeping. I hollered at her, but I haven't seen her," she told Dad, obviously disgusted with me. "Go get her up, Gary. I need to get to work."

I did remember hearing Mom yell at me, but I had rolled over and fallen back asleep. The next sound I heard was the door of my bunkhouse opening, and then my dad's voice booming, "You better be up or your ass is grass!"

I was, instantly! I already had one leg in my jeans when Dad turned the corner into my room. The next sound I heard was the zing of the rope that he had in his hand. I heard it before I felt it and I felt it before I saw it. I was hopping around, trying to get my other leg into my jeans so I could make a run for the barn. A ten-by-twelve room is not nearly a big enough space in which to elude a would-be killer with a thirty-five-foot rope. I was ducking, apologizing, and trying to run past him, all at the same time.

"Get your ass to the barn and help your ma," was the only other thing he said to me as he beat my ass about halfway there, until I finally got my pants all the way up and outran him the rest of the distance to the barn.

"Where's my bunkhouse?" I ask Val after I get my first breath of fresh air. She is still covering her nose with her shirt.

"It was over there," she says in a muffled voice, pointing across the way.

"No bunkhouse, no barn—nothing but a shithole," I say, shrugging. No pun intended.

"Is this where we lived when you shot me with the BB gun?" Val asks as we make our way back to the pickup.

"Oh sure, keep dredging up the past," I say. "Like we haven't had to relive enough of it already. Besides, getting shot with a BB gun isn't that big of a deal."

"It hurt! You drew blood! I still have a scar," she accuses as she pulls up her shirt, looking for a microscopic dot on her waist.

"No bunkhouse," Dad says as we get back in the pickup. "Tam, do you remember the ass-kicking you got that time you slept in and didn't milk for your ma?"

"Yeah, Dad," I say. "Thanks for reminding me. Why does every place we visit have to be about the whipping I got there?"

Valli brings up the BB gun again.

I change the subject. "Why did we leave here, Dad? I think I liked Cody."

He doesn't seem to remember why we left.

"Where'd we go?" Val chimes in, forgetting about the BB gun incident too.

"Let's go back by the calving sheds," Dad says to me, ignoring Valli—again.

Forty-Five

We leave Cody and 1972 behind and we head back into Montana, stopping just outside of Red Lodge in an old mining community known as Bearcreek. This is where Great-Grandma and her husband home-steaded. He came to the United States from Italy, and after their marriage in the early 1900s, they had settled here. When he was thirty-four years old, he died of a heart attack, leaving my great-grandma a widow with four young children, my Grandma Irene being the eldest. She stayed at the old homestead for another five years and never remarried. It's sad that nothing remains today.

From Bearcreek we drive to Boyd, to the farm owned by my great-grandmother's sister Francine and Francine's husband.

This was the farm where Mom used to spend her summers as a kid. It was also the gathering place for Great-Grandma's family. All of the old relatives—aunts, uncles, and cousins— would meet there on Saturday nights for a steam bath. The men would go to the bathhouse first and then all the women and kids would go.

I remember the fat, old aunts and grandmas, with their big, dimpled bottoms, full, soft, round bellies, heavy, sagging breasts with nipples pointing at the floor, and gray armpit and pubic hair. Then there was my mother, with her tiny, perfect, brown body—with no tan lines. Val and I would keep our arms crossed over our chests, hiding our little bee-sting breasts. We would each have our own washcloths, but we all shared the same bucket of cool water, dipping our cloths in it to wash ourselves. We were told to "Wash up as far as possible, then wash down as far as possible, and then wash possible."

There were three levels of wooden benches that we could sit on. The top one was so hot that it surely must have been what hell feels like. Someone would dump a bucket of water on the pile of rocks and the steam would rise up and wrap around us and take our breath away. For a few minutes, we couldn't see anyone, just eerie shapes, like there were fat, big-butted ghosts in the room with us. When we were done, we would run out, wrapped in towels, into the night air, cool or freezing cold depending on the season.

Mom grew up taking the weekly steam bath and looked forward to it each time we visited. Val and I didn't like the ritual, mostly because we didn't want to get naked in front of the old ladies, who looked at our bodies and told us we *were too skinny. I don't recall Dad ever taking a steam bath.*

The farm may have held happy memories for my mother, but my most vivid memory of the place is much more sinister.

I had been spending a week of my summer vacation with the grandmas and I wasn't exactly thrilled when I learned that we were going to Aunt Fran's for the weekend. Great-Grandma and Fran's brother, Elmo, who they hadn't seen in a long time, was visiting from California, so one of Fran's sons had driven my grandmas and me from Billings to the old farm. I was twelve and hanging out with three old ladies who were all deaf as posts and one creepy old guy was not my idea of a fun way to spend one minute of a summer vacation. When my grandmas and Aunt Fran got together, the conversations always went something like this:

Great-Grandma (pointing): "You see that cupboard over there? There is a built-in ironing board in there, but we never use it."

Fran and Grandma Irene nod their heads, sip their coffee, and each take a bite of their cookies.

Five minutes pass.

Grandma Irene (pointing): "There's an ironing board built into that cupboard over there, but we never use it."

Fran and Great-Grandma nod their heads, sip their coffee, and eat their cookies.

Five more minutes pass.

Fran (pointing): "What's in that cupboard over there?"

And so it went.

Elmo was sixty-some years old, heavy, and wore round, wire-rimmed glasses that were as thick as Coke bottles. He wore old-man pants hiked up to just under his armpits and a narrow, brown leather belt with a little gold buckle that hit him at about his sternum. His fat belly was tucked into his pants, giving him what we now call a front butt. A white wife-beater undershirt, revealing a few gray chest hairs, poked out of the neck of his buttoned-up, short-sleeved, old-man shirt, which was wet with sweat stains in the underarms. Dots of perspiration sparkled across his forehead and he was constantly retrieving a hanky from his rear pocket to wipe his brow. His arms were hairy and dotted with age spots.

Whenever we saw him, he would say, "Come give Uncle Elmo a kiss." We would look at Mom, begging, "Do we have to?" with our eyes, and she would give us an "I'm-sorry" nod back, so we obliged just because we had manners.

This time was no different. I endured a sloppy kiss from him, then went outside to play. After lunch, the grandmas and Aunt Fran went outside to drink their afternoon coffee and have one of their meaningful conversations. I came into the house to go to the bathroom and as I was walking out, I had to walk by Uncle Elmo, who was still sitting at the dining room table.

"Come give your Uncle Elmo a kiss," he said as I was passing by him. I pretended not to hear him and kept walking. He grabbed my arm and pulled me down on his lap. At first, I didn't resist. I thought that if I let him give me one nasty kiss, he would let me go. Instead, he locked his lips on mine and forced his tongue into my mouth. I tried

to pull away, but he put one arm around my neck and his hand on the back of my head, pressing my mouth to his. His other arm was around my mid-section, his hand fumbling for my crotch as he held me down and began arching his back, pressing up against me. His breathing sped up and his wet kisses grew sloppier as he continued to force his tongue down my throat. He was pressed into me so hard that I could feel the sweat on his forehead and his nose hairs on my face. I felt a scream welling up from my soul and vomit making its way up from my stomach, but I couldn't get either one to come out. His mouth was silencing my scream and his thick tongue was holding my puke in the back of my throat. The more I struggled, the harder and faster he humped me and the harder and wetter his kisses got.

I couldn't breathe and for a second I stopped fighting him, feeling like I was about to pass out, which turned out to be just long enough for him to come up for air. I felt his body go limp and his grip on me loosen. In that instant, I fought, twisted, elbowed, squirmed, and kneed myself free.

I jumped off his lap and ran for the door, then outside, past Aunt Fran and the grandmas. I didn't stop to answer when they asked, "Where are you going?"

Over my shoulder, I called, "For a walk," as I slowed my run to a skip, trying to pretend that everything was all right. I went down by the old barn, past the hog pens, and stopped to catch my breath, spit, and wipe my mouth with the back of my hand—and to spit and wipe my mouth with the tail of my shirt, and to spit and spit some more, trying to get rid of the taste of prune juice, Polident, and cigars.

To my surprise, the old pervert had followed me to the barn. I was twelve and he was over sixty. I could easily outrun him, which I did, keeping more than two arm's lengths away and ignoring his pleas of, "Just come talk to Uncle Elmo," and, "Nothing happened," and "We don't need to tell your grandmother about this."

I spent the rest of the weekend close to Great-Grandma's side, but I didn't say anything. Uncle Elmo kept an eye on me, wondering if I had tattled on him. I wanted to, but I didn't know exactly how to tell three old deaf ladies a secret, since whispering was out of the question.

When I got home, I told Mom. She was furious and said that I had done the right thing by fighting him off and then keeping away from him. She told Great-Grandma, who told Fran, who said that I was lying. Mom believed me but not another word of it was ever mentioned. I would bet the farm that my dad was never even told about this sinister encounter. If he had been, he and Elmo would likely have had a come to Jesus meeting and Elmo would have met him.

Forty-Six

The trip is finally nearing an end. Melville, Montana, is the last stop of all the places we have lived and we are all in good moods. Val and I are happy because we know that the end is in sight and we have lived to tell about it. Dad is content, I imagine, because he didn't believe that we would ever make this journey, but here we are, twenty-some houses and six days later. He is more chatty than usual.

We moved to Melville sometime in 1965 and moved out less than a year later, right before I went into first grade. Dad knows the way to the place like we are driving home. He notices that there is a new entrance into the Franklin Angus Ranch and he comments on it.

Val and I were three and five when we lived here, so

we remember very little. When we get up to the house, we knock on the door and no one answers, so we peek through the windows. I have a flashback of when we lived here and the Fuller Brush Man would come by and knock on our door and peek through the windows to see if we were home. For the longest time, I thought the Fuller Brush Man was related to the Boogey Man, because every time he came calling, Mom would yell, "Hurry up! Get in the closet and hide! It's the Fuller Brush Man!" We would run for our lives into her bedroom closet, where we would crouch on the floor, not making a peep, except for the sound of our panicked breathing. We would then sit in the dark closet with our eyes as wide as saucers, staring into the darkness, waiting for the knocking on the door to cease.

When Mom was sure that he was gone, we would cautiously creep out of our hiding spot, holding hands and tip-toeing like cat burglars into the living room, where we would steal a peek at the windows. Sometimes the Fuller Brush Man would outwait us (having seen us make a run for it) and he would catch us catching him, peeking through the window, which would send us back into the closet for such a long time that our eyes would finally adjust to the darkness well enough that we could have sorted M&M's by color.

Like most of the other houses we've been to, this place doesn't look familiar. I vaguely remember that, besides hiding from the Fuller Brush Man, we used to bottle-feed bum lambs who had poopy butts, and we had an adopted dog named Blackie.

Valerie doesn't remember anything about this place, but knows that the big scar on her back is her proof that she was here.

Mom had happened to look out the kitchen window in time to see Valli on all fours, crawling underneath a barbed wire fence and into a pasture full of Angus bulls. The bulls were standing near the fence, probably curious about the little, four-legged creature with the long, blonde mane. A couple of them were making their way toward her, ambling leisurely in single file, like bulls do, making that low, slow, humming, I'm-tougher-than-you sound when Mom broke up the cadence by yelling at Valli, "Get the hell out of there!"

Hearing Mom holler got Valli's attention and, as she stood up, she sliced her back open on the barbed wire. She bled like a sacrificed lamb and should have gotten stitches, but didn't, so to this day she has a big, wide, thick scar across her back.

I would have been happy to end the trip and drive away from Melville, Montana, with memories of the Fuller Brush Man, Blackie, shitty lamb tails, and Val's trophy scar. I should have known that we couldn't spend a week on an outing with Dad and not come away with at least one shocker to keep us up nights.

Dad lapses into a story about how Blackie started roaming around at night and was subsequently accused of killing a neighbor's lambs. He tells us that the neighbor knocked on our door and pointed a finger at our fostered pet. He never liked the rambunctious dog, so due to the accusations against our pet, Dad had taken Blackie out and shot him. Three days later, Blackie had come home with a bullet hole between his eyes, near death.

"He just showed up at the door," Dad says, like he is talking about the Fuller Brush Man.

In my mind, I see a young, unsuspecting, forgiving, black Lab with two big, yellow eyes, wet with tears, and a curdled, bloody gunshot wound between them. He came to the only home he had known, surely thinking that the hand that had been feeding him could not be the same one that had pulled the trigger. Regardless, his eyes were begging to be put out of the misery. As usual, Dad was the judge, jury, and executioner, so he obliged, taking the dog out and finishing the job. I don't want to see this horrific image in my mind and I try to block it out by squeezing my eyes shut, hard. It doesn't work. I suddenly feel like I have a fever and I know that this story is going to be haunting me for a long while.

"Good God, Dad, that's disgusting. I don't want to hear any more," I say as my headache sets in.

"Your ma was sure pissed at me," he says, ignoring me. "I had to take him out and shoot him again."

"Dad, just shut up. We don't want to hear any more," Valli echoes my sentiments.

"What?" he snarls. "What's the big deal?"

"Please . . . Dad, please, just shut up about it," she tries again.

"Well, I had to kill the son of a bitch and put him out of his misery," Dad says, still not getting that his daughters would rather jump off a cliff than spend another minute listening to this story. "I mean, he already had a hole in his head and I can guaran-goddamn-tee you he was gonna die anyway."

"Goddamn it, Dad! Just shut up. We don't want to hear any more!" Val snaps. She is shaking and near tears.

"Well, he. . . ."

We don't let him finish. "Guacamole!" we both scream at him, as if we have suddenly been stricken with Tourette's syndrome.

"What? What the hell are you talking about?" He looks at me the way a dog looks at you when it hears a high-pitched noise—like I'm making no sense, which I know I'm not. He wasn't in on our rule-making, so he has no idea why we would suddenly yell the name of a condiment at him.

"It's Mexican for 'shut up,' Dad," I tell him, my voice still raised. I look over my shoulder at Val. She looks back at me and shakes her head in disgust, looking pale, like she has the flu. Tears are already filling her eyes.

Val and I were either too young to remember or we were never told this story, but now, some forty years later, we still think that this is a secret that a father should take to his grave. We are both horrified and sickened, wondering what would ever possesses a man to tell his kids—no matter how old they are—a horror story like this.

I'm squeezing the steering wheel so hard that my

knuckles are turning blue. My insides feel hot, like a scream is welling up in my gut, but I swallow it and add it to the pile that is already stored up inside of me. I feel my own flu-like symptoms set in. I try to use telepathy to get Val to jab the urn-opening screwdriver into Dad's jugular.

I decide that Dad must have a death wish and this time we really do need to kill the SOB. As we drive away from the ranch, I mentally rehearse the deposition that I will surely be subpoenaed to give, while keeping an eye out for a cliff to drive off of. I glare at Dad, thinking that Satan must be his soul mate.

Val and I are both pissed at Dad and he is pissed that we are pissed at him, so now he's pouting. He finally gets it that we don't want to hear anything else about Blackie, mumbles something under his breath, then reaches down by his feet and cracks open a beer. I look back at Val again. She has her head in her hands and she is silently crying for Blackie. Then I look at Dad. His head is turned to the right and he is looking (or pretending to look) out the passenger window. At first I think that his feelings are hurt but then I think, *Wait a minute, what feelings?* No words—just looks—are exchanged amongst us.

Because I can tell that Val is about to ask me, I mentally count how many Valiums I have brought on this trip, trying to decide if I can afford to give one to my sister. I can—and I'm pretty sure that I didn't bring enough.

We forever leave our good moods in Melville, Montana, and we don't talk for the next couple of hours.

Forty-Seven

When I signed on for this trip, I knew that there would be torture, but I didn't know that most of it would be saved for the last two days. A few miles out of Butte, Dad breaks the silence by announcing that we should meet our biological grandfather. Still in a bad mood, I protest and agree with Val when she points out in a rather snippy tone, "It never seemed to matter to Mom that we never met our grandfather." Again Dad ignores us. As we drive into Butte, he says, "We will go meet your granddad tomorrow."

When we get to Butte, Dad instructs me to find a place to stay that will allow us to park at the door of our room, just like he has done every night for the past six. His other prerequisite is that it is cheap. We find just the place.

"Triple A?" the desk attendant asks me.

I slap my American Express card on the counter. "Listen. We're Triple A, we're AARP, and we're AA," I tell her. She doesn't get it. Val and I think this is funny, and we burst into a frenzy of laughter. In fact, we find it hysterical. At this point in the day, after the Blackie story, I'd bet that we would laugh our asses off at dead baby jokes.

Dad is happy when we come back with a room key, forgetting that only a few hours ago we weren't speaking to him.

We settle him into his room and order him everything from the room service menu that is deep-fried. Then we joke to each other that we are still trying to kill him—now with a clogged artery instead of my .38.

"Why don't you girls go out and have a nice dinner?" Dad says to us, obviously sucking up. "I'll be fine. I'm about ready to go to bed anyway."

Our senses of humor need a drink, so Val and I head to the bar for a glass of wine. God, do we ever need this after today. After a second glass, we finally let out a breath and sit at the table and cry like a couple of old winos. We could have gone a long time—like the rest of our lives—without hearing the Blackie story.

We dry our tears, buck up, and on the recommendation of a local, head uptown in search of a Chinese restaurant. When we find it, I send Val up a steep flight of stairs to grab us a table while I park. When I open the door to the restaurant, I am looking down a long, narrow hall with curtains hanging every few feet. Each table is in its own small private room. As I approach,

Val rips open our curtain like she's a magician's assistant displaying a sawed-in-half body. Instead she proudly shows off two glasses of wine.

"Cheers," she says to me, holding up a glass, as I sit down. I can tell that she has a good buzz going.

I look around our personal dining room. "I don't even know what color this is," I say, pointing at the walls. "I've never seen paint this color."

"Salmon," Valerie Martha says. "It's fresh salmon. It's not frozen or cooked salmon, it's fresh. It was very popular in 1998, before pink moved back in." She does a finger gesture, bringing pink in. "Now pink's back in and this is passé." Her thumb ushers salmon out. "But I think this has probably been around . . . oh, by the looks of it, since the '70s." She cracks up at her own commentary.

"And thank you, Martha Stewart," I say, holding half a swallow of wine in the back of my throat, so I sound a lot like Tom Brokaw at the end of a news broadcast.

The waitress brings us two more glasses of wine and our dinner; we settle into a more serious mood, at least for a minute. This little room gives us just the privacy we need. We don't talk about today and we don't talk about tomorrow, we just celebrate that the end of this trip is in sight. We laugh about dumb things, like the salmon-pink walls covered in soy sauce splatter and the curtain that looks like the material for an old pair of panties. We cry a little, for Mom and for Blackie—and because we've had too much wine.

Each time the waitress rips open our curtain, she is in for a show. One time we are laughing hysterically and the next we are crying with the same intensity. Most of the evening is being captured on my camcorder, as are our waitress's startled looks, which always sends us into another fit of laughter.

The food is great and the waitress becomes our new best friend for putting up with our hysterics and stupidity. At the end of our meal, I break open my fortune cookie to find that my fortune says, "You will dance to a different beat next summer." I finally feel good about today!

Drunk, numb, and with swollen eyes, we call it a night.

Forty-Eight

Day Seven

I open my eyes in another motel room and wonder where I am. I wait for my head to pound, but it doesn't. I move my eyes right and left, staring into the darkness of my eye mask, and wait again for my head to pound. It still doesn't. I slide the mask up, onto my forehead, and feel my pupils frantically shrinking to avoid the sudden influx of light. I feel nothing—no headache, no nausea, nothing. I send up a thank you.

I know that I should have a killer headache this morning, but I'm pretty sure that I got a free pass today for all of the suffering that I did yesterday. I wonder if Dad's head is killing him.

"Valli, wake up," I try to say. I don't recognize my own voice. It sounds raspy. "It's Get Out of Jail Free Day."

"Mmmmmm," is all I can make out from her.

"You want me to make the coffee?" I ask, still using my whiskey voice.

"Yeah, make it strong and get me a Tylenol." She's mumbling and barely audible.

"Headache?"

"Mmmmmm . . . you?"

"Nope, I feel like a million bucks," I tell her.

The smell of freshly-brewed coffee and the reminder that this is the last day of the trip finally gets Val out of bed. She's suddenly bordering on perky. My sister is not the praying kind, but as her feet hit the floor I hear her thank God and declare a "Halle-freaking-lujah."

Then reality smacks us in the face. *Oh yeah, today we will meet our "grandfather,"* we think.

We had thought that the worst was behind us, but we had thought wrong. We are still protesting, stating our best case to Dad, as we drive to the grandpa's house.

"Mom never asked us to meet this man," Val reminds him. He ignores her.

"It's not like we will ever see him again, so what's the big deal if we never meet him?" I add my two cents. He ignores me.

"Yeah, what's he ever done to make himself known to us? Nothing." Val answers her own question because it's obvious that Dad isn't about to.

"He didn't even come to Mom's funeral." That's my cue for Guilt to introduce herself to Dad. I'm not sure the two have ever met.

"Yeah, Dad, what kind of a father doesn't even come to his own daughter's funeral?" Val gives it her last, best shot. He continues to ignore her. Guilt refuses to show her face.

The executioner finally breaks his silence, handing down our sentence by saying, "I want you girls to see what you come from."

Not "where," but "what."

We pull up to a little house in a crappy, rundown neighborhood. The weeds are so tall that I think Dad has made a mistake and we are at a house that has been abandoned. We follow Dad up the sidewalk, dragging our feet like we are being led to the electric chair. Dad knocks on the door anyway. Someone inside grunts a half-hearted, "Come in." Dad grabs the doorknob and looks at both of us. The shit-eating grin on his face tells me that we are about to be shocked again, just when I thought it was no longer possible. I did not yet know that I could have added, "beyond belief."

We find two people inside. The carpet is dirty and threadbare. Dishes litter an old coffee table and the floor around it, making me wonder if they have running water. Filthy, tattered fabric, pretending to be curtains, hangs on the windows, faded by the sun and yellowed by years of cigarette smoke. I am certain that a rat will crawl over the toe of my shoe at any second and I'm secretly glad that I'm not wearing the cute, open toe slingbacks that are in my suitcase.

I feel my breathing speeding up and I look at Valli. Her face is calm, but the movement of her chest is a dead giveaway that her breathing matches mine. We are both in our "Buck Up" modes. Thanks to Dad, we have become quite comfortable here.

I understand about living in dumps. We have lived in plenty of them, but living in filth is another thing. No matter how crappy the house that we moved into was, Mom always made sure it was clean. Just because the floors were ripped up and had holes in them didn't mean that we couldn't have eaten off of them.

An old, snowy TV tells me that they do have electricity. On the ratty couch sits a little old man, bald and bare-footed, who I instantly know is my mother's father. He is pale and pasty, with no noticeable hair—or even eyebrows. I can't help but stare at his thick, longish, yellowed toenails. His hands, like two spiny, brittle starfish, lay beached on his chest. He looks just like Mom did—after she died. I feel an ache in my chest when I notice the resemblance. I tell myself, *Don't be a snob. Give the old guy a chance. He is your mother's father and since you don't have a mother anymore, it would be nice to still have a connection to her. Besides, he would probably like to have good granddaughters like us.*

A long-haired guy named Russell, who the snob in me labels a deadbeat, sits in an old chair near him. It doesn't take me long to figure out that he was Mom's first crush—the brother, my uncle. He politely nods at us and says that we are "good-lookers."

The old grandpa on the couch has no idea who we are and seems unsure of who Dad is. Dad reintroduces himself a couple of times without any sign of recognition from the old man, so he finally introduces us.

"These are DiAnne's daughters," he says, repeating it at least three times. He pauses between each introduction to see if a light has turned on in the old guy's head. Dad gives up when the grandpa fails to even acknowledge us. My face remains frozen in a phony smile for about three minutes before I realize that there is no need for it. It's just a good waste of wrinkles because the would-be grandpa isn't going to make eye contact anyway. No nod of the head, no handshake, no hug, or any inheritance is in our immediate future.

Mom's name must finally ring a bell because he seems to suddenly figure out who Dad is. Then he asks, "Where is DiAnne?" For Christ's sake, he doesn't even know that she has died! Dad gives him a few details, such as when she died and that she had cancer. Neither the grandpa nor Russell ask any questions, or even look up; they just stay focused on *Wheel of Fortune*.

Although I have no evidence that would hold up in a court of law, I suspect that a decomposing body is rotting away in another room, perhaps next to some feces. The stench is as bad as or worse than that of the Three Bears' House in Cody, so for the second time in two days, I'm testing my breath-holding capabilities. I feel a panic attack coming on, which is definitely going to interfere with that, so I reach for the doorknob. It feels funky. I steal a glance at it and see that it is covered with several inches of crud, which causes my hand to stick to it.

My sister and I stand pressed against the grungy door while Dad tries to make small talk with Russell.

For a second, I feel truly sorry for these people, living like they do. I'm thinking that they must not have two dimes to rub together, so I wonder if I should drop a small donation onto one of the dirty plates before I leave. Then Dad asks Russell what he's been up to. Russell does have a job, I'm surprised to learn. It's a decent job, which tells me that they live like this by choice. This shocks me even more.

I shift my gaze to the grandpa and see that his eyes are closed, his mouth is open, and he's not moving. I wonder if he has died or just fallen asleep. I am torn between sorrow and shame and hate and hurt. I feel sorry for them—or maybe it's me and Val I feel sorry for. I'm ashamed of them, and of myself, because he is my mother's father and I don't want him to be related to me. I hate him. I hate Dad. I hate myself for hating them and, I'm not sure why, but I hurt for all of us. It's clear to me why, in the fifteen years that we knew about this faux grandpa, our own mother never asked us to meet him.

Dad and Russell can't seem to come up with enough words between them to carry on a conversation, so we all stand here, kind of ducking our heads, as uncomfortable silence crashes down all around us. Valli and I keep our eyes fixed on Dad, like two loyal cow dogs, waiting for a nod of the head. Russell wants to buy a vowel. With no more small talk to be made, Dad finally glances in our direction and gives us the command that launches us into action.

Once again, I buck up and grab the grimy doorknob. I give it a hard twist, knowing that it is our escape to the outside world. I try to sound sincere as I look over my shoulder and give a "nice to meet you" as I walk out the door. They don't say anything back. They're not the warm and fuzzy type and it's clear that our new grandfather doesn't want any new granddaughters, no matter how cute and well-behaved we are.

Valli is hot on my heels and we both hyperventilate all the way back to the pickup. She looks at me and mouths the words, "Can you fucking believe that?" (In Valli's vocabulary, the *F* word always precedes "believe" and "unbelievable," just like I can't say "martini" without putting "Grey Goose, dirty" in front of it.)

Dad doesn't hear her, but he sees her lips moving and asks, "What? What's wrong? How'd you girls like your new granddad?"

I don't know if it's glee that I see on his face because I don't think that my dad does glee, but he seems to be pretty pleased with himself for bringing us together and I have no idea why. What I am sure of is that I will never visit here again; I'm just not that desperate for any new family members.

"Good God, Dad, that was horrible. I can't believe how those people live," I say as we get back into the pickup. "That house should be condemned. It was filthy and it reeks. Did Jeffrey Dahmer used to live there?"

Dad ignores the Jeffrey Dahmer comment, either because he can't remember who he is or he can't remember if he is a distant relative or not.

Instead, he says, "Now you girls know who your granddad is and what you come from." He is still wearing that shit-eating grin and I still don't know why.

We sit in the pickup for a moment with Dad chatting while my hands grip the wheel, anxious to drive away from this place, but too paralyzed to turn the key and pull the gearshift down. I look over my shoulder at Valli to find her face still frozen in the I-can't-fucking-believe-that look. We exchange a quick glance and she shakes her head, telling me with her eyes that she cannot possibly survive one more day of this trip. My eyes tell her, "Ditto." By now we are pretty much able to read each other's minds, so we know that we are both asking the same questions. We aren't just asking the questions, we are demanding the answers—but of course, not out loud.

Why in the hell would Dad make us meet that grandpa—the grandpa who obviously could not have cared less about meeting us? Mormon Bible-beaters or granddaughters, it wouldn't have mattered—we were met with the same enthusiasm and compassion. Hadn't we dredged up enough crap in seven days? Didn't we already know more than we needed to know? Hadn't we relived enough and been exposed to more old wounds than we needed to be? When did sucking it up become as easy as breathing to us? And how did "buck up" become a comfortable place—a place we go to all too often?

I can't help but wonder why Dad felt it necessary to expose us to this one little piece of our past. Couldn't there just have been *one thing* that we really didn't need to know? Does he think that this is our connection to Mom now that she's gone? Had Mom asked him to make sure that we meet her father? Was that her dying wish? Did he think he was covering all his bases, just in case he never got this opportunity with us again, or was it just for shock value?

What I really think is that this had nothing to do with Mom or family or values or dying wishes. Dad wasn't trying to be mean, it was just his way of reminding Val and I of where we came from. He likes keeping us humble, proud, and poor—in the place where he has been in control of us for our entire lives. He taught us to work hard; in fact, he hammered it into our heads, and we did, but he also minimized any little accomplishments that we may have had. At least, to us he did. On more than a few occasions, our mother gushed to us, "Your father is so proud of you!" but we were never sure whose words those really were.

It has taken us forty years, but we are no longer the little, snot-nosed, boot-up-the-ass, knot-headed, hayseeds that he raised.

Whatever his ulterior motives for this little family reunion, I decide not to read more into it than there is and to stop analyzing and caring why he did this. The truth is, I'd love to be mad enough to break a dish or slam a door, but at this point I just don't have it in me. I can't even begin to muster up the emotion.

I refuse to let Guilt have even one word with me. "Go talk to our father," I tell her. "You two have a lot of catching up to do."

As we drive away, I wonder, *Was this Dad's way of reminding us that we are really just white trash in expensive shoes?*

Forty-Nine

It's time to let it go, so I do. This part of our lives is truly over; it is now just another part of our past. We have finally reached the end of this journey, having revisited all of the places that Dad wanted us to see. It's funny how each one was different, but they were always the same. They were places that we called home for short periods, but we never felt like we were actually home—probably because we had no idea of what home felt like. We never belonged to any of them. They were all just temporary stops on a journey that would become our past. Home was always somewhere down the road and we lived our lives with one foot out the door.

I drive us to the Butte airport so I can rent a car and drive home to Wyoming. Dad and Val will head back to

Idaho Falls in Dad's pickup, with him driving them the last leg of the trip.

Dad has already dismissed the events of one hour ago. He's so good at that. Nothing ever seems to haunt him or leave him with lingering impressions. Once the moment is over, it's over. It would be nice to be a little more like that.

He hugs me and thanks me for making this trip. He says he had a good time, and as I hug him back, I tell him that I did too.

Valerie and I stand face-to-face on legs that appear to be attached to a rickety table. With the exception of the obligatory coming and going hugging, we have never been very good at showing one another affection or comforting each other. I hate that I'm more comfortable in a new pair of four-inch, pointy-toed heels than I am hugging my own sister. But now we stand here embracing, holding—truly hugging. We lean into each other in a way that feels more like we are bracing for destiny rather than just saying good-bye.

We know that we are the only two people in the world who understand (but don't *really* understand) our dad, and that we are the only two people who know what living without our mother feels like. I wonder if God took her first so that we would be forced into this relationship with Dad. I intend to have a word with Him about that—someday.

This trip has not just been a pilgrimage of our past, but a learning experience that has explained a lot and taught me even more. It has been a window into our future.

I know that Dad held all the power in life; now Mom holds it in death. Our past suggests that Mom needed Dad—that *she* was the lost, helpless, needy one. The fact is though, that without her, Dad is lost, helpless, and needy. If the situation had been reversed and Dad had been the one who had died, my mother would have shed her cocoon and morphed into a social butterfly. Dad controlled her life, but now she is controlling his.

During this trip, I've seen a side of my dad that I never knew existed. I never knew that he reminisced or that he got lumps in his throat or tears in his eyes. I've felt sorry for him. I know that Valerie and I are all that Dad has left and that all of our jokes about killing him are the outlet we use to make us believe that we are grown-ups and we have *some* control over our lives with him. We also know that we have each other.

Some things I didn't know (and would prefer to have them left that way) or had at least forgotten, until I relived them. I didn't know that my sister and I have so much in common. We may have our differences but not as many as I thought. We do have the obvious, common bond of parentage, but there is much more than that. We share the same life experiences—the same hurts and triumphs. The biggest thing that I have learned, though, is that as different as we are, our pain is exactly the same. That thought has echoed through me, over and over, for the past seven days. It started as a small vibration early in the trip, and has now reached its crescendo, bouncing off the canyons of my soul.

"Drive careful," Dad says, hugging me a second time as I stand next to my rental car. "And thanks for coming," he says, like I'm a customer at a fast food joint.

"Are you being a smart-ass?" I ask, suspicious, as I shut the door and roll down the window of my rented Buick.

"No, I mean it, Tammi. I really did have a good time," he says, patting my arm. "Thanks again, kiddo." He smiles at me, which I think translates to "I love you."

"Yeah, you too, Dad," I say, smiling back.

I drive off and don't dare to look in the rearview mirror. *There is no looking back*, I tell myself.

About thirty miles outside of Butte, I feel my teeth stop clenching. My jaw relaxes and my chin practically hits me on the chest as I release a big sigh and a funny sound. I feel the shakes start to take over my body, like they would when I was a kid and I had been on horseback all day in a freezing rain. I would come in to the house shaking from the cold and Mom would put the oven on broil and open the door to warm me up.

I have to pull over to the side of the road. I switch the dial from AC to heat, trying to stop them. With my head on the steering wheel, I shake uncontrollably for a good ten minutes. Then I feel that familiar burn in my sinuses. It comes from somewhere south of my soul and tries to dry up my tears before they can make their way to my eyes. It's as recognizable to me as the lines on my own face—it feels like family. I am so used to holding that burn back that I have a hard time letting it go, even when I want to. Out of habit, I swallow the burn, but this time it refuses to go down and lodges in my throat, allowing the tears to come anyway. I give in and get out of the car for some air—and to vomit. I throw up the last memory of this trip before I drive home. Dad, Blackie, almond bark, the grandpa, the shit house, the bunkhouses, Guilt, the rescued and sacrificed dogs, Mom, the left-behind cats, Christmases, the uncles (one unknown and one a pervert), frog bacon and other force-fed pieces of food, Tony Lamas, lariats, and the red hills of Richey all spew to the ground.

Sitting in the middle of nowhere along I-90, it occurs to me that our lives have been like that of spawning salmon. Valerie and I have been desperately swimming upstream, struggling to get to wherever it is that we belong, to wherever the end of our journey is.

Mom was like a sparkling lure; she kept us swimming toward her. She was our encouragement—one of the little fish that swam just far enough ahead of us to keep us motivated and on the right track. She did her best to protect us and to lead us on the easiest course through the big rocks and swift current, ultimately sacrificing herself in order to keep us going on this long journey.

Dad has been the grizzly bear, hibernating and quiet one moment, then angry and charging the next—always protective and never predictable. He quietly lurked on the banks, making occasional swats at us, dragging us down from time to time, then pulling us back up, gasping for hope. We have survived by the sheer will of resolve, which he has instilled in us, and we've kept moving on, throwing ourselves against the strong current in the river of our past, refusing to own the fate that we inherited. We have unconsciously focused on the end, which we always believed was in sight. We fought for it, not because we could see it or because we were smart, but because we needed to believe that there was more. We had to stay on course for that big ocean that was our future. It has taken us a lifetime to get this far, but we will never have to make that swim again.

I wonder if Valli is having any kind of a revelation. I switch the dial back to AC, pull the Buick into drive, and get back on the interstate. I cry on and off for the rest of the three-hundred-mile drive home. It's not a poor-me-having-a-pity-party cry; it's a good cry—one that I've needed for a long time. It doesn't burn. It's not like the crying that I've been doing every day for the past three months since Mom died, but a cleansing cry—a forgiving, understanding, and relieving cry. It's a cry that's been pent up for years and has everything to do with grief, but not just grief for my mom; my grief for my father is as certain as it is for my mother. For

Mom, it's because she's gone. For Dad, it's because he left—because he's lost.

I know that as long as my father is alive, I will be dangled off that emotional cliff, only to be pulled back up at the last second before I lose my grip, but I also know that I will emerge stronger every time. He wouldn't dare drop me because he needs me—he needs me to keep him up on that pedestal. I'm fine with knowing that he will never admit that.

I will love and accept him for who he is . . . and for who he isn't. As the tears empty from my eyes, I feel acceptance filling up my heart. I will blame Dad for nothing. I know that he has done the best that he has known how to do, with us and without Mom.

I believe that with all my heart. I will forgive him for everything—for everything he did and for everything he didn't do.

In seven days and 1,800 miles, I believe that forgiveness found me and I am almost at peace with myself. I know that I have a long way to go, in grieving for Mom and in understanding Dad, but I've made a journey that has brought me closer to both.

I know that at home I have two daughters who love me. They adored their grandmother—the loving, doting secret-keeper—and they love their Grandpa Coyote. They love him because I need them to and because he really is a good man who loves them and who has always been very good to them. They forgive me for the craziness and they know that they can count on me to be consistently spontaneous and unpredictable. They don't judge me for my past, they trust me with their futures, and they know that I love them more than anything. They know that if it came right down to it, I would still take that bullet for them. They know it just as surely as they know Alfredo from marinara.

I have a loving husband waiting for me, too. Larry accepts me and my dad for who we are. He accepts our similarities and our differences. He knows us both well enough to know not to question what we do, but to either support or ignore us. He knows when to speak up because I need to hear it, and he knows when to shut up and just listen. He knows my fears and my dreams.

"God, I can't wait to get home!" I say out loud. "Thank you, Lord, not just for giving me this experience, but for allowing me to survive it. And thank you, God, for letting me go home now."

Then I wonder again about Valerie. I guess she is going to have to make her own peace. I mash my foot on the gas pedal, knowing that I'm finally going home. I watch the red needle hit ninety, knowing that Dad won't be able to tell me to "slow it goddamn down."

I'm going home to the stability of a man who is there for me—a man who won't wake me up in the middle of the night to tell me that we are moving, but who will follow me if I tell him it's time for us to move. He doesn't like to watch me squirm, but when I do, he will come to me and wrap his arms around me to bring me comfort. He won't make me shoot my dog or eat fatty bacon. He won't backhand me for disagreeing with him and he won't force me to talk about this trip, but when it's time and I need to talk about it, he will listen. With him, I don't have to bite through my lip to keep from crying—he will cry with me.

When he looks at me, he knows what's behind the designer sunglasses, the Fendi bag, the good cut and color, and the two-carat ring. He knows it even better than I do.

When I look into his eyes, I see eyes that I can trust. They pull me upstream, and I can see the ocean —my metaphorical future. I take great comfort in that and at the end of the day I know that I want my head to hit the pillow next to his.

It feels like I have been gone a lifetime and, in a sense, I have. Now I am finally going to my real home, a home that I belong to.

I'm still like that spawning salmon—hard to pin down, struggling against the current, but always moving forward. It feels good to be like her. She is a big, strong, beautiful fish, one who knows where she is supposed to end up, even if she takes the wrong way—the long way, the hard way. She knows where her home is and, come hell or high water, that is where she is going. I finally have an understanding of the word.

Home is not a place; it is a state of mind.

Part Four

Ashes to Ashes

Fifty

I may have found my home to be a state of mind, but for Dad, home was a person. It was never a place and it definitely was not a state of mind. Home was where Mom was. *Now that she is gone, he is homeless,* I realized.

My revelations were short-lived. While driving home I told myself the trip would bring some closure, but instead, as the days dragged on, I felt orphaned. My heart ached and my soul was restless, looking for a sign from my mother. It had been a few months, but I still couldn't believe that she had left us. I looked for her everywhere—in watermarks left on wine glasses, in the autumn leaves, in toasted baguettes, in soap bubbles while doing dishes, and in the ashes of Larry's cigar. I not only *wanted* a sign from her, I *needed* one. Anything that said she was at peace and that she hadn't forgotten about us would have eased my mind. With each day that passed, I got more and more irritated that she wasn't showing up anywhere that I looked. My doubts were beginning to outweigh my faith.

I finally found her when I wasn't looking for her. A few months after Mom's death, Sierra came down with a case of violent vomiting, which was accompanied by a raging headache. At around midnight on the day that she got sick, I became concerned enough that I thought she should go to the ER. She sat, reclined in the passenger side of her pickup, puking into a Ziploc bag as I drove her the twenty-five miles to the hospital.

The reminder of having done this less than a year ago with Mom brought on my own nausea. I turned the radio up and the CD that I had made for Mom's memorial service was in the CD player, bringing me to the realization of how much Sierra missed her grandma. She was playing a memorial CD rather than one of the many current, popular ones that she owned.

At the ER, Sierra was given an IV that administered anti-nausea and pain meds, and attached to a machine to monitor her vitals. I sat in a chair near the bed, in the semi-darkness, and watched her sleep.

All of a sudden, out of the corner of my eye, I noticed that the cords that attached the monitor to Sierra's body were beginning to move. They moved very slowly at first, gradually speeding up to an even rhythmic, rocking motion, in much the same way that one would rock a baby. I stared at the cords in disbelief, wondering why they were swaying. I watched them for about ten seconds, then got out of my chair and walked around to the end of the bed. I studied the cords, looked at where they came out of the monitor, and saw that they disappeared under the blankets that covered Sierra.

I tiptoed up the left side of the bed, looking back and forth from the swinging cords to my daughter. Sierra never moved, but the cords continued to swing. I tiptoed closer to the monitor and at about the time that I got within one step of it, it let out a loud, fast series of beeps! I almost jumped out of my skin! The cords instantly—not gradually, I mean *instantly*—stopped swaying. Sierra still hadn't moved. I made a beeline back around to the right side of the bed and sat myself in the chair. The beeping stopped just as the door burst open and a nurse rushed into the room. The nurse looked at the monitor, pushed a couple of buttons, looked at Sierra, and shrugged her shoulders at me. I shrugged mine back at her and she left the room.

Then it came over me. At first, the cool room warmed. Then my skin began to feel like I had a slight sunburn—not the sunburn that is so red and hot that your skin feels cold, but the kind that makes you feel like your skin is glowing. I felt a smile start in my heart and then I noticed that it was on my face. Then I knew what it was. It was my mother! I didn't cry; I just felt really good for the first time in a long time.

I got up and went back around the bed to the monitor and studied it. It blinked and did whatever it is that monitors do. I checked Sierra. The sick, pained look that she had fallen asleep with was gone. She was sleeping peacefully, her face relaxed in the same way that babies' faces relax when people rub their backs and pat their bottoms until they fall asleep.

Fifty-One

A few weeks after our road trip, Dad packed up the few belongings that he had, zipped Mom and the little oak urn with the rose into a red duffle bag, and left 240 Dale Street for the Ol' West RV Park. He was lonely, depressed, and doing a lot of self-medicating with alcohol and whatever drugs he could get his hands on. Some had been prescribed but most had not. Some were even Mom's leftover cancer-related drugs. Valli was worried about him, but felt a sense of relief that he was leaving Idaho Falls.

"Do you think you should leave so soon, Dad?" she asked him. "Mom's only been gone for a few months. Maybe you should stay here, where you have family around."

"Three months, four days, six hours, and twenty-two minutes," Dad responded. Valli acted like she was not impressed by his math skills, but inside she was fighting back the tears. Later when she told me about it, I could tell that she was quite upset about the fact that Dad was living in the past—by the minute.

"You know he is going to do whatever he wants so there is no sense in trying to convince him otherwise. Dad only does what is Dad's idea," I reminded her. "Let him go."

He left. I was struggling with my own loss and I was having a horrible time without Mom in my day-to-day life. When the girls did well in rodeos, I wanted to call her. When I got photos made, I sorted piles for her. When my refrigerator needed to be cleaned, I was reminded that Mom always cleaned it when she came to visit. When all the socks without mates made it to the laundry room, Mom always came along and claimed them, saying, "No one is going to see them anyway; I'll wear them." When I opened my eyes in the morning, instead of thinking about what I was going to fix for dinner, I woke up and thought, "Oh fuck, my mother is dead." I couldn't begin to imagine what Dad's days and nights must have been like. I found myself crying for him even more than I did for her. He had been in New Mexico for a few weeks when I wrote him the following letter:

October 9, 2001

Dear Dad,

I hope this finds you well. That statement in itself seems like an oxymoron. I have been so worried about you. All I know is that I have had some terrible moments without Mom in my life and I can't begin to imagine what it must be like for you. Every time I cry for her, it seems like I end up crying even more for you. Anyway, Dad, I hate having you so far away. I know that New Mexico is much more appealing than Wyoming in these winter months, but I want you to consider moving here. I hate thinking that you are sitting there, so far away, with no family around and really nothing much to do. If you were to come here, you could either bring your camper or live in the house.

Dad, if you came here, you would at least have something to do. I'm not sure that you want something to do, but I know that you can't continue to do nothing. Just having a reason to get up in the morning gives some meaning to your day. If you are interested in doing some work, there are always errands to run at the shop, there is inventory to be accounted for, and there are plenty of other miscellaneous chores. You could even be on the payroll and make a few bucks, although I know that isn't really important to you. Even at home, there are things you could do. Savannah needs to be run here and there. There's basketball practice, gymnastics, and dental appointments. There are maids to be told what to do and dinners to be planned. It seems there is always a horse to be hauled to the vet or a horse-shoer to wait on.

There's hay to be fed, barrels and poles to be set up, and that ever-present goat shit to be blown off the deck.

Anyway, Dad, what I'm getting at is that I want you to come live with us. I want you to make a decision to change your life and do something about your health. You are still a young guy and it is not too late if you want to make a change. I want you to quit smoking, start being more active, and become more of a participant in our lives. After all, Dad, we are all you have left. If you don't want to or can't quit smoking, it is OK with me and you are still welcome in our home. I love you regardless. Right now, I am so afraid of losing you. I won't pretend to tell you how much it hurts to have lost Mom, because I know that you know more than any of us how horrible these last four months have been. I know it is hard to get on with living right now, but you really do have me and Valli, Larry, Saul, and the grandkids to think about. You and Mom have both been such a big part of their lives that I hope you want to continue to be a part of their upbringing. I do know that that is what Mom would have wanted. They still need that old school wisdom, however warped we sometimes think it may be.

Anyway, Dad, please think it over. Larry and I and the girls really would like for you to come live with us. I think it would be good for all of us. You wouldn't be alone, we could use the extra help, and it would give you something to do.

Take care, Dad, and let me know if you want to come here or if there is anything I can do.

I love ya,
Tammi

I didn't hear anything back from him, which didn't surprise me. I continued to call him every few days to check on him and not once did he mention my letter. Finally, about a month later, I asked him if he had gotten my letter.

"Yes," was all he said.

I just said, "Oh."

Not "OOOOOh," as in, "No big deal," or "OOOOhhhh?" indicating that it was his turn to say something back, or even "Ohhhh," as in, "That's a bummer,"—just "Oh."

Fifty-Two

Larry, the girls, and I went to New Mexico a few days before Thanksgiving. When we got there, we found Dad drunk, drugged, and miserable, but glad to see us—as far as I could tell. I spent the days sorting through doctor bills, doing laundry, paying bills, grocery shopping, and cleaning Dad's camper. Each night we went to the Holiday Inn, where I sat in the bathtub, drank wine, cried, and wrote out my will. Larry and the girls weren't invited to my pity parties, so they watched TV and ignored me because they didn't know what to say to me. From time to time, one of the girls would knock on the bathroom door, saying that she needed to pee. I would grunt a "come in," then catch her stealing a glance at me from the toilet before she slipped back out the door. I wouldn't get out of the bathtub and crawl into bed until after the TV was off and everyone was asleep. The next morning I would put on my happy face and go back to Dad's camper.

Using his little three-burner stove and miniature oven, I made a Thanksgiving dinner of turkey and ham and all the trimmings. Thanksgiving has always been my favorite holiday. When I was a kid, I liked it because I was never disappointed. I wasn't anxiously waiting for some phony, dreamed-up character to come through with wonderful surprises. At Thanksgiving, there could be good surprises that maybe I didn't expect, like marshmallows on the sweet potatoes, blue punch instead of red, green olives with no pimentos, or deviled eggs loaded with nothing but yolks. It was all about the food—especially the turkey—and I knew it would be the real deal. A real turkey just can't disappoint like a fake Santa can. We could count on that big bird to be in the middle of our table more than we could ever count on Santa Claus to leave something under our tree.

When we were kids, Thanksgivings were always at Grandma Wanda's house. She would buy the biggest bird she could find and every year she was on a mission for a bigger one than the previous year's. Plus, there was the ham. It was never the kind that's packed in water, but a big, bone-in one, which she would wrap in a piece of bread dough that was about the size of a bed sheet. Then she would seal it up and bake it until the dough turned into a beautiful brown crust that was so thick we had to crack it with a hammer and pull it away in chunks.

There was also every trimming that we could possibly think of, plus about a dozen pies. She set two beautiful tables—one for the adults with her good china, and one for us kids, with her not-so-good china. Then she invited anyone who didn't have a place to go, which sometimes included homeless drunks who were still sleeping it off at the bar across the street from her house.

One of my fondest memories is of watching her create a giant batch of homemade punch, which consisted of dumping in any can or bottle of pop or juice that she happened to have on hand. The concoction went into a massive punch bowl that had about twenty cups hanging off the sides of it. She would break it out every Thanksgiving and we would stand over it, ooohing and ahhhing while she dazzled us with gallons of liquid rainbows.

After Grandma passed away, Mom took over the Thanksgiving chores. Now the torch was being passed to me, unceremoniously. I was being promoted from the kids' table to the grown-up table. I had even inherited my grandmother's punch bowl a few years before—in anticipation of the big day, I suppose.

"I can't believe it's been almost six months that Mom has been gone," I said to Dad, while peeling potatoes.

"Five months, eight days, two hours, and forty-three minutes," Dad replied, glancing at his watch. It was 12:53 p.m. on November 22, 2001.

Dad has always had the ability to stump me, or at least to leave me speechless. I didn't know what to say to that and decided to do the math later so I just said, "You want whole or jellied cranberries? I got both." He ignored me, electing to stay in his arithmetic trance.

Les, Dixie, and all the rest of the residents of the Ol' West RV Park, which was seven people, plus my family of four, helped us cart the food to the clubhouse/ secondhand store. We all gathered around three card tables that each had four mismatched chairs. Forced small talk was made by everyone except Dad, who was silent and looked like he had nothing in the world to be thankful for. I was thankful that I was going home in two more days. All of that drinking, writing, soaking, and sulking was about to kill me.

There was one noticeably empty chair that made everyone noticeably uncomfortable. This Thanksgiving wasn't about the turkey, or the punch, or the olives, or the pies. The realization came crashing down on me— it didn't matter if it was a fake Santa or a real turkey, holidays aren't about presents and the food. They are about people—and not just the people you share them with, but the people you don't. That's why you get together: to be thankful for the people who come to your table, and to pay some sort of homage to the people who can't—the ones who are having dinner at that big table in the sky.

There I sat in a room full of people who lived in campers and kept their excess belongings in a community clubhouse, and this Thanksgiving had nothing to do with them being there, except that their presence was the reason that I made all the food. It had everything to do with Mom not being there. I don't remember dinner or even eating it. I only remember that eleven out of twelve chairs were filled. My turkey could have been exchanged for tofu and I wouldn't have noticed. I was lost in a holiday-induced, sage-and-rosemary-scented chasm. It was the worst Thanksgiving of my life.

Dogs couldn't care less about holidays. Leftovers are leftovers and it doesn't matter if they are turkey, bacon grease, or horseshit. To them, every day is a holiday—unless they're in Deming, New Mexico, over Thanksgiving. I had brought Captain on this trip and then felt bad for inflicting this on him. Each evening when we left for the Holiday Inn, I left him chained to the old storage trailer. He and Dad seemed to be on the same page. Both were edgy, depressed, and miserable when I left them in the evenings, and then both were happy to see me when I returned in the mornings, when they knew that they would get my undivided attention—and breakfast.

On the day that we left New Mexico, Captain stayed close to my side, constantly using his nose to place my hand on his head, begging me not to leave him there. When it came time to go and I released him from his storage trailer prison, he got to the pickup before anyone else, staked his place in the front corner of the box, and crouched down with his nose pressed in the far corner, trying to be as unobtrusive as he could possibly be. Only when we were a good hour down the road did he poke his head up. He looked serene, resting his chin on the edge of the box, eyes closed, his head not moving, his nose twitching back and forth, sniffing the smorgasbord of smells that the road was serving up. The air got cooler and crisper as we headed north, which told him that we were leaving Deming behind. If dogs can be melancholy and relieved at the same time, I sensed that he was. I felt exactly the same way. We both hoped never to return but only one of us got our wish.

Fifty-Three

Deep down, I always knew that someday Dad would need me. In February of 2002, he hit rock bottom. He called me saying that he thought he was having a heart attack and Les was going to take him to the ER. Les called me later in the day to say that the doctor had told him that it was just the alcohol and drugs, that there was nothing wrong with Dad's heart. I knew that wasn't true; I knew that Dad's heart was shattered.

"Dad, do you want me to come and get you?" I asked him after he had been sent home. I didn't give him a chance to answer before I fired off the next question. "Do you want to go into treatment?" I was still afraid to say the *T* word, but I sensed his hopelessness and took advantage of it.

First there was silence. Then, "Yeah, I guess you'd better," he said, sounding like a lost little boy. I had the go-ahead that I had needed, so I jumped into action before he could change his mind.

"I'll be there tomorrow, Dad," I told him as I hung up the phone. The next day, February 23, Larry took me to the airport. Two Valium later, I was on a tiny plane from Sheridan to Denver. After another flight to El Paso, I rented a car and drove to Deming. Dad was fidgety, testy, anxious, and miserable, but, once again, glad to see me. I helped him pack up what he wanted to bring, loaded it into the back of his pickup, and locked up his camper. We left Deming less than twenty-four hours after my arrival.

He didn't thank me for coming to get him; he didn't have to. Just having him admit that he needed me to rescue him made up for a lot.

As soon as we got back to Wyoming, I made an appointment for him with a doctor who referred him to a heart specialist in Billings, whom we saw the following day. That doctor made arrangements for him to go to the treatment center in Cody. It was a huge step—one that was long overdue.

During the one-hundred-mile drive to Billings, we made small talk. Mom's name came up and I said that I couldn't believe how much time had passed, that it had already been eight months since she passed away.

Dad replied, "Eight months, thirteen days, one hour, and six minutes." I felt the weight of my tears pressing against my eyes. I looked at the clock on the dash and did the math in my head, thinking that he couldn't possibly still be living in this clock-watching, minute-counting trance. He was. He was dead-on. We both remained silent for the last twenty miles.

At the hospital, he went through a plethora of tests. Then we spent the afternoon in the parking lot, waiting for his next appointment time to come so I could go in and get his test results.

"Dad, do you want to die?" I asked while we were sitting in his pickup, listening to the radio.

"No, no not really," he answered, as if he had just been asked if he wanted fries with that.

After a long pause and a deep breath, I heard myself say, "Would you ever kill yourself?" I wasn't sure it was me, but it sounded like my voice.

"Hell no!" he said, shocked that I would ask such a dumb question. "If I did, then I wouldn't ever see your ma again. I know she's in heaven and you can't get to heaven if you commit suicide."

I said nothing. I just let it sink in. I would never have said that Dad was a spiritual man, but he believed in Mom and Mom believed in God, so in a roundabout way, I guess he believed in God too. I just figured that he had never thought about the afterlife, but for the first time, it occurred to me that, not only had he thought about it, he had a plan: he planned on getting into heaven so he could be with Mom again. I was glad, for his sake, that God is a forgiving God.

Fifty-Four

It was the day that we had all waited for—the day that Dad would go into rehab. My only regret was that Mom wasn't there to see him take that step. She would have been so hopeful and so proud of him. Instead, she was sitting on a table in my formal dining room, next to a picture of her and the grandkids in Mexico, all wearing big sombreros.

When I drove Dad to the treatment center in Cody, we shared a room at the Holiday Inn and stayed up late, talking, watching TV, and drinking vodka—his straight out of the bottle, mine mixed with cranberry juice. We ordered our dinners from the room service menu.

We both had a restless night, in anticipation of the next day, I supposed. Dad snored for part of the night, he tossed and turned for most of it, and he made a strange whimpering noise when he wasn't tossing, turning, or snoring. We were both awake early.

"You get any sleep?" he asked me.

"Yeah, a little," I lied. "You?"

"No, your snoring kept me awake," he said.

"I'll make the coffee," I said, getting out of bed.

I was standing at the counter, putting my makeup on, when Dad went to get his clean shirt, which was hanging on the rack by the door. He stopped beside me to look into the mirror, shirtless, with his big, round belly hanging over his belt, huge bags under his eyes, his teeth yellowed from fifty years of smoking, and his hair thinning.

"Ain't it something that a man can turn out to look like this?" he asked, shaking his head.

We were standing side by side, looking at his reflection in the huge bathroom mirror. Memories of Dad when he was young and so handsome flashed through my mind, and I understood what he meant.

"You don't look so bad, Dad." I said, lying to him for the second time in less than twenty minutes.

"I got a belly so big you could hide a bull in there," he grumbled as he pulled his shirt on, still shaking his head in disgust. I looked away from the mirror, feeling sorry for him.

I drove him to the treatment center and got out of the pickup.

"You want to me come in with you?" I asked.

He said, "Nah, it's probably not necessary," so I handed him his bag, gave him a hug, and turned up the collar on his coat to keep out the cold Wyoming air, as if he was my son and I was sending him off to his first day of school. His suitcase looked like an oversized lunch box as he walked off slowly, with his head down, wearing the red and black, plaid Woolrich coat that I had bought for him and slip-on shoes instead of his usual cowboy boots. His Wranglers sagged down off his butt and an S&T Trucking cap was pulled down over his head.

"Good luck, Dad. Call if you need anything," I said as he walked away. He didn't look back and he didn't answer me. It was March 4, his sixty-second birthday.

Fifty-Five

I answered the phone and heard the automated operator ask if I'd accept the charges for a collect call. When the recording instructed, "State your name," I heard Dad say, "Her dad." This was five days after I had dropped him off at the treatment center.

"Oh shit," was what I thought, but "Yes," was what I heard myself say. Then, sounding perky, I added, "Hey Dad, how's it going?" I could hear him ticking, about to explode.

"They're a bunch of dumbasses here," he said, detonating his anger. He didn't sound happy and he didn't give me time to say anything back.

"They want me to go to some bullshit group therapy class and talk about why I'm depressed. Why the hell wouldn't I be depressed? They can read my goddamned paperwork. I don't need to talk about it. And there's a bunch of little juvenile, drug-dealing, punk-ass kids here who just need their asses kicked. They don't need therapy for Christ's sake; they just need their old man to put a boot up their ass. How the hell am I supposed to be able to talk about my problems with fifteen-year-old Indian kids who got busted sniffing paint and drinking Lysol?"

He had a point. I finally interrupted him. "Do you have to participate, Dad, or do you just have to attend the sessions?"

More fallout. "I don't know, but I can guaran-goddamn-tee ya I'm not going to any more of this group therapy bullshit."

"OK, Dad. Who's your doctor? I'll call him in the morning." Realizing that this was the first time in sixty-two years that my dad had followed any sort of rules, I changed the subject and tiptoed around everything else. No one, before this, had ever told him what to do.

The next day I called his doctor and, like a mother getting her asthmatic son out of PE class, I got Dad excused from group therapy.

I heard from him a few days later and he sounded a little less angry, but he still said that his doctor was a "goddamned touchy-feely dumb son of a bitch who hasn't ever been cold or hungry a day in his life or ever had to work for a living and who wouldn't know the ass-end of a cow from a hole in the ground."

"You gotta stick it out, Dad," I told him, interrupting his rant. "It's been a week and a half. You must be making progress."

"Progress, my ass," he snapped. "What do you call progress? I can't sleep in here. Does that sound like progress? This place is full of kids and crazy women. There ain't no one like me in here."

Ain't no one like you anywhere, I was thinking, but in my best upbeat voice I said, "It'll be OK, Dad. You can get through this. It's only a few more weeks."

The next day, Dad ended up in the hospital, where he stayed for three days. Detox was what I suspected, but Dr. Touchy-Feely used other big words when he called to tell me. "Anxiety" was the only one that I recognized.

In anticipation of Dad completing the treatment, I scheduled our "Family Visit" for the week of April 3 and got busy recruiting my sister for the big day. It was a date that we wouldn't need to worry about keeping.

At the start of week three, Dad called me again. "Get my pickup and get your ass over here," he said when I accepted his collect call.

"Dad, it's only one more week. You—"

"I'm walking out today. Now get your ass over here and get me!" he demanded.

I fell apart. Then I pulled myself together, all in the same three seconds. I took a deep breath and said firmly, "No, Dad. I'm not coming to get you."

"What?" he hissed and I swear bolts of lightning shot through the telephone at me.

"No, Dad, I can't. I'm not coming to get you!" I stood my ground but felt like there was an earthquake going on under my feet. He hung up on me.

"I'm done with him," I yelled at Larry as I slammed

down the phone. I was pissed, pacing, crying, thinking it through out loud, and on the verge of hysterics.

"God, what have I done? I need to get his pickup over there to him. I should go get him. No, I'm not going. I can't. I better go. Where will he go when he walks out? Shit, I have to go get him. Damn him! Why is he so selfish? Why Mom instead of him?"

Larry stopped my ranting and raving by coming to me and wrapping his arms around me, then holding me tight so that I couldn't pace anymore. He held me until I quit trying to get away from him and then he convinced me not to run to Dad, saying, "Tammi, your Dad needs to help himself. You've done enough. You've done everything you can but you can't do this for him."

I knew he was right and feeling his arms wrapped tightly around me convinced me that Dad had to do this on his own. I felt so guilty for not going to him but I knew that I couldn't. It felt like we had both let Mom down.

The next day, Larry, bless his heart, arranged to have Dad's pickup delivered to the Holiday Inn in Cody. Dad was there, pacing anxiously, waiting for it. He had walked out of the treatment center the previous day. Actually, he hadn't walked. Dad doesn't walk anywhere. He had talked a janitor into giving him a ride to the hotel after he'd hung up on me.

Dad stayed at the Holiday Inn for a couple more days, then called me to say that he had decided to go back to New Mexico, but would stop and spend the night at our house on his way. I was dreading his visit, as I was sure that he was still mad at me for not coming to get him. I was only half right. He was still on the fight when he got to my house, but not so much with me. He was mad at the system, telling Larry and me that the doctors were "dumbasses" and that the whole thing was "bullshit." He wasn't drinking, though, so I took that as a good sign. I put an apple-and-walnut-stuffed pork loin in the oven, then took a bottle of wine upstairs to my bathroom, where I sat on the toilet and said a prayer that went something like, "Please God, don't let him pick a fight with me tonight—and if he does, please let him choke to death . . . slowly . . . on a walnut." Then I raised my glass.

The next day, before he drove me crazy, he drove himself back to Deming, New Mexico, leaving Mom sitting on a table in my formal dining room.

Part Five

One Year Later

Fifty-Six

I woke up, thought about my mother, mentally dropped the *F* bomb, then rolled over and spooned Larry in an attempt to wake him. "Honey," I whispered, "I think I want a little sports car." It was Sunday, June 9, 2002.

"Huh?" Larry replied as he tried to wake up and decipher the words that he thought he had just heard. "What do you mean?" he asked, rolling over and sitting up on one elbow. "Did you just say you wanted a sports car?"

"Yeah, I want a sports car," I said, putting the process in motion.

"What kind of sports car?"

"Oh, I don't know—something fun."

"Like a Mustang?" he asked.

"Yeah, that's a good idea! A Mustang would be fun!"

"Well, you want a convertible, don't you?"

"Oh my God, that's even a better idea, honey! A convertible Mustang would be so fun to take on our trip!"

"OK, I'll do some checking tomorrow," he said, not sounding the least bit surprised that I would wake up and say something so off-the-wall.

Truth be told, I *had* thought "convertible Mustang" about two days prior, when the crazy notion of owning a sports car first popped into my head. After twenty-four years of marriage, Larry is still accepting of my compulsiveness—that's one thing I love about him. And after twenty four years of marriage, if there's one thing I know how to do, and do well, it's how to plant the seed to make whatever it is that *I* want, be *his* idea.

It's like magic: I think of something and sprinkle it with a little uncertainty, then he waves his better-idea wand over it and—POOF!—it materializes. He lay back down, wrapped his arms around me, and within a couple of minutes, was snoring. I lay there smiling and thinking about my new car. The poor bastard never knew what hit him.

Monday morning, around ten, a brand-new, gray Mustang GT showed up at my office. On Wednesday morning, I called Valli and said, "I'm on my way and I'm bringing something fun for our trip."

"Book on tape?" she asked.

"No, more fun than that," I assured her.

"OK, whatever. Come by the store. See you later."

Another trip. This one was to be a pilgrimage of sorts: just Val and I on the first anniversary of Mom's death, taking her to the place that she said she had always wanted to go to—the Lewis and Clark Caverns.

I pulled up in front of Valli's store, top down on my new car, wearing my Jackie O shades and a leopard scarf, and called her from my cell phone.

"Thelma, it's Louise," I said.

"What?"

"I'm outside your store," I told her. Valli came out with the phone still up to her ear, looking for my SUV. Then, I assume, she recognized the perfect, toothy smile parked just outside.

"What the hell are you doing in that?" she asked into the phone.

"Told you I was bringing something fun for our trip," I said, trying not to sound giddy.

"Sweeeeet," Dustin said when his Mom and I picked him up from his job at Albertson's.

"Aunt Tammi, have you wanted a Mustang for a long time?" he asked as he slid over the side and into the backseat.

"Yep, ever since Sunday," I replied.

The trunk of a Mustang doesn't hold much but we didn't think we needed much for our three-day trip. On

Thursday, we packed a tent and sleeping bags into the trunk. Mom, in her oak urn, was tucked into the Harley Davidson backpack in the backseat of the Mustang, when we left Idaho Falls.

We drove to wherever the Lewis and Clark Caverns are—somewhere in western Montana— and then that afternoon, we pulled into the Lewis and Clark Caverns Campground and began to set up camp. The only problem was that neither of us knew how to pitch a tent. We wrestled with the sticks, which were attached by strings and bent in every direction. We kept trying to fit them into holes and bend them into the shape of something that resembled a tent. When they wouldn't, we would erupt in fits of laughter. Valli, the tent, and I kept ending up in a pile on the ground.

Throughout our two-hour ordeal, we kept an eye on a guy who was keeping an eye on us and who, in my opinion, had the misfortune of camping in the site next to ours.

"Don't make eye contact," Val told me when she saw him watching us. "He could be a mass murderer. Nobody camps alone except weirdos and mass murders."

"We're related to weirdos," I pointed out.

"Well then he's probably a mass murderer because I'm sure he's not family," she said, still wrestling with the double-jointed sticks.

We fought with the big piece of canvas and the collapsing sticks for another half hour before the weirdo/murderer made his way over to our campsite and said,

"I can't stand it for one more minute. Let me help you ladies set up your tent."

"No," Valli said immediately, "we don't need any help."

"Are you completely out of your mind?" I blurted out, a little too hysterically. Then, more discreetly and composed, and through clenched teeth, I pointed out, "We don't know what the hell we're doing."

"We can do it!" she cried, like she was rallying a camping team. I looked at her, dumbfounded, like I was the fat kid on the bench who had just been put into the game. I half-expected her to call a huddle, whisper a play, high-five me, and then smack me on the ass as I stumbled, clueless, onto the field.

The helpful camper/killer got the memo. "Oookkkk," he said, backing off, hands raised like she was pointing a gun at him. "Well, if you want coffee in the morning, I'll have some made."

Those were the magic words! We looked at each other and realized, instantly, that neither of us had brought coffee. We volleyed responsibility. She shot me a look that suggested that the coffee was my obligation. I played it back to her and she missed.

"I brought the car," I said. Game point.

"OK," she told the camper/killer, "you help us set up the tent, we'll share our wine tonight, and you share your coffee in the morning."

The deal was made! He set up our tent while we opened the wine and watched him. We gave him a glass, sent him on his way, and went to bed. It then became clear that coffee was not the only thing we had neglected to bring. An air mattress would have been nice and a flashlight would have been useful. However, I did remember to bring my pillow, my eye mask, and my .38.

Fifty-Seven

June 14, 2002.

It's amazing what a difference one year can make. What's even more amazing is the difference it doesn't make. I'd spent the past year alienating my husband, daughters, and friends who were there for me, or at least tried to be. I had become emotionally bankrupt, spending every ounce of energy I had worrying about my father, who wasn't there for me and didn't seem to care what price I had paid.

One year later, my grief was still as heavy as a cast-iron skillet. I still cried every day, for my mom and for my dad. I could barely say Mom's name, talk about her, or see her handwriting without my heart sinking like a soufflé that's fresh out of the oven.

We awoke to find that the camper/killer had made coffee, as promised. I distracted him with small talk while Val put her urn-opening skills to good use, pouring some ashes in a sandwich bag so we could take Mom to the caverns. After our coffee, the three of us hiked the mile or so uphill to the caverns. At the opening of the cave, Valli fumbled with the baggie while I tried to block the view of the ten or so other spelunkers who were about to enter the hellhole with us. Our new best friend eyed us curiously, trying to determine the goal of our covert operation, while Val tried to spread some of Mom's ashes discreetly. He saw the baggie, his eyes met mine, and I saw a question forming on his lips. I offered no explanation and gave him a don't-even-think-about-asking-me-or-I'll-have-to-kill-ya look instead. It must have worked because he suddenly decided to take an interest in kicking rocks while waiting to enter the cave.

When Val and I walked into the dark, dank cave, we heard the squeaking of bats, smelled the bat guano, and felt them buzzing over our heads. One or both of us may have cussed Mom about then, wondering why in the hell she wanted to come here rather than, say, Cancun or Paris.

"I'm sure she said the Lewis and Clark *Tavern*," I said, trying to convince Val. "We could leave now and be there for happy hour."

She was acting like Dad—ignoring me—so we trudged on. Somewhere deep in the cave, shortly after we had slid on our butts down a steep rock, and right before it was necessary to walk like a duck through a small passage where something sticky dripped on our heads, we lost the camper/killer and we all got our wishes. We finally saw daylight and Mom finally made it completely through the Lewis-and-Goddamned-Clark Caverns.

A few hours later, we pitched our own tent near Big Sky, Montana. We didn't need a man to help us, but we *were* wondering where our morning coffee would come from. We figured out the magic sticks, but it still took us a couple of hours and a bottle of wine to get the job done.

We then went a few miles up the road to one of the local joints. We had envisioned ourselves enjoying a leisurely meal and then lingering over wine while we patted ourselves on our backs. Our reflection in the bar mirror showed us looking smug with satisfaction as we celebrated what we perceived to be one of our greatest accomplishments. We had taken our mother to the Caverns, fulfilling one of her last wishes, and there was no denying that we felt good about it. Not every daughter gets to do that for her mother. Instead we found that self-satisfaction is a lot like a fish out of water. It only lives for a couple of minutes.

Guilt managed to overshadow all of our warm, haughty feelings, and there she was, sitting, uninvited, with her elbows on our table, staring us down. We could have—should have—been better daughters. We should have stood up to Dad. We shouldn't have gone to the Bahamas. We should have spent that last Christmas with Mom; we should have taken her to that Indian faith healer that she had wanted to see. We should have stood up to Dad.

Thoughts of Dad, all alone on this day, also weighed heavily on us. We were wondering what Dad was doing on this anniversary, but we were afraid to call because we had no idea what we would say to him. We were even more afraid of what he would say to us.

"Do you think this makes us bad daughters?" Val asked. I didn't really want to answer because I wasn't sure that I would like what I heard.

"Hell yes," Guilt answered for me. We both heard it loud and clear, but neither of us was willing to step up and make the call. We drowned Guilt with a second bottle of wine and told ourselves that at least we were good at being bad.

By the time we made it back to our campsite, it was completely dark outside. We then realized that we had neglected to bring matches—another essential camping tool.

"Someone has been in our tent!" I whispered as I entered, staring into complete darkness.

"How do you know?" Val asked.

"Because I didn't leave my sleeping bag like this. I left it laid out, ready to crawl into." I was sure of that. "Oh my God! Our tent has been ransacked," I said in a high-pitched whisper, as if I could actually see my sleeping bag and the inside of the tent.

Valli, being the liberal that she is, has always been against me packing a gun (except for when Dad told the Blackie story), but now, scared of whatever had ransacked our tent, she wanted to know if I had it on me.

"Shit! It's in the Mustang," I said. "Don't you have your wine opener with you?"

"Yeah, why? Do you think they'll want to party?" She laughed at her own joke, but was still too afraid to let go of my arm.

"Well then, Sister Mary Valerie Margaret, be the good, Catholic sister that you are and get it out, in case you need to poke an eye out to save our sorry asses." I tried not to giggle because I really was sure that our tent had been ransacked.

We managed to scare each other enough to decide to get out of there and get a room at the lodge up the road. We fumbled in the dark just long enough to get our make-up removers, hairdryers, and pajamas, then high-tailed it five miles up the road and checked into Buck's T4 Lodge at about midnight.

The next morning while standing in the shower, I began to think about the previous night's events and I wondered where my purse was. With my hair still full of complimentary shampoo and my body soaking wet, I bailed out of the shower and tried to pull on my pajamas, while at the same time wrapping a towel around my dripping hair. I searched the room.

"Goddamnit, Valli! Get up and help me find my purse," I demanded. "I can't remember when I last had it."

While she was climbing out of bed, I slipped on my shoes and ran outside to check in the Mustang. The top was still down, so I took a quick glance inside. No Fendi bag!

"OK, shit. Help me find my car keys," I said, still panicking as I burst back into our room. She tossed my keys to me and I took off down the highway, back to our abandoned campsite.

I found our tent and marched by the real campers, who were eyeing me curiously. Not only had I just screeched up in my car, I was wearing a towel on my head, soaking wet pajamas, and leopard heels. I entered the tent cautiously, half-expecting to meet Big Foot or a camper/killer. In the broad daylight, I found the tent to look remarkably similar to how we had left it the evening before—except that we had ransacked our suitcases in our haste to make our getaway.

There, dropped in the middle of our tent, was my Fendi bag. I ripped it open and shuffled through my cash, though I had no idea how much I had been packing. I counted out 1,129 dollars—enough to convince me that it was all there.

"I hate camping!" I shouted, ignoring all of the eyes that were on me and no doubt wondering why I was wearing a wet shortie set, a towel, and cute shoes, and packing an expensive bag. "What are you looking at?" I started to bark. Then I smelled our neighbor's coffee and remembered that my sister and I would need to suck up to someone in order to have ours, so I just smiled and waved—and tried to fit in.

"Be back in a minute. Keep the coffee warm." I said, imagining myself decked out in camo and hiking boots. I tried to leave in less of a scene than I had arrived in.

A day later, Val and I parted company and went back to our homes, our families, and our lives. We never did call Dad, who was still lost in New Mexico like he was the last man on Earth.

Fifty-Eight

One year had passed since Mom's death and I had been inducted into a secret club—Daughters Without Mothers—and I felt like I was stuck in a waiting room. I was waiting to be able to look at a picture of Mom without choking up or bursting into tears. I was waiting for that stinging feeling behind my eyes to go away. I was waiting to be able to look at a wig without feeling like I needed to throw up. Most of all, I was waiting to be able to stop crying myself to sleep at night.

I had been waiting for a year and I was still waiting for someone to give me the password to the next room, which I hoped would be the Second-Thought-I-Have-in-the-Morning Room. I really did want to go back to my old life, when my first thought of the day was "What should I fix for dinner?" I just wanted to open my eyes and think something other than "I don't have a mother!" I really didn't even care what the second room was; I just wanted out of the goddamn waiting room! I wondered why my friends who had lost their mothers had never told me about this secret club. Was it part of the initiation? The answer is yes. You have to figure it out on your own. You have to find your own way out of the waiting room—and you won't find that after just one year.

I know I'm good at instigating and carrying out the occasional pity party, but I'm even better at cracking the whip and getting the job done. I've always said, "Don't put me on a committee unless you want me to run it." And there I was, unable to delegate myself the job of getting my shit together enough to even want to crawl out of bed on some mornings. I knew I wasn't special; I wasn't the only person on earth to feel like that. My sister felt exactly the same way but for some reason I still felt very much alone. I ached everywhere and I just needed to go home.

I sucked my straw cowboy hat down on my head and put the top down on the 'stang. Once again, I found myself on I-90, driving too fast, anxious to get home. The hot, one-hundred-mile-an-hour wind pushed my tears down my cheeks and back toward my ears, turning them into ghost tears.

Part Six

Last Call

Fifty-Nine

The rest of 2002 seemed like a blur. I went through the motions of living, working, eating, and breathing, but deep down I felt like someone had taken over my body and I was locked somewhere deep inside. I barely recognized myself in the mirror and I became a stranger to my family and friends. I saw the worried glances and I ignored the hushed whispers. The world around me had turned into a cold, barren place with no color, and I couldn't believe that it was still turning without my mother in it. How dare it?

Not long after our trip to the Caverns, Valerie announced that something other than Mom was missing from her life.

"I don't know what it is yet, but September is going to be life-changing," she told me.

"What is it, and why September?" I asked. I could

sense that she had a secret that she was dying to share. I took the bait. "All right, spill your guts. What's going on?"

"Oh, I don't know. Nothing terribly specific. I just know it's time to make a life-changing decision," she said, gazing into her crystal ball.

"So you're serious? This isn't just about switching from half–and-half to non-dairy creamer again?"

"No, I mean something like a career change," she said. I swear I heard tarot cards being shuffled.

"I need a career change too," I practically demanded, and I wasn't referring to anything that involved my other, less–talked-about obsession: vacuum cleaners. I'm going to spill my guts here and admit that not only do I love vacuum cleaners, I love to vacuum. I went through a phase during which I actually kept the vacuum cleaner in the garage because—I shit you not—I vacuumed my way out of the house every morning. Sometimes I even came home from work in the middle of the day to vacuum rooms that no one had been in. Sick, I know. The height of my mania came when we lived in Pompey's, which corresponded with the height of Dad's drinking. Coincidence? I think not. The roaring of the vacuum cleaner drowned out the replays of our arguments, slightly muting the screaming in my head.

Not only did I get really good at pushing vacuum cleaners, I have a God-given talent for fixing them. If I wanted to (and I'm pretty sure I don't), I could be a vacuum cleaner repair person—and a damn good one. Truth be told, I would much rather my gift be playing the piano by ear, but it's not. It's overhauling vacuum cleaners. After weighing my options, I decided that it wasn't a career that I was quite ready to trade my day job for, so I dropped the thought and told Val to let me know when she figured hers out, because maybe then I could figure mine out, too.

Valerie figured hers out. A few weeks later, she telephoned me to say that she had gotten the calling. No, not *that* calling, for God's sake. She didn't want to become a nun; she wanted to be a nurse!

"I liked taking care of Mom, so I'm thinking of selling the store and enrolling in nursing school," she said.

"I want a calling," I sulked, still chained to my desk at our trucking company. I glared at the stack of my business cards, which were piled neatly on the corner of my desk, like they were to blame. I listened patiently as Val chattered on, spelling out her new career plan and telling me that in four years she would be an "RN." After twenty years, I had gotten my own hard-earned letters behind my name. Granted, I had put them there myself, but I had a big fat "NDBA" in bold type, italics, and all caps on my business card, affirming my important position. If anyone asked me what it meant, I told them the truth: "No Degree, Boss Anyway."

Sixty

Dad left New Mexico in the fall of 2002. He went to Seattle and stayed with Uncle Dean, where he pretty much stayed on the hooch 24/7. After a few months, his bingeing caught up with him and he landed in the hospital. Before he went in, he told me that he was checking into a sleep clinic, which I bought (because I can be a clueless dumbass), knowing that he had been suffering from insomnia for years. When I couldn't reach him for several days, Uncle Dean finally clued me in to the fact that he was actually in some sort of dry-out facility. He stayed for a couple of weeks. It wasn't exactly rehab—he'd been there, done that. Let's just say he wasn't completely dried out, but still damp when he left the clinic and Seattle, and returned to New Mexico for the last time.

In May of 2003, he left New Mexico for good and took his camper to the Mustang Ranch, a horse-boarding facility in Colorado that we own. Sierra was living there while attending CSU. It was ironic that my daughter and her grandpa would end up on a ranch together again. They were no longer poaching deer, but they remained partners in crime by scoring bulk grocery items at the local food bank. The two of them defended their low-income status to me by claiming to be a partnership composed of a disabled old guy living in a camper and a poor college student who picked horseshit for a living. They did have a point, so I overlooked the fact that they got cases of canned and dried goods for free.

My father and my daughter shared a sassy, you're-not-the-boss-of-me type of relationship. Dad would tell Sierra that the horse shelter that she was attempting to build was "all wrong," and that she couldn't "run a hammer for shit." She would respond by telling him to either pick up a hammer and help or go back inside his camper if he was going to criticize her work. She worked, he supervised. When he got on her last nerve, she told him where to go. She monitored his alcohol intake and he monitored her social life. They both tattled on each other to me. He cooked for her and she cleaned for him. He grumbled about the rate of speed at which she drove the tractor and she complained about the rate at which he created laundry. They hung out together and looked after each other. It was a match made in heaven.

Before we knew it, June 14, 2003, had come and gone. That fall, Dad decided to leave Colorado and move to Idaho. He was still able to recite the number of years, months, days, hours, and minutes that had passed since Mom died. After three years, four months, and seven days, he left his camper in Colorado and tried to move back into the apartment at 240 Dale Street. Thank God it was not available.

"Why would he want to move in there?" I asked Valli, horrified at the thought of ever having to set foot in that place again.

"He's coming here to die. I just know it," she said. "This is where Mom was and, for some crazy reason, I think he wants to die where she did."

I had no idea what his reasons were. I had decided long ago to stop analyzing why my father did the things he did. Unconsciously, I had also made the decision not to go to see him anymore. I'm not sure why. It seemed I just couldn't bring myself to make that drive back to Idaho Falls.

Because I never inherited the Christmas-loving gene and because I can be a thoughtless, selfish bitch, I abandoned Dad and Valli and let them suffer through the holidays together. I took my family to the Cayman Islands for a week and acted like everything was fine.

The only resolution I made for 2004 was to continue the charade. I went to Florida in February, California in March, and then in April my friend and I went to Italy, where we took cooking classes and toured Rome, Pompeii, the Amalfi coast, and Capri. I was either planning trips or taking them. The paranoias were after me, so it took a Grey Goose dirty martini (or two) and a valium (or two) for me to muster up the courage to get on a plane. I spent most of the year traveling to anywhere except Idaho Falls. The only things exceeding my frequent flyer miles were my credit card bills. I was pretty much absorbed in my own mind game of Liar's Poker. I told myself that as long as Dad had Valli around it was OK for me not to be. I made up for it with Prada and Gucci for everyone. I even bluffed Guilt.

June 14, 2004, passed us by. Valli, Dustin, and Sierra were all in college. Savannah and Hannah were in high school. Larry and Saul were in neglect, Dad was in hell, and I was in denial.

Sixty-One

I finally went to visit Dad in September of 2004. It had been over fourteen months since I had seen him. What the hell was I thinking? I should have had my butt kicked for deserting him and Valli for that entire year. I must have finally found some wisdom in the bottom of my Sangiovese glass because I quit the globetrotting and began spending my spare time driving or flying between Wyoming and Idaho.

I will admit to being a somewhat slow learner, but I finally got the memo that families really should spend time together, especially over the holidays. I visited again in October and then Larry, the girls, and I went to Idaho Falls for Christmas. Mom's birthday was November 28 and Dad pretty much stayed shit-faced from then until Christmas. A few days before the holiday, he fell down and cracked some ribs and was more depressed than usual, refusing to come to Valli and Saul's house for Christmas dinner. We spent three days walking on eggshells around him, then my family and Valli's family went to Mexico for a week. We invited Dad to come along, but of course he wouldn't, so Guilt tagged along instead.

As Dad's emotional health began to heal, his physical health began to decline at a rate usually reserved for lab animals. He became more and more housebound and more and more demanding of Val, keeping her and Saul in a marathon of crazy demands on a daily basis.

"Fifteen black garbage bags, the ones with a tie, not draw strings and not white ones."

"A vanilla cake mix—not white cake, but vanilla."

"Four pounds of prime rib, cut into no bigger than half-inch-thick slices."

"Vella box wine—burgundy, not merlot or cabernet."

His requests were very precise and he wasn't happy with anything that wasn't exactly what he had asked for.

Not long after Dad moved to Idaho, Uncle Dean decided to move there too. That was good news and bad news. The good news was that Dad would have another family member around. The bad news was Uncle Dean drank and smoked even more than Dad did, which meant that Dad's own habits escalated. His house was filled with such a haze of cigarette smoke that it looked like someone had filled it with dry ice and then poured water over it. Dad never walked the six doors down to Uncle Dean's apartment; Dean always went to Dad's house, dragging his oxygen bottle along.

By now, Dad was on oxygen too, so Val became the oxygen police; she had her work cut out for her with two repeat offenders who were under house arrest. They constantly smoked with their oxygen on and when she reprimanded them, they ignored her. She warned Dad about storing the oxygen bottles in his pickup in the 105-degree summer heat, but he ignored her warning, saying, "I ain't gettin' them out. Let 'em blow up. We could use some excitement around here." She had her hands full with the two of them and she didn't have a lot of sympathy.

At least once a week Dad made Valli go to the cigarette store to feed his and Uncle Dean's habit. Valli once told the lady at the cigarette store, "These are for my Dad. He can't come to get his own cigarettes because his emphysema is too bad and he's on oxygen." People who smoke don't really find this funny, and that gravely-voiced, leather-skinned sourpuss was no exception.

I showed up at least every other month, armed with a cooler of food. I brought Wagyu steaks, ahi tuna, fresh herbs, my saucier pan, my spice kit, and my chef's knife. I cooked, I cleaned, I fussed over him, I drank wine with him, and I monitored my blood pressure and oxygen levels with him. I would stay for four or five days and then give back custody to Valli.

We replayed it over and over: Dad picked on Valli; Valli bitched to me about Dad; and I agreed with her. I went to Idaho; Dad bitched to me about Valli; I cooked for him, drank with him, and agreed with him. When I left, Dad went back to picking on Valli. Uncle Dean was Switzerland.

Sixty-Two

I think my breakthrough came at about year five. I was still in the Daughters Without Mothers Club but I had made it out of the waiting room, through the Second-Thought-I–Have-in-the-Morning Room, past the Pity Party Hall, and out through the Acceptance Foyer. There was no getting out of the club, but at least I had found my way out of the clubhouse. Oh, I still had some much needed cries for Mom and I still missed her terribly, but my faith assured me that I would see her again, so I clung to that and found some comfort. I also had one more encounter with her, which gave me the real peace that I had been searching for.

At first I blamed it on the wine. Finally there was just no denying it. I awoke one night to the feeling of Larry spooning me. His arms were wrapped tightly around me yet he was holding me gently. It was such a warm feeling that I completely succumbed to it. His knees bent at the exact same angle as mine and our hips aligned perfectly. His arms cradled me and his hands cupped my heart, which beat into his palms. I felt his breath in my ear as I fell deeper and deeper into a peaceful sleep. I plunged my whole body into his hug, letting go of hurt, denial, and anger. Sleep came back.

I don't know how much time passed, but I awoke to feel him pushing me away. *Why is he pushing on me?* I resisted at first, clinging to the feeling that I had fallen asleep with. Then our bodies began to undo and I felt my heart chill as it was placed back inside my chest. *Why is he pushing me away?* I wondered. I was still not completely awake but awake enough to move away from the force of his push. He pushed harder, waking me a little more and causing me to move closer to my own side of the bed. *Why is he still pushing on me? Wait a minute—Larry's not in bed with me, I am home alone.* I was now fully awake. I sat up and looked around my bedroom, confirming the fact that I was indeed home and in bed alone. I shook it off and told myself that it was only a weird dream. My head hurt and my heart had a throbbing that I had not felt before. I blamed it on the wine from the previous evening and forced myself to lie back down, close my eyes, and go to sleep.

The next morning I woke up alone in my bed with a slight hangover, wishing that Larry was home to bring me my coffee. Just to be sure he wasn't, I rolled over and checked the other side of the bed. Then I listened for the sound of water splashing all over the bathroom, only to hear the silence of being alone. Gradually the strange dream started coming back to me, first in random flashes, then in vivid detail, but the memory of it was like a jigsaw puzzle scattered all over a table. I could imagine it all put together, I just didn't know which piece to pick up first. Then I realized that all of the pieces were the exact same and they all fit together. It then became crystal clear to me that my mother had paid me a final visit. She came to my bed, she hugged me, she held me close for a little while, she felt my heart ache, and then she pushed me away. It was her way of telling me that I needed to get on with living my life and let her go. I finally understood. I knew that my heart would always have a special ache for her, but she would hold me again one day.

I wasn't sure about Valerie. According to the last conversation that we had about heaven, she didn't believe in it, so I guessed that she was going to have to figure that out on her own. I knew that she had always had a closer relationship with Mom than I did and I imagined that Dad's demands on her had made her long for Mom even more. We both had plenty of why-her-instead-of-him moments, but as the months rolled by I found myself getting closer to and caring and worrying more about my father. My stomach still did that flip when I heard his voice on the phone, but I truly loved him with all my heart.

By this time, my relationship with Dad had evolved enough that I actually got to play the part of a grown-up. Our bond seemed to be forged with food and nostalgia.

We talked about old recipes, old relatives, old horses, and old dogs. We rehashed the old cowboying days, remembering the good times and turning the not-so-good times into not-so-bad times. He was appreciative of my cooking and he wasn't judgmental about any of my impending travels. He was interested in and supportive of things that I would have normally been cautious to bring up. We stayed up late at night, sipping our drinks and visiting like two long-lost friends. He was able to tell me he loved me and that he was proud of me. Oh, I still sucked up to him, because that's where I shined. Besides, it was my starring role in life and I knew all the words by heart, plus I was still gunning for that Lifetime Achievement Award.

As much as I hated to admit it, I knew that I would never have had that relationship with my father if my mother had still been alive. Dad would probably still have been screwing up and Mom would still have been covering up. I had to be strong—at least on the outside—for Dad's sake. He expected a certain amount of toughness from me and I didn't want to let him down so late in his life. We needed each other and I still wanted to be his right-hand man.

Sixty-Three

M om would kick your butt if you didn't come," I told Dad one day over the telephone.

I was referring to Savannah's upcoming wedding.

"I know she would," he said, sounding sad. I could almost see him sitting there in his apartment, oxygen tubing plumbed into his nose, a smoke dangling between his first two fingers, and a coffee cup full of Burgundy sitting in front of him.

Savannah was getting married on August 25, 2007, and I expected Dad to be there. He had not left his apartment in months, but he said that he would come. On August 20, he told me that he would come on the twenty-first. Then on the twenty-first, he said that he would come on the twenty-second, and on the twenty-second, he said the twenty-third. Larry bet me that he wouldn't come—period.

I collected ten bucks from my husband on the afternoon of August 23, when Dad, Uncle Dean, and Dean's son Matthew (the DD) all showed up at our house. In anticipation of his arrival, I had moved his camper from Colorado to our place in Wyoming and parked it next to the creek. It was clean and stocked with glasses, coffee cups, ash trays, ice, new pillows, and fresh bedding. Minutes after their arrival, I showed up at the camper door with a basket full of fresh fruit.

"We don't need that," Dad said as I entered the camper announcing, "Welcome Wagon, this is your complimentary welcome basket." Ignoring him, I put the fruit down on the table. Within minutes they were picking at grapes and Matthew was peeling a banana.

"We got ice?" Uncle Dean asked, pulling a jug of whiskey out of a bag. I opened up the freezer, showing off a full bag of ice. Cigarettes were lit, whiskey was poured, and I pulled up a chair and felt right at home.

"Dad, the four-wheeler parked outside is for you and Uncle Dean to use to get you from the camper to the house. And I rented you a wheelchair, plus I have a golf cart for you for the wedding," I told him, hoping that all of these forms of transportation would make him realize that I expected him to be *at* the wedding. His emphysema was chronic and full-blown and he could hardly take two steps without having to rest. He wasn't drinking or smoking nearly as much, but he hadn't completely given up either habit.

That evening, when they refused to make the five-hundred-yard drive from the camper to the house to join the rest of us for dinner, I delivered a Caesar salad and lasagna. The next morning, in spite of the fact that I had ten people staying at my house, I immediately went to the camper with a carafe of coffee and a cream cheese strudel. They still refused to budge for lunch so I took pizza to them. The big welcome and rehearsal dinner was that evening and I told them come hell or high water, I expected them to come to the house for that. The three of them finally cooperated and left the camper. I dished up Dad and Uncle Dean's plates with barbequed ribs, chicken, and all the other fixings, and they dined and dashed.

The next morning, the day of Savannah and Shane's wedding, I delivered bagels, muffins, and donuts, along with their coffee, and instructed them to be at the Big Horn Equestrian Center by four o'clock.

"Or your ass is grass!" I said, having never gotten the chance to say those words to my father.

"We'll be there!" he said, giving me one of his shit-eating grins. I had my doubts.

Dad was there, though, to see the first of his four grandchildren walk down the aisle. Larry and Savannah both cried as they made their way up the aisle, and I cried, too. I cried, first and foremost, because my mother was not sitting in the front row next to me . . . and a little bit because I was sure that all those checks that I had written were about to clear.

As much as I wished that Mom could have been there to see her little Vanni get married, I knew that she was watching from above and I was sure that she had something to do with the perfect, cloudless day. I was even more certain of it after the Big Horn Mountains were painted with the most spectacular August sunset that anyone had ever seen.

They stayed for one more day and Dad paid me two compliments as they were leaving. He said that I was a good hostess and that I really knew how to throw a party. I was sure that his words translated to, "You're a good daughter." I hugged him and looked at him and said, "I love you, Dad."

He didn't just mumble, "Uh, uh, yeah, uh yeah, me too." He hugged me, patted my back, looked me in the eye, and said, "I love you too, kiddo."

I helped him into the pickup and watched as they drove off. He looked back at me, stuck his arm out the window, and waved goodbye. I was surprised by that. Looking back has never been a habit of his.

Sixty-Four

Y ou're an asshole!" Valli said that she had screamed at Dad. She was now repeating it into my ear, her voice two octaves higher than normal, and I could tell that she was about to cry.

"What'd he do?" I asked.

"He's just mean to me. I've been nothing but nice to him and he is just a fucking asshole." She spit the words out as if they had left a bad taste in her mouth.

Dad was in the hospital. He had been taken to the ER by Saul, per his request, because he was feeling "really bad." Saul and Val spent ten hours in the ER with him while he underwent every test that a person with Medicare can get—which is every test that can be performed.

"Nothing is wrong with him," Valli told me. "It's just his COPD, but he wants some sort of diagnosis—some drugs, surgery—something to make him feel better, but there is nothing. It's just a progression of his COPD."

Three days earlier, Dad had informed me that he had MS or diabetes, or maybe Parkinson's.

"How do you know?" I had asked.

"Because I have all the symptoms," he'd said, like I was the village idiot.

"Well Dad, the good news is that MS and Parkinson's take about thirty years to kill you. I think your breathing is what you need to worry about." I was sure that that was not what he had wanted to hear.

Now here he was in the hospital, and all tests had confirmed that he did not have MS, diabetes, or Parkinson's—just carpal tunnel in his wrist. He was pissed; he needed a diagnosis to validate why he felt like he did. And he thought that he needed some drugs to make him feel better.

"Maybe he feels like shit because he gets hammered every day and smokes too many cigarettes," Valli said without the least bit of sympathy. "Maybe if he didn't wake up with a hangover every morning, he wouldn't feel so bad. I'm telling you, I am nothing but nice to him and he's just an asshole," she repeated, as if that was part of his diagnosis.

"It's just because you're there," I tried to tell her. "I'll come stay with him when he gets out of the hospital. In the meantime, just stay away from him if he's mean to you."

Five days later, he was out of the hospital and I was making the 475-mile drive to Idaho. "Meals on Wheels," I announced when I walked into his apartment. He looked good—really good—and had baked a cake, which told me that he felt good. By then, he and Val had made up, although making up with Dad never involves an apology from him. He just acts like nothing ever happened and he's nicer than usual for a day or two. I actually found him to be a lot nicer than usual.

There are just some things that we are reluctant to tell our Dad: things that cause him to make a face, shoot a stink eye at us, and say, "Oh, for Christ's sake." Even though over the course of the past year I had found him to be a kinder, gentler father, I hadn't planned on telling him that I was trying to get tickets to an Elton John concert. I just didn't want to listen to him gay-bash and tell me how dumb I was for spending $89.50 on a ticket. Since I was still hitting redial on my cell phone every three minutes when I got there, though, I told him.

"Well, I don't really approve of his lifestyle," he said as if he was Dr. Phil, "but he does have some pretty good music."

"OK, who are you and what have you done with my father?" I asked. He didn't get it—or if he did, he didn't answer me. Then I wondered, *What's Valli talking about? He's not a mean, asshole Dad.*

"Dad's not being a mean asshole. He's being really nice," I told her when she called to see if I had gotten there, "and he didn't make any fag remarks when I told him I wanted to go to the Elton John concert."

"You must be at the wrong house," Val said. "It's been awhile since you've seen him. Our dad is the mean one smoking a cigarette, chained to an oxygen machine, with a box of wine on the kitchen counter. Apartment 23."

"I'm at the right house, but I must have the wrong dad 'cause this guy isn't smoking, drinking, or gay-bashing."

"Something must be wrong. I'll call 911 and be right over," she said, ending our call.

"Oh sure, he's nice to you because you're the Disney-daughter," Val pointed out while I was searing the ahi steaks for our dinner. "I'm here all week for all the crap and then you just drop by on weekends and it's like you're the parent who just shows up to take her kid to Disneyland." She was half joking, but I knew that she was right and there was nothing I could do about it.

I had a love/hate relationship with the Disney-daughter syndrome. I loved that I felt validated because I was responsible for making life fun again, but I hated that it came at the expense of my sister. I loved to make Dad happy by showing up on his doorstep with my cooler of food, but I hated that it meant that we were going to bash vegetarians, environmentalists, and liberals.

"Well, you're the one who wanted to be a nurse," I reminded her. "I've always been the party girl."

I spent five rather enjoyable days with our father, and he was appreciative of the cooking, cleaning, and laundry that I did for him. When I got ready to leave, Valerie said, "I'll be mixing up his drugs again so he'll be back in the hospital in a week and then you can come back and nurse-maid him."

"I'll be on to you," I warned her.

"I'm just calling to bitch," Val said. That was how a lot of our conversations had been starting lately.

"What'd he do now?"

"I went to get his grocery list and do his shopping. I even took him cookies and he just picked a fight with me. I swear I did nothing to provoke him. He started by making remarks about my jeans because they had holes in them, and then he started going on about you going to see Elton John—called him a faggot. I lost it and said, 'Dad why do you have to be so mean?'

"Do you know what he said? He said 'Whatever meds you're on, you need to up your dose.' Then I really laid it on the line. I told him that he was verbally abusive and that he needed to learn to treat me with respect. He never gave one inch or took once ounce of responsibility. I said, 'Dad, I'm nothing but nice to you. Why can't you just be nice back and be appreciative of all I do for you?'

"Then, do you know what he said to me? He said, 'It's because you're a goddamn Democrat and you need to get off your donkey.' What the hell does that have to do with anything? We got into a screaming match and as I was leaving he told me not to come back."

Valerie was beyond upset—again. She was raising her voice—again and I could sense that she was on the verge of tears—again.

"What if I never see him again, Tammi? I mean, what if he won't ever talk to me again?"

"He'll be sucking up to you the next time you see him," I reassured her. "I think he's turning you into Mom. He's ornery. He picks a fight with you and then he sucks up—like he used to do with Mom when he'd fall off the wagon."

"I just want him to acknowledge my feelings, to say he's sorry and that he knows that I do a lot for him."

"That's the problem, Val. He's not going to do that—not now, not ever. You need to realize that and accept that. Stop trying to turn him into somebody he's not. He can be an asshole and he can be unpredictable and downright mean, especially when on the hooch. We know that. Accept it, forgive it, and just let him be who he is. He's too old to change, so all you're doing is setting yourself up for disappointment and setting Dad up for failure."

There was dead silence on the line for ten seconds or so. I waited her out.

"I know you're right," she said, "but I just want a nice dad." Another ten seconds passed. "In fact, I think

I'll put an ad in the paper. It'll say, 'Good daughter, attentive and loving grocery-getter, needs a mother and a new dad. Old dad mean and ungrateful.'"

I laughed with her and we made up several ads for a mom and a new dad, knowing that we were stuck without one and with the other.

"Listen, I'm busy next week. I can't come to Idaho, so don't be messing with his drugs," I warned her.

"Like I'd do that," she said.

Sixty-Five

"I just told Dad to go fuck himself," Val said. She sounded less frantic than she did when she told me about the time that she told him to kiss her ass.

"Shit, Valli. What'd he do now?" I wasn't really surprised. Their relationship seemed to be going downhill faster than a roller coaster with a psychopath carnie at its controls.

"Well, I'm just not going to put up with his radical bullshit and his racism. He was using the *N* word and I'm just not going to put up with it," she told me, defending her position.

"Fine, then continue to fight with him."

"Well, do you think it's OK for him to talk like that?" she fired back.

"No, I don't, but why do you let him pick fights with you? Just ignore him or walk out of the room."

"Well, I'm going to stand up for what I believe in!" She had climbed up on her soapbox and mounted an attack.

"Valerie, when are you going to figure out that he just says that stuff because he knows it pisses you off? If you wouldn't react to it, he wouldn't say it. It's like wrestling a pig in mud—the pig enjoys it! You know he's wrong, but do you want to be right or do you want to have a relationship with your father?"

"Well I'm not—" She was preparing her defense.

I didn't let her finish. "Sometimes he says stupid shit! You can ignore it or you can get into a stupid shit-throwing contest with him!"

"But why should I—"

I cut her off again. "He's not going to have an argument with himself, so if you just shut up, then he won't be able to pick a fight with you. It only took me forty-five years, but I've finally figured that out! For God's sake, Valli, he's been ignoring what we say for years. It's not that hard. Just don't open your mouth!"

It wasn't what she wanted to hear but she knew that I had a point. If she was going to have any kind of relationship with our father, she needed to stop being the victim and just shut the hell up!

From that day on, Valli seemed to finally get it. Dad still said things to upset her, but she set some boundaries and learned to walk away when he crossed them. He seemed to respect that and finally quit pushing her buttons when he figured out that by doing so, it caused her to walk out the door.

That became evident on my next trip a few weeks later. I was at the stove, stirring shitake mushrooms, red bell peppers, carrots, ginger, and cilantro into bow-tie pasta, when Val and Saul arrived. They greeted me and then Val immediately turned to Dad.

"You don't look good. Do you feel OK?" she asked as she put a hand to his forehead. I expected to see her produce a stethoscope and a thermometer.

"I feel like I always feel," he said, trying to dodge her temperature-taking hand.

"Are you dizzy, Dad?" she persisted with real concern.

"I don't feel any worse than normal," Dad said.

"Let me see your legs," she continued.

Dad hiked one leg of his sweatpants up, revealing a puffy, white limb that looked like it belonged to a corpse.

"They look swollen. Are they achy?" she asked as she tried to pinch some skin between her thumb and forefinger.

"Don't you go dying on me before dinner," I said, slicing the flank steak and plating it on top of the Asian pasta.

Valli switched her attention to Uncle Dean. "You don't look so good yourself. Your face is red."

"Yeah, what's new?" Uncle Dean asked.

"Are you taking your blood pressure meds?"

"Are you writing a book?" he answered with a question of his own.

Valli refused to be offended or ignored. She went about her business of evaluating their conditions with poking fingers and probing questions. I smiled to myself, enjoying the fact that they hadn't been able to get under her skin as they wise-assed their way around her health questions. She was rolling with punches and I could see that Dad and Uncle Dean were enjoying the attention. I also liked that this dialogue seemed normal and relaxed—like pleasant small talk.

"If anyone is dying here, at least have the courtesy to wait until after we eat," I warned as I set dinner on the table.

Sixty-Six

He's driving me crazy with his grocery demands," Valli told me on her way to pick up cases of green beans, corn, mushrooms, peas, tuna, mac and cheese, and other nonperishables.

"He wants twenty pounds of rice!" she added in disbelief. "I told him, 'Dad, with your health, you shouldn't be buying green bananas, let alone twenty pounds of rice.'"

"Where's he going to store all that?" I wondered out loud. I was sure that the "use by" dates would be way past Dad's expiration date.

With the exception of an occasional relapse, Dad had pretty much stopped picking on Val, probably because he couldn't get much of a rise out of her anymore. She had finally decided to follow my advice and not go down that path with him. Every few days, Val called me to report on his behavior or his latest demand.

"Dad's making his funeral arrangements," she said, as if he was making Jell-O shots. She said it like it was something that he did, just not something that he did every day. Then she continued, "He said he wants to go pick out his urn, so I asked him what he wanted done with his ashes. Do you know what he said? He said, 'I don't give a shit what you do with them. As mean as I've been to you, you'll probably want to flush them down the toilet.'"

"Owwwww. What'd you say?"

"I told him, 'As mean as you've been to me, Dad, I was planning to stick a hot dog up your ass and let the coyotes eat you.'"

"You did not!" I said, shocked, but not so sure that she wouldn't have said such a thing.

"No. I didn't say that, but I thought about it. I said, 'I thought you wanted your ashes mixed in with Mom's.'"

"Oh God, does that mean we have to take another trip?" I asked.

"We should take the kids," Val said, sounding like she was already planning one.

I changed the subject, not ready or willing to entertain the thought of retracing those steps. "Why is he making funeral arrangements? Is he feeling really bad?"

"I don't know. He just told me that he wanted to do it because if you did it you would pick out something too fancy and too expensive," she said.

"Ah, the chair, he hasn't forgotten about the chair," I said. "The chair" was a one-thousand-dollar bomber leather recliner that I had insisted he buy for himself. He had said that the only reason it was comfortable was that he was no longer sitting on that wad of cash that had been in his wallet prior to paying for the chair.

"But he loves that chair," I defended my good taste to Valli.

"Well, he wants to pick out his own urn, so just let him."

What could he possibly want next? I asked myself as I hung up the phone.

"I want you to get me some marijuana," Dad told me over the phone. He said it as nonchalantly as if he were requesting Vitamin C.

"Why do you want to smoke pot, Dad?" I asked, not that I would have been surprised by anything that he said.

"I want to see if it makes me feel better—and oh, bring me about five thousand dollars in cash when you come. I want to pay for my funeral."

A month later I kissed my hubby good-bye, saying, "I'll either see you in eight to ten days or eight to ten years, depending on if I get busted or not for running drugs."

"Don't be speeding," Larry warned me.

"I'll be out in five for good behavior," I reassured him as I prepared to back out of the driveway. "Besides, that shade of orange washes me out, so there's no way I'm going to risk having to wear that for more than a day."

"It's not funny, Tammi," he cautioned. "You could get in serious trouble."

"I'll be good. I promise." I gave him a wink, blew him a kiss, and left him shaking his head in my rearview mirror. I was fully aware that the .38 concealed under my seat, along with the cash, the weed, the pipe, the papers, and my small stash of valium would not help my case, should it come before a judge. I imagined myself trying to explain, "Really, Your Honor, it's not mine. It's for my dad, swear to God!" I had failed to notice that I was also driving on expired tags. Eight hours later, I showed up on Dad's doorstep with an ounce of weed, drug paraphernalia, a sack of cash, and a salt-cured Virginia ham.

"Are you going to get him a whore and some coke if he asks for that?" Valli asked. I'm sure she was thinking that she would rather insert catheters than take care of our father when he was stoned.

"Oh, what's the big deal if he smokes a little weed? It's not like it's going to kill him. He might even be nicer to you when he's high," I pointed out.

She wasn't exactly impressed with my reasoning. Her look told me that if I got busted for smuggling any more illegal substances to our father, I wouldn't be able to count on her for bail money.

After that, Dad started to get obsessive about his funeral plans. He wanted me to look through Mom's "funeral bag" and get the name of the guy who had helped us with her arrangements. That would be Mr. Tall-Dark-And-Somber, who I'm sure was just the employee who had happened to draw the short straw the day we walked in. I relayed those thoughts to Dad, but he insisted and when I failed to deliver the real name of the guy, he went over my head to Valli. He made her go to the funeral home to try to actually find out who the guy was and make an appointment with him.

"Well, I just made Dad an appointment to get cremated," Valli announced to me, as casually as if it were an appointment for a teeth cleaning.

"Can you do that? When's he doing that? Better yet, does he know he's doing that?" I asked. The craziness of her statement sank in and I found myself laughing so hard that I could barely speak.

"Yeah, I told him," Val said, now laughing herself, as if she had suddenly realized how absurd that sounded.

"What'd he say?" I tried to ask.

"He said it would be his last big smoke." She could barely get the words out.

Once the arrangements were made and paid for, Dad didn't want to get too far away from Woods' Funeral Home. I begged him and Uncle Dean to come spend a few weeks with me in Wyoming. I even tried to bribe him with a promise of being his private chef and personal maid, but he was unwilling and no amount of USDA prime, dry-aged, perfectly grilled beef was going to pry Dad away from his prepaid urn.

"He won't go to your house," Valli told me. "He said he needs to stay close to the funeral home in case they need to come get him. He thinks it's extra if you croak when you're out of town, and he didn't pay for that option."

I promised him that if he kicked the bucket on my watch, I would put him on ice and get him back to Idaho Falls. Still he resisted, even when I pointed out that I was quite proficient at making the trip with a cooler full of something dead on ice.

Our behavior was childish, our gallows humor ghoulish, and we knew it. Laughing on the outside was our way to keep from crying on the inside. Our survival for these past few years may have meant plotting his death, but secretly and without saying as much, we were preparing our hearts for our future.

As difficult as it had been with Dad as our main focus in life, it was even more daunting to imagine our lives without him. Our relationships with him had come a long way and, although it wasn't the easy way if felt like the right way, and I was glad that we had made the journey with him. We got to know Dad from a perspective that likely would not have been possible if Mom had still been running interference. We were there for each other when it counted and we were a family. He was finally able to look us in the eye and tell us that he loved us and that he was proud of us—words that before we had only heard secondhand.

"Listen, I'm planning on coming for his birthday. Can you reschedule the cremation?" I asked Val.

"I'll check with Dad and see what he wants to do," she said. I could tell that she was trying her best to keep a straight face.

Sixty-Seven

It was March of 2008 when I went to Idaho Falls for Dad's sixty-eighth birthday. Uncle Dean insisted that he pay for king crab legs, which is what they wanted for Dad's birthday dinner. The only problem was that Uncle Dean didn't have much money. What he did have was a food stamp card, so armed with that, I hit the grocery store.

I stood at the checkout wearing Burberry and shame as king crab, at $18.99 per pound, slid across the scanner. I made eye contact with the checker, daring her to judge me as I handed over the food stamp card.

Back at Dad's, I prepared the birthday feast and Val and Saul arrived with a cake. I lit the votive candles under the butter-warmer things that I had bought to go with our crab leg birthday dinner, then tapped my fork on my water glass, which was doubling as a wine glass on this special occasion. "I'd like to propose a toast," I said. "Here's to Dad on his sixty-eighth birthday." I raised my glass.

I made the announcement with a certain amount of ceremony, as if I was making a toast at a dinner party with fifty hoity-toity guests, rather than the Clampets. Valli and Saul raised their glasses; Dad and Uncle Dean ignored us. King crab legs spilled over the edges of our paper plates.

"May you live . . . ohhhh . . . another six months or so, Dad," I added. Valli and I instantly cracked up; Saul tried not to choke on his mouthful of wine. Uncle Dean never even looked up—he just kept right on cracking crab legs.

Dad cracked a smile. He raised his own glass and looked at me, then Valli, then back at me, and said, "Goddamn, I hope I don't have to put up with you two for that much longer."

Epilogue

Nine years can disappear real fast. My father would disagree with that statement because the past nine years of his life have dragged on like they were shackled to his ankles. They have slowed him down, tripped him up, worn him out, and brought him to a complete standstill. That's what finally landed him in the Old Folks Home for ten days, five of which he sat in a wheelchair, doped up to resemble a catatonic quadriplegic, staring at the toilet. He refused physical therapy, declined to bathe, and waved away the insipid, unidentifiable food.

It was during this time that Valerie insisted that I come.

"He just looks so sad and pathetic," she informed me. "And he is so weak he can't even stand, let alone walk." This was one of the moments in which she would be sympathetic.

I had a hard time even picturing this. In my mind, my dad has always been this strong, ruggedly handsome man with so much pride and determination. Unstoppable, really. Even when he was falling-down drunk, pathetic was not an image or word that I associated with him.

The next phone call from my sister was to report that he may be drugged and staring at the wall, but he was still an ornery son-of-a-bitch.

"And when are you coming? Call him and call me back."

It occurred to me that in most of my conversations with Valerie in the past nine years that she never says goodbye. She always just says, "Call him and call me back." I don't say good-bye either. I always reluctantly say, "OK, I'll call him."

So that was how it went down. And I have to admit: I was forty-nine years old, my larger-than-life dad was weak, helpless, and in a nursing home, and I was afraid to pick up the phone and call him. But I did, and then I did what I have always done. I went to him.

I found him sitting in a wheelchair staring at a wall of reality. He has ached for the loss my mother for too long. Grief has fought a hard, long, and valiant battle, leaving Dad maimed and broken and deeply scarred. Each tick of the clock was like a fingernail picking at a scab, leaving a wound that time can't heal. He wouldn't tell you that he has wasted these last nine years; he would tell you it's been more like the last twenty.

The key to the lock that kept the ball and chain of grief tethered to him was found at the bottom of a bowl of bland soup. A day after my arrival at the Old Folks Home, he stopped waving away the tasteless food and instead started refusing the pain meds, the anti-depressants, the sleep aids, and the anti-anxiety drugs. His eyes conveyed a determination that his body dared not question. He got himself up out of that wheelchair and he walked.

"Ya gotta get me out of here, Tammi," he said. "Tell Valli to call my doctor and get me released. I just need to go home now."

Was it an order or a plea? I didn't know. But just like he has always called the shots and determined the course of our destiny, Dad decided when he was ready to go home for good, leaving Val and me staring in disbelief down a road we'd not yet traveled.

After eight years, ten months, six days, sixteen hours, and thirty-seven minutes, he and my mother were together again. When the dust finally settled, I saw them riding hell-bent for leather through the green, green grass of heaven.

"I hope the grass is greener on the other side
an' he's got good horses to ride."

From the song "Good Horses to Ride"
by Trent Wilmon

About the Author

Tammi Littrell finally quit her day job at her trucking company. She, her husband, and their two Chihuahuas, Elvis and Gracie, currently live aboard their catamaran in the British Virgin Islands, where they can be found entertaining friends and family. She is still food-obsessed and can knock out an impressive six-course dinner in her little galley. She has traded in her cute leopard heels and Fendi bag for flip-flops and a backpack; her .38 and her collection of good jewelry have been replaced by a mooring stick and seashells; her good cut and color is now barely noticeable under a baseball cap; and her latest fashion accessory is a headlamp, which she thinks looks pretty darn good on her. (It really doesn't.) She thinks it may even catch on as a trend. (It won't.)

Tammi and Larry still have their home in Dayton, Wyoming, which is where they live during the summer. She also writes a blog about food, travel, and other random, useless things, which can be found at www.saucedujour.blogspot.com. *When the Dust Settled* is her first book.